The Railways in Assam
1885–1947

The Railways in Assam 1885–1947

Sarah Hilaly

PILGRIMS PUBLISHING
◆ Varanasi ◆

The Railways in Assam 1885-1947
Sarah Hilaly

Published by:
PILGRIMS PUBLISHING

An imprint of:
PILGRIMS BOOK HOUSE
B 27/98 A-8, Nawabganj Road
Durga Kund, Varanasi-221010, India
Tel: 91-542-2314060
Fax: 91-542-2312456
E-mail: pilgrims@satyam.net.in
Website: www.pilgrimsbooks.com

Cover Design by
Dushyant Parasher
Layout & typesetting by
Astricks, New Delhi 110070, www.astricks.com

ISBN: 81-7769-422-7

Printed in India at Pilgrim Press Pvt. Ltd. Lalpur Varanasi

For my mother
and
my son Imroz

Foreword

Karl Marx had foreseen that, despite its devastating effects on the 'old' Asiatic Society, British colonialism would also be the agent of 'regeneration' in India. In other words it would lay the material foundation of Western Society, the features of which would be introduction of private property in land, stronger and regular linkage with the world market through steam navigation and establishment of a railway network. He felt that the railways would increase the productive powers of the country by promoting internal exchange, equalizing prices between regions and extending irrigation. Most important of all it would lead to the development of modern industries. Marx had admitted that though the chief motive of the colonialists in introducing railways was to draw from India cheap cotton and such raw materials, its effect nonetheless would not be contained to such drainage only; there would be positive ramifications too. From railway locomotion would arise the necessity of application of machinery to those branches of industry, not yet immediately connected with railways. Socially too, it would dissolve the hereditary division of labour and caste system and take to the rural areas the knowledge of modern technology to enable the traditional artisans modernise their age old crafts. Such was the importance assigned to the railways by this modern Seer. Whether it actually dissolved the division of labour and diluted the caste network is debatable but there is no doubt, that railways had played a pivotal role in the limited economic regeneration that India experienced before independence. John M. Hurd in his contribution to *The Cambridge Economic History of India 1757– 1970* (Dharma Kumar and Meghnad Desai (eds), Cambridge in association with Orient Longman, 1982, pp. 760–61), says, *'without them (railways) freight shipment would have been much more expensive, more resources would have been used to ship goods and fewer goods would have been transported to internal and overseas market. Railways led to increased agricultural output, the growth of modern industry and mining, new jobs — although many jobs were lost, the redistribution of the urban population, higher incomes for some segments of the population and numerous other economic changes'*. The impact of railways on the political history of India cannot be underestimated. Through physical connectivity, it helped the generation and spread of the ideology of nationalism.

Yet Indian railways have hardly been given their due in the conventional historiography of modern India. Even when it is discussed it is relegated to the narrow confines of economic history, not always a popular fragment of history. In this context the present book by Sarah Hilaly is an important step, more so because it deals with the development of railways in the strategic north-eastern region. The north-eastern region of high mountain ranges and gigantic rivers had been connected and integrated with the rest of the subcontinent through a wide network of railways by the British. But partition and the consequent disruption of this network rendered this region into a 'remote periphery'. The 'turbulence' with which this region is identified with in the post-independence period has a lot to do with this remoteness. Sarah Hilaly's work does not extend to that period. Still it not only provides enough material to understand the advent and spread of the railways in north-east India but also its role in the drainage of valuable raw material like coal and oil from the region. It has sections that assess the impact of railways on the beginning of ceaseless immigration of impoverished peasants and tribals to the wastelands and tea plantations of the region. These emerged to be very important issues in the post-colonial history of the region. This book stands out not just because it is the sole book on the subject in the region, but also because it depicts it just as *'history'* without relegating it to the realm of any fragmentary disciplines.

Sajal Nag
Professor in History
Assam University
Silchar

Preface

The forms of economic exploitation of India as a colony can be understood by analysing the roles of various tools used in the process. Railways were one of the most remarkable achievements of the Industrial Revolution and were used as an important tool for the transfer of technology over indigenous technology. Railways were instrumental in securing greater political and economic control of the resources of India.

Assam, which came under colonial rule in the first quarter of the nineteenth century, was subjected to the changed economic operation of Industrial Capitalism. Its economic transformation under colonial rule was traumatic, as it was marked by drastic changes from a quasi-feudal economy to a market economy. Railways as a tool of economic exploitation of the resources of Assam have not been studied in depth.

In various works pertaining to Assam, H.K. Barpujari in *The Comprehensive History of Assam*, volume IV, has detailed the history of railways in one of the chapters. Amalendu Guha has extensively contributed in highlighting various aspects of the society, economy, and polity of medieval Assam. In *Planter Raj to Swaraj: Freedom Struggle and Electoral Politics in Assam 1826–1947*, he has highlighted the proportion of investments for railways in Assam. Shyam Bhadra Medhi's *Transport System and Economic Development in Assam*, is a pioneering work on the study of railways in Assam as a means of transportation. The early history of the railways have been dealt with at length as a prelude. The growth and development of railways has been analysed from a purely economic standpoint, the primary thrust being on their role as an instrument of economic growth during the post-colonial period. In P.C. Goswami's *Economic Development in Assam*, railway development of the post-colonial period has also been studied. These works give us the basic data as well as an analysis of the issue of railway development in Assam.

An attempt has been made to comprehensively understand the processes involved in the initiation of railway projects in Assam; aspects of construction, financial management, and impact on the economic resources of India as a colony. The railways role in fostering economic development of the province, an analysis of the actual benefits of the railways on the socio-economic development of the indigenous population, and an understanding of the phenomenon of immigration into Assam in the last quarter of the nineteenth and first half of the twentieth century has also been attempted in the light of the expansion of the railway network.

This book is divided into eight chapters.

The first provides the geographical setting of Assam with an overview of the socio-political and economic structure at that time. The process of the political annexation of Assam as a part of the great Indian Empire and the visible economic changes during the pre-railway era have been examined.

The second chapter deals with the existing channels of communication during the pre-colonial period, both in terms of overland routes and navigable waterways. It lays out the changes initiated by the British in improving communications of both modes with their advantages and limitations, and the changes brought about in the light of economic transformation.

The third chapter focuses on the factors responsible for the introduction of railways in India. It covers the official correspondence on the issue and pressure groups like British investors looking for investment opportunities abroad. The factors responsible for the sanctioning of railways as feeders for steamers, the survey of trunk routes by the colonial government and the stage at which railways were introduced in Assam have been discussed in detail.

The fourth chapter gives details of railway lines constructed in Assam. Contracts specific to Assam have been analysed to see whether they were in line with terms followed over the rest of India. The technical aspects and financial management of the various railways operating in Assam have been studied to understand the role of these railways as feeder lines. The dynamics of the construction of trunk lines and their role in economic development have also been covered.

The fifth chapter deals with the human component behind the railway projects, labour — its composition, nature, and wage structure. It covers land settlements initiated with a view to retain the body of labourers for future maintenance and construction activities. The role of this force in the national movement has also been examined.

The sixth chapter details the various industries which developed along with the growth of the railways and their symbiotic relationship. It also describes the role of railways in the development of the agricultural sector.

The seventh chapter studies the impact of the railways on the socio-economic life of the people of Assam. It tries to link processes like the growth of an internal market, equalization of trade and development of urban centres, and human movements fostered by the railways, alongside the inducements of colonization schemes. An assessment of the actual gains to the peasantry by the railway network has also been made.

The eighth chapter summarizes the major findings of this study.

Acknowledgements

During the course of my research I was helped by many people and institutions. I am indebted to Professor Sristidhar Dutta, for guiding and patiently bearing with me during my research. Dr David Syiemlieh, Dr Dipankar Banerjee and Professor Amalendu Guha offered valuable suggestions in the formative stages of the project. Dr J.L. Dawar and Dr N.C. Roy contributed by offering suggestions on certain aspects of my research. Dr S.K. Patnaik helped me with the maps and Dr A.K. Das with botanical names.

My thanks to Ms Aienla Longkumer for allowing me to borrow her computer for typing the first draft, Dr H.M. Upadhyaya for valuable inputs during the last stages of my work, and the help of Mr J. Thakuria in typing out the manuscript.

This book would have been unimaginable without the encouragement and enriching stimuli of my family. My friend and companion Ranendra Prasad painstakingly taught me the nuances of editing. He was there all along, putting in innumerable man-hours and bearing with my emotional outbursts. Without his steadying presence I would not have been able to complete it.

I express my gratitude to my parents, especially to my mother who has been an immense source of inspiration. She has helped in ways which cannot be detailed. My son Nedaye Imroz has helped me in innumerable ways. He bore with my absence during the fieldwork as well as at home ungrudgingly. He has helped me with his skills on the computer. I am immensely indebted to my 'little angel' for his inputs.

I would like to express my sincere thanks to the staff and workers of the various libraries and archives from where I collected my data — The National Archives of India, New Delhi; The Nehru Memorial Museum and Centre for Contemporary Studies Library, New Delhi; National Library, Calcutta; The West Bengal State Archives, Calcutta; The Assam State Archives, Dispur, Guwahati; The Directorate of Historical Antiquarian Studies, Guwahati; Central Library North Eastern Hill University, Shillong; and the K.K. Handique Library, Guwahati University, Guwahati.

During the process of publication I have incurred debts to people I need to make special mention of. My greatest friend Professor Sajal Nag was instrumental in introducing me to the publishing house. Dr O.P. Kejariwal helped me at every stage. Profuse thanks are due to the publisher, Mr Rama Nand, for accepting my manuscript and according me the privilege of authoring their first academic book. I would be failing in my duty if I did not mention the contribution of Hartej Baksh Singh, without whose meticulous copy-editing, the book would not have taken its present shape.

Sarah Hilaly

Contents

List of Tables

List of Maps

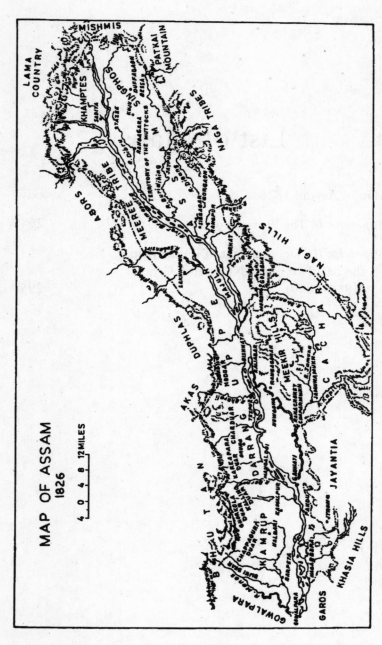

Map of Assam: 1826 (Source: The Comprehensive History of Assam, vol. III, H.K. Barpujari (ed.))

1
Introduction

GEOGRAPHY

The present state of Assam lies between latitude 22° 19′ to 28° 16′ North and longitude 89° 42′ and 97° 12′ East, and has three natural divisions — the Brahmaputra Valley, the Barak Valley and the intervening ranges of North Cachar and Karbi-Anglong hills. Assam, when it came under British occupation in 1826, comprised the territory lying on both sides of the Brahmaputra. Bounded on the north by a chain of hills, it was inhabited successively, from the west to the east by the Bhutias, the Akas, the Duflas (Nyishis), the Abors (Adis) and the Miris. The hills inhabited by the Mishmis swept around the top of the Brahmaputra Valley. On the extreme east, the hills that separated Assam from Burma (Myanmar) and China, were inhabited by the Khamptis, Singphos and various Naga tribes. The hills in the south of Assam ranging from the east to the west were inhabited by the Nagas, the Khasis, the Jaintias, and the Mikirs. The states of Cachar and Manipur were on the south-west, and to the west lay the province of Bengal.[1]

Nature has been lavish in bestowing its beauty on Assam. The landscape stands out from the rest of the country, offering a pleasant sight to lovers of nature. The river Brahmaputra, through a greater part of its course down the valley, is bounded on either side with vast stretches of land covered with thick grass interspersed with patches of cultivated land. Further inland, on the higher reaches are found considerable forests. The smaller rivers pass through gorges of exceptional beauty debouching upon the plains. The valley is dotted with numerous swamps and lakes.

The Brahmaputra with its numerous tributaries causes heavy floods and inundations along its course. The sub-tropical forests bordering the river result in excessive precipitation, which in turn cause heavy rainfall and humid conditions.

Throughout the rainy season, the land is generally swampy, which deteriorates further during floods, making it a breeding ground for malaria. Smallpox, kala-azar and dysentery were once endemic.[2] A seventeenth century visitor referred to Assam as 'a wild and dreadful country, abounding in danger'.[3] Early British accounts on the province of Assam are replete with details on the enervating effect of the climatic conditions on the lives of the people. They attributed it as a cause for making the people averse to hard work and consequently ease loving:

> but its climate is damp and relaxing so that while the people enjoyed great material prosperity, there is a strong tendency towards and physical deterioration. Any race that has been

1. Cachar became a tributary of the British from 1824. Barring a small portion of its territory, it was annexed to the British Empire in 1832.

2. Edward Gait, *A History of Assam* (Calcutta, 1906), p. 133.

3. Shihabuddin Talish (1662) as cited in Gait, *A History of Assam*.

a resident there . . . would gradually, become soft and luxuri-
ous, and so after a time, would no longer be able to defend
itself against the incursions of the hardy tribe behind
them . . .[4]

Bounded by hills on all sides Assam virtually remained
isolated from the rest of the country. Centuries of isolation
resulted in Assamese society developing an insular social
structure. The Brahmaputra formed the vital highway of communication between Assam and the world outside. Navigation
along the river was uncertain and perilous. Overland routes
to the neighbouring province of Bengal were subject to the
vagaries of nature and extremely unreliable. Communication
bottlenecks bred geographical isolation, which in turn bred
insularity.

The limited interaction, which took place through the
numerous passes and river routes, with the inhabitants of the
neighbouring hills, did not have any profound impact on
social formations in Assam.

PRE-COLONIAL STRUCTURE

Political Situation

History is a continuous process. It is not possible to study a
particular period in history without studying the preceding
period. To understand the history of the colonial period it is
imperative to examine the history of the pre-colonial period.

Before the advent of the British, the Ahoms ruled Assam.
The Ahoms were an offshoot of the Tai or great Shan[5] stock

4. Gait, *History of Assam*, p. 7.
5. H.K. Barpujari, *Assam in the Days of the Company: 1826–1858*
(Gauhati, 2d ed., 1980), p. 7.

of South-East Asia. They inhabited the northern and eastern tracts of Upper Burma and Western Yunnan.

This group came to Assam through the Patkai range under the leadership of Sukhapa in the thirteenth century. They soon subjugated and conquered the petty tribal chiefdoms that existed in the area. The powerful Chutiya kingdom was absorbed within the Ahom kingdom in 1523. The Ahoms successfully repulsed the repeated attempts of the Mughals to extend their sway over Assam, in the seventeenth century. Consolidation of their kingdom was achieved by holding the Kachari state to vassalage and absorbing Kamrup into its kingdom. At its zenith, the Ahom kingdom extended from the easternmost extremity of Assam to river Manas on the west.

At the close of the eighteenth century the *Moamaris* a socio-religious sect, took up arms in protest against religious persecution by the Ahom rulers and for various other reasons. The weak Ahom regime failed to check the uprising. Imposition of puppet kings and counter-revolutions did not retrieve the situation, but on the contrary led to fresh uprisings. Unable to quell the rebellion the reigning monarch, Gaurinath Singha (1792–94) sought British help, which came in the form of Captain Thomas Welsh's expedition in 1792. Sir John Shore succeeded Lord Cornwallis as the Governor General — propounder of the non-intervention policy — soon thereafter. He recalled Captain Welsh in 1794. Assam, once again relapsed into a state of misrule and anarchy. Kamaleshwar Singha (1795–1810) made efforts to restore peace and order. His successor Chandra Kanta Singha (1811–18) was unable to reconcile with the powerful *Burgohain* and in desperation invoked Burmese assistance.

The Burmese who had an eye on the westward extension of their dominion seized this opportunity and virtually remained rulers of Assam between 1819 and 1824. The Burmese interlude was the last nail in the coffin of the Ahom rule. A reign of terror was unleashed in Assam, during which plunder, devastation and murder was rampant. The efforts of the Burmese interlude can be gauged from the following extract:

> parts of the country which had been thickly populated were now wastes of elephant grass. Everywhere the effects of two generations of anarchy were visible in the ruined homesteads uncultivated fields and huge areas of jungle.[6]

Economy

The Ahoms introduced wet rice cultivation into Assam, which superseded the primitive dry paddy cultivation which had been practised by the tribal groups inhabiting the region. Through collective effort, the Ahoms reclaimed marshes and made them suitable for wet rice cultivation. All such lands, which were jointly reclaimed, became community lands and were distributed amongst various families.[7] Their earlier experience in wet rice cultivation, superior iron implements and buffalo power made them well equipped for the task. The essential prerequisites for this form of cultivation — slope and water control — was achieved by cutting down and uprooting forests and the levelling of undulating surfaces. This marked the beginning of a flourishing agrarian economy, which Assam developed over the centuries.

Further, embankments were constructed and maintained for overall water control. These works necessitated a collective effort on a wider scale that could not be left to peasant initiative

6. *Note on the History of Past Settlements of Assam*, p. 1.

7. Amalendu Guha, 'Land Rights and Social Classes in Medieval Assam', *Indian Economic and Social History Review*, vol. III, no. 3, (henceforth *IESHR*), September 1966, p. 221.

alone. A huge militia under the *paik* system was organized for this purpose.

Militia System

Payment of revenue under the Ahom's was by an insistence on the labour services of the free adult male population between the age of 15 to 60, who were known as *paiks*. Their services were mostly utilized in the realm of defence. In times of peace, their services were utilized for construction and maintenance of public works. To effectively utilize the services of the entire community in a phased and organized manner, four *paiks* were organized into a *got* or unit. A number of *gots* constituted a *khel* or guild.

A *paik* received from the state two *puras*[8] of wet rice lands free of tax. In lieu of tax, each *paik* had to serve the state for three months in a year.[9] Therefore, in rotation, one *got* completed within itself one year of manual service to the state. Reclamation of wastelands (*khats*) was permitted. The Ahom aristocracy and a section of the Ahom officials were excluded from this organizational set up. As there was no regular army, the *khels* were led by a gradation of officers, which formed the crux of the Ahom militia. The militia system was the basis of Ahom society, polity and economy.[10]

Like any other medieval society, the economy of Assam was primarily agrarian, with land as the primary means of production. Land of all denominations theoretically belonged to the State. The king, who represented the State, exercised all rights and claims over cultivated or wastelands, forests,

8. A *pura* is equivalent to 1.33 acres.
9. Gait, *History of Assam*, p. 240
10. Sajal Nag, *Roots of Ethnic Conflict: Nationality Question in North-East India* (New Delhi, 1990), p. 7.

woods, ferries, mines, etc.[11] The monarch gave two types of land grants: one to the nobility and the *paiks* in lieu of their services to the state and the other, rent-free lands for religious purposes. The nobility were granted rent-free estates as well as *paiks* to cultivate their estates. These estates practically became the private property of the recipients.

A *paik* possessed three types of lands: homestead (*bari*), garden (*bori*) and inferior land suitable for plough cultivation. For holdings of the first two categories, the *paik* had no obligation to the state, as they were treated as private property, subject to a degree of control by the clan. Inferior lands, because of their abundance were hardly acquired as permanent private possessions. However all wet rice or *rupit* lands called *ga-mati* — the most prized possessions — belonged to the State, which a *paik* was entitled to in lieu of his obligatory service to the state. The wet rice lands which were given to the *paiks*, were not hereditary and were redistributed on their deaths.[12] Even the hereditary homestead and dry land were not saleable because transfer of lands outside the clan was not permissible.[13]

In its efforts towards proselytization, the Ahom government gave land grants to Brahmins for temples and other religious purposes. These were known as *Brahmottar, Devottar* and *Dharmottar* land grants respectively. Servitors, called *likchous*, were gifted to these religious institutions along with the land grants. The state, however retained the power to

11. Gait, *History of Assam*, p. 270.

12. For details on the *paik* system refer to S.K. Bhuyan, *Anglo-Assamese Relations 1771–1826*, pp. 10–12; Edward Gait, *A History of Assam*, pp. 247–50, and Amalendu Guha, 'Land Rights and Social Classes in Medieval Assam', *IESHR*, vol. III, no. 3, September 1966.

13. Guha, 'Land Rights and Social Classes in Medieval Assam', September 1966, p. 230.

confiscate the wealth of such institutions and withdraw the
likchou service granted to them, whenever deemed necessary.

Agriculture

The agrarian economy of medieval Assam was characterized
by a subsistence level of production. For the peasant, the
family was the unit of production, and production was limited
to goods required for the unit's consumption. Surplus
production was not extensive. It was only during the fifteenth
and sixteenth centuries, with the expansion of the Ahom
territory and intensification of feudal relations, that surplus
production increased.[14] The average landholding was small
and agriculture was highly individualized.

The plains of Assam lagged far behind the rest of India
technologically. An abundance of land sparsely populated,
continuous migration from the hills to the plains, combined
with a slow-down in the transition from shifting hoe cultivation to permanent plough cultivation, was responsible for
this. In areas where plough cultivation was practised, it was
of a shifting nature spread out over large areas of the sub-
montane and riverine belts of the plains. Ploughshares of
areca nut trees or bamboo existed alongside iron ploughshares.[15] The use of iron, bricks and wheeled carts was extremely limited.[16] Potters did not universally use a potter's
wheel.[17] Iron was neither used in building houses nor building

14. Amalendu Guha, 'Medieval Economy of Assam', Appendix 1, in
Tapan Raychaudhuri and Irfan Habib (eds), *The Cambridge Economic
History of India: 1200–1750*, vol. I (Cambridge, 1982), pp. 478–535.

15. Amalendu Guha, 'The Geography Behind the History', in Amalendu
Guha, *Medieval and Early Colonial Assam: Society, Polity and Economy*
(Calcutta, 1991), pp. 23–4.

16. Ibid.

17. Guha, 'The Geography Behind the History', pp. 23–4.

of boats. The level of technology employed in boat building was primitive. Dugout canoes with sails were mainly used.

Division of Labour

Because of limited growth in trade, the division of labour, both in terms of the number of castes and in terms of actual occupational specialization did not emerge strongly in Assamese society. Like the rest of India, nucleated villages with servants integrated into the dominant caste group through *jajmani* relations were conspicuously absent. Efforts in this direction, to found new villages of composite caste groups including artisans, were made by Pratap Singha (1603–41).[18] The bonds of brotherhood formed the basis of the functional *khel* system, and institutionalized by the administrative machinery inhibited the growth or autonomy of the village.

Weaving and spinning were not caste specific, but universal with all Assamese women irrespective of caste or status. Extraction of mustard oil, *gur* (molasses), and rice pounding was carried on in individual households.[19] An exception was found in Kamrup where certain villages were entirely settled by oilmen or weavers, with agriculture as a secondary occupation.

The members of the *Kalita* caste, who were essentially peasants, formed diverse occupational groups. They were wheel-using potters, blacksmiths, bell-metal artisans, carpenters and boat builders, and weavers.[20] Certain classes, reduced to the level of untouchability, were the *Hiras* who fashioned earthen pots without using the wheel, the *Britials* (goldsmiths),

18. Guha, 'Medieval Economy of Assam', p. 486.
19. Guha, 'The Geography Behind the History', p. 24.
20. These groups tended to form sub-castes, but did not finally emerge in the social structure as sub-castes.

and the *Nadials* who were net-using fishermen.[21] Under Mughal influence, new crafts were introduced like making granulated sugar, tailoring, brass-work, etc. In Lower Assam more occupational castes appeared. They were the *Ganak* or *Acharya* (astrologers and fortune-tellers, respectively), *Napit* (barbers), *Bej* (village physicians), *Kumar* (blacksmith), *Keot* (fishermen), *Sonar* (gold/silver smiths), *Dom* and *Deori* (an order of priesthood).[22]

Trade — Internal and Extraterritorial

Very little information is available about the extent of trade, crafts and circulation of money in Assam in the period between the thirteenth and seventeenth centuries. There are no inscriptional references to coinage or use of money during that period, nor have coins of that period been found. There are inscriptions however referring to cowries (conch shells) being used as money.[23] Nevertheless, barter remained the primary mode of exchange, alongside the use of cowries and coins from Bengal which came into the region through trade.

The concept of isolation and self-sufficiency in those times was a myth. The economy of the plains of Assam was integrated with that of the hills surrounding it. This symbiotic relationship was maintained through a chain of foothill fairs and marts where both sides met. The Mishmis, who occupied the hills north of the Sadiya brought with them a few Tibetan swords and spears, a little musk, a considerable amount of vegetable poison, a few deer skins and some ivory, which they

21. The *Morias* who were originally Muslim settlers came as prisoners of war, and formed the occupational sub-caste of braziers. They made utensils out of brass sheets and were socially treated as untouchables.

22. Nag, *Roots of Ethnic Conflict*, pp. 20–1.

23. Guha, 'Medieval Economy of Assam', vol. I, p. 487.

exchanged for glass beads, cloth, and money.[24] Similarly, the Adis (Abors) and the (Miris) Mishings brought down some amount of pepper, ginger, *munjeet* (a red dye plant), and wax, which they exchanged for produce of the plains. The Singphos traded in ivory. From the southern confines, the Nagas frequented the markets at Nagura and Cacharihat where they exchanged their cotton, ginger and considerable amounts of salt for rice and beads.[25]

The Khasis brought down iron implements, cotton, honey, red chillies, and potatoes, which they exchanged for cloth and silk.[26] The Garos who frequented the foothill marts exchanged their main staple of cotton, for cows, fowls, rice, and dried fish. The total volume of this trade however, was very small.

External trade links existed across the hills between Eastern Assam and Upper Burma, Bhutan, Tibet and probably Southern China, throughout the thirteenth and fifteenth centuries. Assam imported salt from coastal Bengal. In the exchange, unable to match the value of salt, there was an outflow of gold (collected from river sand) and also of slaves.[27]

Concrete and detailed information on the region's economic condition, growth of trade and crafts, and advances in monetization and specialization is available from the latter half of the sixteenth century. The biographies of a number of sixteenth century Vaishnava saints contained in the *Katha-guru-Charita*,[28] mention the participation of these saints in their younger days in trade. Merchants, according to the

24. William Robinson, *A Descriptive Account of Assam* (Calcutta, 1841, reprinted, Delhi, 1975), p. 243.

25. Ibid.

26. Ibid.

27. Guha in *Medieval and Early Colonial Assam*, p. 22.

28. This treatise dates back to 1716, whose author has not been identified. In 1952, U.C. Lekharu edited and published it. (Nalbari, 1952).

author were classified into three categories: (i) shopkeepers dealing in gold and jewels (ii) those dealing in a variety of silk and cotton fabrics, and (iii) those dealing in commonplace articles like salt and *khar*.[29] The first two categories dealt in luxury items, while the third in daily necessities.[30] Casual references in this source on the scale of transactions, was said to have ranged between Rs 1 to Rs 4 lakhs.

Within the indigenous caste structure, there was no existence of a separate trading class. In Upper Assam, where trade was primarily confined to exchange at the foothills, such a class was conspicuously absent. However, in Lower Assam a small trading community called the *Vaishya-Saud* had carried on trade in the remote past. The boat owning *sauds* carried on trade as far as Bengal.[31] The merchandise comprised mustard seeds, areca nuts, betel leaves, ornamental umbrellas, silk, black pepper, elephant tusks and gold.[32] The people of Barpeta were described as vigorous traders.

In the early seventeenth century, a few enterprising merchants of Assam carried out trade with Bengal by the river route, as far as Dacca or followed on the overland route across the Jaintia Hills to Sylhet.[33] Regular trade relations existed between Mughal India and the Ahom Kingdom except when it was suspended on diplomatic grounds. Elephants and *agar* or aloes wood was in heavy demand by the Mughal administration. Shihabuddin Talish (1662) writes:

29. An alkaline substance made from the ash of plantain trees and generally used as a substitute for salt.
30. Guha, 'Medieval Economy of Assam', vol. I, p. 488.
31. These inferences have been made from sixteenth century folk literature. Chand Sadagar of medieval folklore is said to have belonged to this caste, cf. Amalendu Guha in *Medieval and Early Colonial Assam*, p. 21.
32. Guha, 'Medieval Economy of Assam', vol. I, p. 489.
33. Robinson, *A Descriptive Account of Assam*, p. 252.

quantities of aloes wood, pepper, spikenard, musk, gold and silk were exchanged for salt, sulphur, saltpetre and several other products of Mughal India at the Ahom–Mughal out-post.[34]

Salt accounted for an overwhelmingly large part of the imports into the Ahom Kingdom. In 1750 the total salt imported was to the tune of 120,000 maunds ($\approx$ 4,408.18 tons). Assamese diplomatic envoys visiting Tripura thrice between 1709 and 1715, noted important trade centres where produce from Assam was found.[35]

The earliest estimates on the composition of the Ahom Mughal trade can be comprehended from the customs check-post returns of the year 1808–1809. Exports to Bengal included raw cotton, stick lac, mustard seeds, *muga* silk thread, elephant tusks, slaves, bell-metal utensils, iron hoes, pepper and miscel-laneous forest products to the value of *Sicca*[36] Rs 1,30,900 only. The primary imports from Bengal were salt (84 per cent), and muslin (5 per cent), the rest being luxury items valued at *Sicca* Rs 2,28,300.[37] The trading pattern reflected that there was a trade surplus, generally in favour of Mughal India.

From early times overland trade seemed to have existed across the frontier with Bhutan and Tibet. Towards the end of the Ahom rule, the Bhutan trade was conducted under the supervision of an official of the Ahom government, called *Wazir-Barua*, who resided at Simlibari. A well-established mar-ket at Seelpothah in Darrang district was the centre of external trade. The *Wazir-Barua* did not levy duties on the merchandise,

34. Gait, *History of Assam*, p. 144.
35. Guha, 'Medieval Economy of Assam', vol. I, p. 490.
36. The nomenclature for the currency used by the British East India Company.
37. Francis Buchanan-Hamilton, *An Account of Assam . . . 1807–1814* (Gauhati,1940; reprinted 1987), pp. 47–8.

but received presents and acted as a mutual broker between the Bhutias and Assamese. In 1809, Hamilton estimated this trade, even under the most disturbing political conditions, to be valued at Rs 2 lakhs per annum.[38] The primary exports from Assam were lac, *munjeet*, silk, *muga* and *endi*, and dry fish while the imports were woollen clothes, gold dust, rock salt, musk, ponies, Tibetan cowries and Chinese silks.[39] Under adverse political conditions, in the first two decades of the nineteenth century, trade declined. Yet, preceding the Burmese incursion, the Bhutia merchants brought down gold amounting to Rs 70,000 which was principally exchanged for *muga* and silk.[40] In 1833, when the Burmese overran the province, only two merchants were registered to have come down for trade.[41]

There was considerable frontier trade with Tibet. The Tibetans brought down silver bullion amounting to Rs 1 lakh and a large quantity of rock salt. They exchanged this with the Assamese, for rice, silk, lac and iron found in Assam, and otter skins, buffalo horns, pearls and corals imported from Bengal.[42] Tibetan pilgrims carried items like smoking pipes of Chinese manufacture, woollens and rock salt. In exchange for these, they got musk, ivory, *Beesa* (a vegetable poison), and Assamese slaves, who at one time formed a considerable trade item.[43] M'Cosh mentions of the existence of a reasonable amount of trade with China and Burma. The imports mentioned were nankeen, silks, lacquered and Chinaware, lead, copper and above all things silver.[44]

38. Buchanan-Hamilton, *An Account of Assam*, p. 76.
39. Ibid.
40. Robinson, *A Descriptive Account of Assam*, p. 243.
41. Ibid.
42. John M'Cosh, *Topography of Assam* (Calcutta, 1837, reprinted, Delhi, 1975), p. 66.
43. Ibid.
44. M'Cosh, *Topography of Assam*, p. 66.

The Ahom monarchy conducted and controlled the external trade with Mughal India and the hill frontiers through some specially appointed officers like the *Duara-Barua, Sadiya-Khowa Gohain* and the *Baruas.*[45] The custom-houses (*Chaukis*) towards Bengal were farmed out to *Baruas.* The chief custom-house, Kandhar or the Assam Chauki as referred to by the English was situated at Hadira, opposite Goalpara. There were seven subordinate custom-houses on the banks of the river and several others on various routes by which goods could possibly pass. All duties were paid at Kandhar and the other subordinate houses to prevent illicit trade. The *Baruas* annually paid a sum of Rs 54,000 to the king and were permitted to levy a moderate duty of 10 per cent on all exports and imports.[46] The Mughals were not allowed to enter into the territory and all trading activities were limited to the Ahom–Mughal outposts.

Internal trade in medieval Assam was essentially barter oriented. It was not until the sixteenth century that internal trade acquired a limited level of specialization. The *Katha-Guru-Charita*, an important treatise of the sixteenth century, provides an insight into the nature of trade.

A certain degree of locality-wise specialization in the production of a single commodity was achieved.[47] In the local weekly or bi-weekly *hats*, betel leaves, areca nuts, earthenware, piece-goods, etc., were exchanged. In the 1660's in the Ahom capital of Garhgaon, there was a small daily bazar on

45. S.K. Bhuyan, *Anglo-Assamese Relations: 1771–1826* (Gauhati, 1949, reprinted, 1974), pp. 51–3.

46. Buchanan-Hamilton, *An Account of Assam*, pp. 43–7.

47. It was noted in the *Katha-Guru-Charita*, that there were concentrated orchards of betel-vine and areca nut in the villages of Kupajhar and its vicinity. Paralhat served as a marketing centre.

a narrow street. The only sellers there, as Shihabuddin observed, were betel-leaf sellers.[48] At the weekly mart of Nazira-
hat, located outside the city gates, women vendors amongst
others, brought in head-loads of various provisions. Village
potters went out with boatloads of earthenware for sale. Some
older villagers eked out a living by making a variety of bamboo
baskets, fishing appliances and containers, which were bar-
tered for salt, oil, areca nuts, rice and other necessities. Occasional sale of vegetables, mustard oil and fuel wood was also
recorded. Besides, the *Kalita* craftsmen of Kamrup, primarily
silk-weavers and bell-metal artisans sold their specialized
products as itinerant traders all over Assam.[49]

Exchanges within the limitations of a basically barter and
cowrie economy, were mostly intra-local on a petty scale and
at a peddlers level. In such an economy, sellers were more often
buyers as well as producers or gatherers of the goods sold.
Traders, whether big or small, were not independent of their
agricultural roots.

The small range of trading activities could be attributed
primarily to: (a) the surplus, that largely took the form of
labour-rent, as rent-in-kind was appropriated by the ruling
class (b) household consumption was not by production
within the household. An organized grain market was absent,
nor were there a chain of intermediaries both vertical and
horizontal to intervene in the market.

Money

From the late sixteenth century — the period of steady
consolidation under the Ahoms — there was a rapid rise in
surplus production. Concrete information about the region's

48. Gait, *History of Assam*, p. 50.
49. Guha in *Medieval and Early Colonial Assam*, p. 21.

economic condition is available for this period. Some advances were made towards monetization and specialization. Ahom coinage was believed to have been initiated by Suklengmung around AD 1543–44. They are now attributed to a king who ruled more than a hundred years after Suklengmung.[50] The earliest coins issued under the Ahom monarchy were in AD 1648 (Saka 1570) during the reign of Jayadhvaja Singha.[51] After Jayadhvaja Singha, Ahom coinage was struck at regular intervals by Chakradhvaja Singha, Gadadhar Singha, Rudra Singha, Siva Singha, Pramatta Singha, Rajesvara Singha, Lakshmi Singha, Gaurinath Singha, Kamaleshwar Singha and Chandakanta Singha. Coins struck by two rebel Moamaria rulers — Bharata Singha and Sarvananda Singha (AD 1818) are also known.[52] The coins of the Ahom Prince Brajanath Singha (AD 1818) were in line with those of the rebel rulers.[53] Jogeswara Singha was the last Ahom king to issue coins.[54] Siva Singha introduced a regular gold currency.

The earliest extant Koch coins — the Narayani coins — were issued in AD 1555.[55] The earliest coin minted by the Kachari king had a date equivalent to AD 1583.[56] Coins found in the Jaintia Kingdom were minted in the beginning of the seventeenth century. By the end of the seventeenth century, half-rupee and quarter-rupee silver coins were in circulation and by 1750

50. Jai Prakash Singh, 'Coinage in North-East India: An Overview', in Jai Prakash Singh and Gautam Sengupta (eds), *Archaeology of North-Eastern India* (New Delhi, 1991), p. 186.

51. Jai Prakash Singh *et al.*, *Archaeology of North-Eastern India*, p. 187.

52. Ibid.

53. Ibid.

54. Ibid.

55. D. Nath, *History of the Koch Kingdom 1515–1615* (New Delhi, 1989), p. 158.

56. Gait, *History of Assam*, p. 252.

one-eighth rupee and one-sixteenth rupee coins were extensively in circulation throughout the region.[57] Gaurinath Singha issued coins of the lowest denomination, $1/32$ of a rupee.[58] A standard Ahom coin weighed two-fifths of an English ounce. In the absence of copper coins and coins of smaller denomination, cowries were used to meet the needs of petty trade. Coins were also minted for making religious donations after the conversion of the Ahom kings to Hinduism.[59] The increase in money circulation was an indicator of an expansion in exchange and trade by the end of the sixteenth century.

SOCIAL STRUCTURE

Based on a natural economy and in the absence of urbanization, medieval Assamese society was stratified into distinct classes: (a) the king was at the top of the pyramidal hierarchy, (b) the privileged aristocracy — both secular and spiritual — who were not obliged to be under any kind of manual service to the state or its economy, (c) the peasantry — including fishermen and artisans — who were required to render such service or to pay a tax, in lieu of it in kind or cash, and (d) the servile classes constituted of slaves, serfs and bondsmen, all of whom owed no service to the state but were to serve their respective masters.

The categorization remains incomplete without assessing their respective roles in the production process. The secular aristocracy comprised of the king, vassal chieftains and the seven leading Ahom clans (*Satgharia Ahoms*) who monopolized

57. Guha, 'Medieval Economy of Assam', vol. I, p. 488.
58. Gait, *History of Assam*, p. 243.
59. J.N. Phukan, who has worked extensively on the economic conditions under Ahom rule, endorses this view.

all the important offices. They had hereditary estates on which slaves, bondsmen and tenants carried on cultivation. While in office, this class was apportioned crown lands as per their requirement, along with a number of *paiks* denominated as *likchous* for cultivating these lands.

The spiritual aristocracy constituting temple priests, *goswamis* and *mahantas* of approved *satras* — the Vaishnava monasteries, and the Brahmins were all favoured with land grants. Revenue-free land grants were made in favour of three categories of grantees: (a) Temple-gods, (b) religious institutions like *satras*, and (c) learned Brahmins. Throughout the Ahom period large tracts of land with or without serfs attached to them, continued to be donated by the rulers. The first two constituted the unproductive classes.

The peasantry, primarily the productive class, constituted the largest class in the hierarchy with a certain degree of stratification within it. Artisans and fishermen who had cultivation as their major or subsidiary occupation were incorporated into the peasantry. They cultivated their own holdings, which were subject to rendering service to the State. This service was for a specified period annually, or payment of a compensation in lieu of it. Alongside cultivation, multiple occupations like fishing, collecting forest produce, weaving, spinning, basket-making, etc., were integrated into household activities. Activities like harvesting, house-building, etc., requiring concerted efforts were carried out with mutual help. The peasant enjoyed inalienable rights over his homestead and garden lands. Traders and artisans had not yet crystallized into a distinct social class.

Slaves constituted the lowest rung in the social hierarchy. They were both domestic and agricultural. Prisoners of war, persons purchased from the hill tribes, condemned criminals and persons born of slaves constituted a major section of the servile class. Slaves were an object of merchandise in the trade with Bengal, Bhutan and Upper Burma, though no organized markets existed for such transactions.[60] They often featured prominently as a marriage dowry of rich men's daughters.[61] There was no distinction between serfdom and slavery in the absence of the classical dehumanized form of slavery. Serfs and bondsmen often lapsed into conditions of slavery in course of time. The slaves, serfs and bondsmen constituted approximately between five to nine per cent of the population.[62] This social stratification remained stable till the eighteenth century, when it was upset by new social developments. The momentous development was the evolution and growth of Vaishnavism, under Shankardev and his disciples. Vaishnavism operated through *satras* (monasteries), which were centres of power. Simple ideals, incorporation of peripheral tribes and caste groups, in contrast to the rigidity of Shaktism, propagated by the state machinery, appealed to the masses.

Religious preceptors or *gossains* commanded a great deal of authority over their followers. In due course, *satras* became prosperous, with certain *gossains* commanding a gradation of officials and servitors, besides regal paraphernalia. They enjoyed all royal privileges with the exception of royal sedans and elephants. The *gossains* practically ran parallel governments. This was considered as a threat to the ruling authority as well as an instrument for upsetting the existing social order. Peasants increasingly identified themselves as servitors to the monasteries to escape compulsory militia service. The militia, which formed the core of Ahom polity, economy and society

60. Guha, 'Medieval Economy of Assam', vol. I, pp. 488–9.
61. Ibid.
62. Ibid.

was threatened, having a weakening effect on its effective operation. A systematic persecution of Vaishnavism with the view to minimize its threat to the Ahom State, led to a peasant rebellion in a religious garb known as the Moamaria Revolution. This rebellion shook the foundations of Ahom rule.

COLONIAL PERIOD — PRE-1887

British policy in India was marked by certain distinct phases. At the outset, the East India Company began its operations in India as a purely commercial concern. It endeavoured to secure a monopoly over the supply of products from India for a ready market in England and Europe, which would yield rich profits. To strengthen its monopolistic nature, the East India Company transformed itself into a military power and began to expand its territorial limits in India. A systematic plunder began through the monopoly in trade and maximum extraction of land revenue, which drained the wealth out of India. This phase of economic exploitation of India is referred to as 'Merchant Capitalism'.

The Industrial Revolution that took place in England was regarded more as a product of the plunder of India, rather than a mere extension of the Renaissance. Once the task of industrial production began, it became imminent to find new outlets for the flood of manufactured goods. It necessitated a revolution in the economic system, from the principles of mercantile-capitalism to the principles of free-trade capitalism, involving a complete change in the methods of the colonial system. The new system required the creation of a free-market in India, replacing the old monopoly system. It was therefore imperative to transform India from an exporter of finished goods to an importer of machine-made goods.

The monopolistic privileges enjoyed by the East India Company had to be curtailed. The Industrial class in Britain campaigned relentlessly for abolishing the trading privileges of the East India Company, whose imports of superior Indian fabrics posed a serious competition to manufactured goods. The 'Charter of 1813' put an end to the monopoly of the East India Company's trade with India and marked the ascendancy of Industrial Capitalism. It transformed India into a market for finished goods as well as a source of raw materials. With the ascendancy of Industrial Capitalism, the British policy in Assam received a specific direction.

With the grant of the Diwani of Bengal in 1765 to the East India Company, Assam became a neighbour to the newly acquired British dominion of Bengal, Bihar and Orissa. The political situation during the second half of the eighteenth century and early nineteenth century has been dealt with earlier. The British came into Assam at the invitation of the rulers of Assam in the wake of the Burmese reign of terror, as saviours. During the initial years, there was confusion over the policy to be adopted for administering Assam.

The Burmese war was said to have 'added thirteen million to the India debt' and 'the territory taken from the Burmese in 1826 cost as much more'.[63] Coupled with the debts, there was an apprehension of loss in profits in trade with China — especially the monopoly on the trade — in the wake of reduction of the East India Company's power by the 'Charter of 1833'. The East India Company therefore insisted that the entire cost of British administration was to be henceforth borne out of the Indian revenues. As soon as Assam came under British occupation — in conformity with this policy —

63. Karl Marx, 'War in Burma', in Marx and Engels, *On Colonialism*, 1981, pp. 75–6.

David Scott began to investigate into the revenue possibilities of Assam. Scott's investigations revealed that under provisional administration the gross revenue yield of Lower Assam was about Rs 30,000.[64] The revenue yield was considered adequate for covering the administrative expense; therefore Lower Assam was annexed to British India in 1828.

Initially, Upper Assam was not annexed. A major reason assigned was that the revenue of the region was estimated at around Rs 1 lakh, which was just enough to meet the allowances of the Ahom royal family and the gentry. The population of Upper Assam did not exceed 300,000 of whom about 40,000 were *paiks* subjected to a capitation tax yielding a revenue of about 1,20,000 *Rajmohari* rupees — the depreciated Ahom currency.[65] Upper Assam was restored to the Ahom ruler Purandar Singha. Meanwhile, the British authorities set themselves on exploring about the wealth and resources of Assam. The fateful discovery of tea, prompted the British to discredit the native rule on grounds of mismanagement and justify the annexation of Upper Assam.[66]

The devastated Assamese economy had very little to offer to the British for exploitation. They turned their attention to land as a major source of public revenue. Immediately on the annexation of Lower Assam in April 1828, a regular survey and review of the former revenue measurements were taken up. David Scott was instrumental in introducing revenue payments in cash, replacing the hitherto system of payment in

64. Nirode K. Barooah, *David Scott in North-East India: A Study of British Paternalism, 1802–1831* (New Delhi, 1970), p. 103.
65. Barooah, *David Scott in North-East India*, p. 141.
66. Hiralal Gupta, 'An Unknown Factor in the Annexation of Assam', in *Proceedings of the Indian History Congress*, 22nd session (Gauhati, 1959), pp. 412–19.

labour service. This was the first step towards monetization of the economy of Assam.

He pitched the demand at about one-fourth of the rate of land revenue levied by the *zamindars* of Goalpara and of the adjoining company territories.[67] The areas in which revenue was assessed were Kamrup, Darrang, and Naduar, lands occupied by the Rajas of Dimarua, Beltola and Rani. In the district of Kamrup the principle followed by Scott in the settlement of land revenue, was to double the assessment on inalienable land.

The whole of Kamrup was divided into twenty-six *paraganas*, each in charge of *Chaudhuris* who were on the same footing as their counterparts in Bengal before the Decennial Settlement.[68] The *Chaudhuris* were not owners of land but official rent receivers, who drew their expenses from their collections. The hitherto rent-free religious grants of the *Devottar*, *Dharmottar*, and *Brahmottar* lands were brought under assessment.[69] They were assessed at a rate half of that levied on arable land. In Central Assam (Nowgong, Darrang and Raha) and Lower Assam, a tax of two rupees, called *gadhan* was imposed on each *paik* for their entitled three *puras* of arable land or *ga-mati*. The *kharikatana* or poll tax, introduced in Kamrup during the Burmese interlude was revived and extended to Nowgong and Darrang, and generally charged under different names and at varying rates.[70] House tax, which was first introduced by Raja Chandra Kanta Singha in Lower Assam, was continued.[71]

67. Barooah, *David Scott in North-East India*, p. 92.
68. Bengal Secret and Political Consultations, 1827, 5 April, no. 27, Scott to Swinton.
69. Barooah, *David Scott in North-East India*, p. 92.
70. Barpujari, *Assam in the Days of the Company*, pp. 28–30.
71. Barooah, *David Scott in North-East India*, p. 92.

In both the above-mentioned geographical divisions, professional tax was imposed on the braziers, silk-weavers, gold-
washers, fishermen, etc. Duties on *hats*, *ghats* and fisheries
continued to be levied as under the former government.[72] The
revenue in Upper Assam was principally raised from capitation tax; 'thus every *paik* is assessed at a rate of rupees three
per head'.[73] To expand the land revenue base further, Scott
resorted to reviving the Ahom Government's practice of levy-
ing a tax called *barangani*. This tax was levied only towards
the end of Ahom rule, on rent-free lands to cover emergency
expenses, when the state exceeded its ordinary receipts. The
barangani to be levied was to be between 6 to 8 annas on the
gross collection. In addition, the *paiks* were required to pay
six-and-a-half per cent to the *Chaudhuris* as *mufassil* expense,
one per cent to the treasurer for profit and loss, and half per
cent as commission.[74] Scott therefore levied taxes on every
source, which had ever been taxed either by the Ahoms or by
Mughals for augmenting land revenue. There was an insistence on payment of revenue in cash, replacing the earlier mode
of payment in labour-rent or kind.

The concept of taxation was completely alien to the peasants of Assam and was therefore wholly incomprehensible to
them. Settlements were made and taxes were levied without
taking into account the resources of the country, coupled with
the capability of the peasants. There was a massive drive towards monetization of the self-subsisting economy of Assam
and pushing it into a path of capitalistic development. As there
was very little money in circulation in the erstwhile Ahom

72. Barpujari, *Assam in the Days of the Company*, pp. 28–30.
73. Bengal Government Papers, file no. 298 of 1876, p. 62.
74. Cited in B.C. Allen, *Assam District Gazetteers*, Kamrup (Shillong
1905–1907), p. 39.

State, the peasants found it difficult to pay taxes in cash. Amalendu Guha noted, 'the collection of land revenue in cash created a severe strain on the hitherto money-short barter-oriented economy of Assam'.[75]

When the British took over the administration, the royal mint of the Ahom Rajah was put out of operation. For the convenience of peasants and for facilitating trade, the *Narayani*[76] currency, in circulation in Lower Assam was replaced by the East India Company's *Sicca* Rupees. The British-Indian currency did not flow into the area in sufficient quantities. Statistics on the external trade in the 1830s show an excess of exports over imports. This could barely retrieve the situation of money shortage in Assam, where trade was barter-oriented, with goods being exchanged for salt. The trade surplus which accrued, mostly went outside the province to the non-indigenous salt trader. The revenue collection in local currency was remitted to Calcutta for re-coinage. With practically no flow back of currency into Assam, their economy was faced with an acute money shortage.

Shortage of money in circulation resulted in circulation of spurious coins. Multiplicity of currency in circulation — *Rajmohari*, *Narayani*, *Ferracabad* and *Sicca* coins — with their fluctuating and conflicting exchange values further aggravated the crisis.[77] The peasants increasingly turned to the merchant-usurer to pay off their dues.

Changes in the land revenue system, particularly the large increase in the revenue demand and its method of collection

75. Guha, 'Medieval Economy of Assam', vol. I, p. 488.
76. The coin was originally minted by Maharaja Nara-Narayan of Koch Behar (1540–1584).
77. Amalendu Guha, 'Colonisation of Assam: Years of Transitional Crisis 1825–40', *IESHR*, June 1963, p. 131.

had a negative effect on agriculture. The revenue demand between 1824–25 and 1849–50 was said to have increased by a drastic 480.72 per cent.[78] A negligible portion of the revenue came from confiscated estates of the nobility and rent-free land reclaimed from the spiritual aristocracy. A bulk of the revenue came from the large increase in land revenue demand.[79] The peasants suffered from improper taxation by the *Chaudhuris*, as well as by their insistence on reclamation of wastelands by the peasant. This resulted in large-scale migration of peasants from old locations to wastelands in remote areas, to evade taxation, and a consequent stagnation in cultivation followed. The British administrators justified this heavy assessment on ordinary cultivation, on the grounds that, 'if ordinary cultivation was heavily taxed, the ryots would be forced to leave their farms to work for the cash crop oriented capitalist farmer'.[80] No attempt was made to improve agriculture on scientific lines. The peasants had to remain content with poor breeds of cattle, lack of manure and irrigation, ignorance of potential cash crops, absence of multiple cropping and paucity of food grains.

Large tracts of wastelands were a prominent feature of the landscape in Assam. In an attempt to broaden the tax base and secure an influx of much needed capital, a generous policy for grants of wastelands was envisaged. Preliminary surveys undertaken by Captain Mathews in 1827, showed that in Lower Assam, of the 1,659,694 *puras*, 529,735 *puras* were cultivated,

---

78. B. Chaudhuri, 'Agrarian Relations: Eastern India', in Dharma Kumar and Meghnad Desai (eds), *The Cambridge Economic History of India: 1757–1970*, vol. II (Cambridge, 1983), p. 120.

79. To cite an instance, in Kamrup between 1828 and 1852–53, the rate of revenue on land under wet rice cultivation per *pura* had increased by 25 per cent and that on highland by 75 per cent.

80. Guha in *Medieval and Early Colonial Assam*, p. 149.

with the rest being wastelands.[81] Under the Ahom monarchy, the high officials were remunerated by grants of wastelands or *khats* at nominal rates of revenue. Scott outlined the conditions for encouraging settlement on wastelands. However, he did not live long enough to implement them, but they became the basis of the future wasteland grants later. The terms were:

i) That the grantee bring one-fourth of his allocation in cultivation by the expiration of the third year; an additional fourth on the expiration of the sixth year; another fourth on the expiration of the ninth year; after that period that grantee should be entitled to hold land in perpetuity on paying the *pargana* rates upon three-fourth of the whole.

ii) That the tenure created should be liable to be transferred by sale or otherwise, subject to the condition of the grant, and that where the revenue ultimately assessable amounted to fifty rupees or more or the holder voluntarily agreed to make it up that sum, he should be entitled to pay it directly into the public treasury.

iii) That the applicants for land on the above terms should be required to deposit or give security for the first two years of revenue, to be forfeited to government and the land resumed if the terms were not complied with on the expiration of the fourth year after which the land holding should be liable to sale for arrears for revenue in the usual manner.[82]

Scott insisted that the speculators should be allowed a free hand in choosing any crop of their choice. He felt that the wastelands could be effectively utilized for production of

81. A.J.M. Mills, Appendix 'A', 'Statistics of Assam, 1853', *Report on the Province of Assam* (Gauhati, 1984, 2d ed.), p. 56.
82. Barooah, *David Scott in North-East India*, p. 104.

commercially viable commodities like opium, *muga* and mulberry, which was already cultivated in individual households all over Assam.

T.C. Robertson (1832–34), who succeeded David Scott, formalized the wasteland rules conceived by Scott. As per the formulation, occupants of the grants were allowed to hold land rent-free for a period of three years. A graduated system of taxation was introduced. According to its provisions land tax was to be paid at the end of three years and subsequent three years, until the end of a ten-year span. At end of the tenth year, the land was liable to be assessed at full rates. Failure of the occupants to cultivate wastelands empowered the government to resume these grants.[83]

The stipulations of the grant could not attract wasteland settlement on a large scale, nor yield revenue. There was scope of land being occupied and abandoned before it was assessed at full rates. This was because the existence of unlimited wastes permitted the occupants to shift their holdings and evade taxation at full rates. The duration of the grants was too short to allow the grantee to improve the condition of their estates.

Jenkins, a true representative of the new school of industrial capitalists, devised and executed a policy for maximum utilization of wastelands. He set upon himself the task of gathering systematic data on wastelands and their agricultural potential. Information was drawn from the District Officers, on the extent of the wastelands and their commercial prospects. In the district of Goalpara, the available wastelands were found suitable for cultivation of indigo.[84] Its cultivation had however been restricted by the orders of the government,

83. Barpujari, *Assam in the Days of the Company*, p. 235.
84. Letters issued to Government, vol. no. 14, 1846–48, no. 73 of 27 March 1846, para 7.

while cultivation of mustard was permitted. In Kamrup, the inundated wastelands were considered unfit for commercial cultivation on a large scale. On the other hand, 'Darrang, Nowgong, Sibsagar and Lakhimpur divisions had the best tracts of wastelands adapted for the culture of sugar cane and offered many superior advantages.'[85]

Jenkins was very much in favour of encouraging Europeans and Americans to hold land in Assam, as the natives neither had the capital nor the required manpower to utilize the wastelands profitably. He hoped that, 'their settlement would be attended with the most beneficial effects in hastening development of the resources of this highly fertile tract and improving its communication with the vast countries immediately beyond to the North and the East.'[86]

The discovery of tea and the prospects of its successful culture in the soil of Assam provided the final thrust for formulating the policy on wastelands. The East India Company's activities in China centred on the monopoly in tea trade. In the eighteenth century, tea was one of the major items of trade, as it had a ready market in Europe and America. The rigid closed-door policy adopted by the Chinese and the consequent strained relationship between the Government of China and the East India Company led them to desperately search for alternate sources of tea. In 1823, the discovery of tea in Assam opened a new avenue for the East India Company. An important feature of the 'Charter of 1833' was that Englishmen were permitted to acquire land in India on a large scale on long-term leases or freehold rights to set up plantations in India.[87] Tea

85. Letters issued to Government, vol. no. 2, 1835, no. 46 of 3 June 1835, para 1.

86. Ibid.

87. Rajani Palme Dutt, *India Today* (1st ed., 1940, reprinted, April 1986, Calcutta.), p. 124.

was therefore a deciding factor in the final annexation of Assam, apart from the often-cited 'strategic factor'.

A Tea Committee was appointed in 1834 to ascertain the practicability of growing tea in India — at the foothills of the Himalayas, the Nilgiris and the valleys and slopes of the North-Eastern Frontier.[88] In response to the encouraging report of the Tea Committee, a government sponsored experimental tea garden was started in 1836. In December 1837, the first successful manufacture of 'Assam Tea' took place. The experiment was deemed to be successful after two successive seasons of steady production. The government decided to encourage private enterprise in tea cultivation. The 'tea factor' made Jenkins' 'scheme of colonization of wastelands' acceptable and the policy received its final shape.[89]

The Board of Revenue in consultation with the Commissioner of Assam submitted a detailed scheme with slight variations of the Sunderbans Grants to the Bengal Government. In 1836, the Government of Bengal approved the scheme and gave Assam the first set of wasteland rules. The earlier efforts of Scott and Robertson had not been implemented successfully.

In this scheme the wastelands were broadly divided into three categories: (a) forest lands; (b) reed and grass wastes and (c) grasslands amongst cultivated lands. Of these, the first category was to be allowed to be rent-free for five years, and the third, for twenty-one years. For four years subsequent to the rent-free period, a graduated manner of assessment was to

88. Letters issued to Government, vol. no. 2, 1835, no. 46 of 3 June 1835, para 1.

89. Here it is necessary to mention that the first set of rules for granting wastelands in India was applied in Gorruckpore [*sic*] District. These set of rules were used for making similar grants in the Sundarbans. The Gorruckpore Rules were the basis of all wasteland grants over the rest of India.

be introduced, from 8 annas per *pura* to Re 1–8–0 per *pura* for twenty-one years from the ninth, fourteenth and twenty-fourth year, respectively, for each category of land. From the twenty-first year of the grant, lands were to be assessed at full rates till the end of the total grant period of thirty, thirty-five and forty years on all three categories.[90] The wasteland rules were revised in 1854. Although these rules did not discriminate openly against non-indigenous inhabitants, apparently they had been framed to exclude them from any concessional grants. An applicant in possession of capital worth Rs 3 per acre was allowed to occupy the grant, with a minimum limit being fixed at 100 acres.[91]

The rules thus permitted only Europeans to avail such concessions. The industrial capitalists had their policy for India clearly defined to make India an agricultural colony, supplying raw materials and a market for buying manufactured goods. To enhance production and export of raw materials from India, modernization of agriculture was imperative. In Assam too, Jenkins sought to commercialize agriculture. In a letter to the Sudder Board, he emphasized on the need for commercialization in agriculture, for enhancing the trade potential of the province as well as to augment the land revenue base, by taxing areas under specialized crops. He believed that it would enhance the paying capacity of the peasants. Increased cultivation of easily marketable crops would also create a class of speculators who could be instrumental in exploiting the natural resources of Assam. In 1836, he expressed his desire to convert 'these wastes and haunt of wild beasts into fruitful fields of sugar cane, mustard, mulberry, lac, tobacco and vegetables.'[92]

90. Barpujari, *Assam in the Days of the Company*, p. 236.
91. Guha in *Medieval and Early Colonial Assam*, p. 154.
92. Bengal Political Consultations, 10 July 1836, no. 84.

The earliest instance of trade between the mercantilist East India Company with Assam dates back to 1765, when Clive formed the 'Society of Trade', permitting the Company's officials to carry out internal trade in 'salt, betel nut and tobacco'.[93] The 'Society' was short-lived and ceased to exist in August 1768, when an exclusive monopoly was created for Europeans, infringing upon the natural rights of the local merchants. Several attempts were made in subsequent years to revive the trade, but the fluid political situation acted as a deterrent for such ventures. Captain Welsh was despatched to quell an internal rebellion within the kingdom, in response to the Ahom ruler Gaurinath Singha's appeal to the British administrators in Bengal. The British capitalized on the opportunity and strove to promote trade ties with Assam. They were keen on recovering the expenses incurred on the expedition.

The agency and the officials appointed by the Ahoms at the trade outpost at Kandhar had become a centre of corruption. The officials (*Duara-Baruas*) colluded with corrupt ministers, monopolizing the entire trade, thus depriving the government of a large share of its lawful revenue. The *Baruas* virtually monopolized the Bengal–Assam trade in salt. Captain Welsh was impressed by the volume of the salt trade and sought to monopolize the trade. Consequently, a commercial treaty was signed establishing 'a reciprocal and entire liberty of commerce between the subjects of Bengal and those of Assam for all singular goods and merchandises'.[94]

It stipulated that all imports and exports were to be

93. A.C. Banerjee, 'The East-India Company and Assam', in H.K. Barpujari (ed.), *The Comprehensive History of Assam*, vol. ii (Gauhati, 1992), p. 302.

94. C.U. Aitchinson, *A Collection of Treaties, Engagements and Sanads relating to India and Neighbouring Countries*, vol. xii, part ii (Calcutta, 1929), p. 134.

subjected to a duty of ten per cent. Two custom-houses, one at the existing entrepôt — Kandhar and the other at Gauhati were established. Agents were authorized to keep twelve per cent of their collections. The expected turnover was estimated at over one lakh rupees, after deducting the agents' commission and a payment of Rs 26,000 to the Ahom monarch. The rest was credited to the British treasury. British subjects were free to trade in commodities other than salt all over Assam, on payment of a duty at the rate of ten per cent. Permanent residency in Assam however was not granted to European merchants.[95] The broad guidelines for trade were rendered ineffective in the aftermath of the withdrawal of the military detachment under Welsh. Three decades of political instability subsequently, virtually led to a total cessation of trade.

The annexation of Assam in the aftermath of the Burmese war, and restoration of administration, created an ideal political environment, which boosted trade within and outside the province. Restoring the frontier *hats*, the centres of trade, revived trade with the neighbouring hill tribes, which had ceased. These *hats* in course of time became centres for collection of raw materials for export, primarily of forest products, and also distribution centres for British machine-made goods. These foothill markets were also a source of revenue. *Hats* — which the tribes frequented to exchange their produce for salt — came to be used as an instrument to exert political power. They were closed in instances of recalcitrance amongst the tribes. This measure of economic blockade helped in keeping the tribes under control and maintaining British paramountcy.

Frontier trade in the province of Assam under changed

95. Aitchinson, *A Collection of Treaties, Engagements and Sanads*, pp. 112–15.

political conditions became an exclusive domain of Marwaris. They came in as a class seeking avenues for trade, and in the absence of a local trading class, soon gained a foothold over the entire gamut of trading activities. At the frontier *hats* they exchanged salt, opium, tobacco, betel nut, and machine-made clothes for gold dust, ivory, amber, musk, *daos*, Burmese cloth, Chinese silk and other Chinese wares. They also received forest products like lac, rubber and cotton from the hills.

The volume and content of Assam's extra-territorial trade with Bengal in the early part of the nineteenth century is available from the survey of Buchanan-Hamilton. In the immediate aftermath of annexation, the custom duties payable at the Kandhar *Chauki* were retained and brought under direct control. Duties levied earlier were continued. The situation was altered with the renewal of the 'Charter of 1833', which permitted free trade and destroyed the monopoly of the East India Company. Accordingly, in 1835 the Kandhar and all other *Chaukis* in and around Goalpara were abolished. Customs tariffs had a devastating effect on the native merchants.

CONCLUSION

The Ahoms held sway over Assam for six centuries preceding British rule. At the outset they encountered several tribal formations like the Chutiya and Kachari kingdoms, and a large number of petty non-tribal and armed land controllers (*Bhuyan/Bhaumik*) — the latter mostly concentrated in the central and western part of erstwhile Kamrup.[96] The powerful Chutiya kingdom was absorbed; the Kachari Kingdom was pushed back; the westward thrust was into the land of the *Bhuyans*, while the *Morans* and *Barahis* were assimilated into

96. Guha, 'Medieval Economy of Assam', p. 478.

their fold. The Kingdom reached its zenith at the close of the seventeenth century. Simultaneously, along with the Ahom expansion in the early sixteenth century, certain other tribal state formations like the Koches and Jaintias emerged. The structure of the Ahom polity was quasi-feudalistic with a largely tribal base.

A dominant feature of the economy was the role of the Ahoms in altering and improving the rice economy. Traditionally, the tribes living in Assam practised dry cultivation. It was superseded under the Ahoms by wet rice cultivation for which marshes were converted into fields on the basis of their prior experience. Innovations like use of superior iron implements, buffalo power and knowledge of the techniques of gravitational irrigation, for sloping sub-montane tracts equipped them for the task. The flourishing rice economy, sustained the Ahom state over the centuries during its political expansion. The economy was sustained by collective effort, institutionalized by a militia, which was intrinsically integrated into the economy and formed the core of its defence system.

Theoretically, all land belonged to the king, whether cultivated or waste. He assigned land both to the nobility and the freemen or individual *paiks* in lieu of their services to the state. Land grants were made for religious purposes along with servitors. The pyramidal social structure that emerged was stratified with the king at the apex of the pyramid. The privileged aristocracy — both spiritual and secular — formed the middle rung. The large peasantry and the several classes consisting of slaves, serfs and bondsmen formed the lowest rung. The first two were the unproductive class, with the last two being direct producers. In general, the caste rules were less — rigorous, specialized, elaborate and inhibiting.

The growth of Vaishnavism with its mass appeal had its

impact on the existing social order. Monasteries and religious preceptors became centres of power and practically ran parallel governments which threatened the very foundations of the weakened Ahom monarchy. The Ahom monarchy faced with both internal and external crises sought British aid, which was short-lived. Unable to tackle the crises, the weakened puppet monarchs invoked Burmese assistance. This was the last nail in the coffin of the Ahom kingdom. The Burmese stayed and unleashed a reign of terror for six successive years, having a devastating effect on Assam.

The British in order to save their dominions in Bengal from Burmese expansion as well as to exploit its natural resources intervened and freed Assam from the clutches of the Burmese in 1824. The colonialists inherited a depopulated and ravaged area. They brought in changes in administration and economic polices, which uprooted the existing social formation. The imposition of capitalism on a quasi-tribal, quasi-feudal society resulted in the disintegration of the existing social order.

The absorption of Assam into the British Indian Territory was achieved in a phased manner. Lower Assam, with a substantial revenue was politically annexed in 1826 and Upper Assam was resumed back to the old monarchy. The fateful discovery of tea was instrumental in the final annexation of Upper Assam in 1838.

The system of collecting land revenue was changed. The tax base was widened with the inclusion of other sources. Wasteland grants were awarded with the thrust on inducing peasants to cultivate cash crops. The plantation industry took its roots in the province. The barter-oriented economy was transformed into a monetized economy, and efforts were made to expand trade and commerce.

Increase in trade and more so the growth of the tea industry made it imperative to link Assam with world markets. A vital requirement was improvement in communications by land and water. Major Adam White, the Political Agent of Assam in 1835, in a letter to the Commissioner of Assam attributed the languishing condition of the trade to the lack of an efficient network of communication. He states:

> which if expended in improving the land communication between Rangpur (Bengal), Sylhet, Cachar and Gauhati would have opened a channel for the influx of trade and population that would have effected a wonderful change in the production of this province.[97]

97. Bengal Government Papers, file no. 298 of 1836, p. 105.

2
Pre-Railways
Transport and Communication —
Roadways and Waterways

The 'Charter Act of 1833' marked the transfer of economic power from the monopolistic East India Company to the Crown. Deprived of its major role in foreign trade, the East India Company was willing to finance ventures for export-oriented products, in order to ensure regular remittances to London. Liberal wasteland grants devised by the representative of the East India Company in Assam facilitated large-scale investment in India's plantation industry, which had taken roots in Assam, and was a major sector for the investment of European capital.

The efforts of the colonialists in transforming the subsisting agrarian economy of Assam, into an export-oriented economy was achieved by 1840, though on a limited scale. To set the economy on the path of capitalistic development, the colonialists sought to link Assam with world markets to maximize their benefits. A major bottleneck in exporting the agricultural produce from the province was the absence of a reliable means of transporting bulk goods.

Captain Jenkins — the initiator of the major economic policies of Assam — realized that unless communications, both by land and water, were effectively developed, trade as well as the all round development of the province would be hampered. In a letter to A.J.M. Mills in 1853, he emphasized the need for improved communications:

> The measure for accelerating the progress of the Province. . . .
> A systematic improvement of the main roads is one of the obvious means we have. . . . A great obstacle now to the clearing of wastes is the want of communication between these tracts and the cultivated districts. . . . The outlay on the roads, if the works be regularly conducted and permanently established and be not again allowed to fall to disrepair, will as certainly be returned to Government by increase in revenue. . . . The people cannot [live] amongst wastes that are cut off from all communication with the present villages, but wherever the jungles are opened out, colonization does and will take place.[1]

A relative degree of political stability had set in by 1840. The five undivided plain districts of Assam proper — Kamrup, Darrang, Goalpara, Nowgong and Cachar, had come under direct British administration. The neighbouring hill areas of the Khasis and Jaintias were brought under British administration in the years 1833 and 1835 respectively. The hill tribes beyond the Sadiya and the Naga frontier had to be effectively controlled.

1. Mills, *Report on the Province of Assam*, Appendix 'B', no. 275 of 1853, from Colonel Jenkins to A.J. Moffat Mills, para 2.

David Scott as early as 1826, had entered into formal agreements with the chiefs of the frontier tribes, who accepted British suzerainty. They also undertook to abjure future relations with either the Burmese or any other foreign power.[2] In order to secure the confidence of the tribes the British ensured them a supply of rice and other necessities. A Political Agent was appointed in Upper Assam, for exclusively managing relations with the frontier tribes. With the annexation of Upper Assam in 1839, the headquarters of the Assam Light Infantry was shifted from Bishenath [*sic*] to Sadiya. The Khamptis attacked the cantonment within three days of the shifting of troops, which revealed the vulnerability of the North-East Frontier. The urgent need for improving lines of communication for strategic purposes was realized.

The initial thrust of the British, after the annexation of Assam, was on maximizing land revenue by increasing it manifold. The desired result not being achieved, the industrial capitalists were desirous of commercializing agriculture to make it export-oriented. The authorities in Bengal instructed the government in Assam to encourage cultivation of cash crops, particularly opium, which was grown commonly in homesteads. By encouraging cultivation of cash crops, it sought to create a class of speculators to exploit the natural resources of Assam. The results of the efforts are visible from Table I, the export returns of 1852–53 on selected items.

The table shows an increase in the export of commodities like mustard, silk, lac and cotton. Rice did not feature as an export item except in Lakhimpur. New items like jute and *til* appeared in the trade statistics.

---

2. Barooah, *David Scott in North-East India*, p. 119.

TABLE I: Exports from Assam on Selected Items, 1852–1853[3]

Commodities	Goalpara (1852)		Lakhimpur (1852)		Sibsagar (1852)	
	Qty (Mds)	Value (Rs)	Qty (Mds)	Value (Rs)	Qty (Mds)	Value (Rs)
Lac	7,000	36,750	–	–	–	–
Muga Silk	600	2,622	385	51,850	315	50,400
Mustard Seed	400,000	824,000	7,000	6,000	17,000	17,000
Cotton	50,000	175,000	600	1,800	12,609	36,500
Ivory	100	18,750	25	3,750	17	2,550
Rice	–	–	4,250	3,378	–	–
Jute	20,000	20,000	–	–	–	–
Silk Cloth	4,000 pieces	16,000	1,050 pieces	1,050	–	–
Rhino Horns	7	1,680	4.5	2,000	1.5	600
Munjeet	2,500	9,375	500	8,000	–	–
Wax	300	82,500	100	2,500	12	240

An Indian maund, which was the standard of weight in British India was equal to 82⅔ lbs avoirdupois or 40 *seers*.

ROADWAYS

As early as 1835, Major White the Political Agent of Upper Assam in a letter to Captain Jenkins, urged that improved communication was an essential prerequisite for the expanding volume of trade:

> improving land communications between Rangpur (Bengal), Sylhet, Cachar and Gauhati would have opened a channel for the influx of trade and population that would soon have effected a wonderful change in the condition of this province.[4]

3. Mills, *Report on the Province of Assam*.
4. Bengal Government Papers, file no. 298 of 1836, p. 105.

As mentioned in the earlier chapter, there was a considerable increase in produce coming from the hills, which was facilitated by a network of foothill markets. Items like cotton, lac, rubber and *munjeet* came to feature as important export items from Assam. To extract the maximum benefit from the hill trade, it became imperative to maintain and construct new roads in and around the markets. Strategic needs, as well as the pulls of external markets provided the thrust for rebuilding and expanding the existing road network in Assam.

Early Roadways

Assam's earliest commercial relations with the outside world were with the province of Bengal. From very early times it was maintained through the river Brahmaputra, M'Cosh mentions of the existence of three overland routes to Bengal:

> The first was via Murshidabad, Malda, Dinajpore, Rangpore, [sic] Bugwah and Goalpara . . . the second road was via Dacca, Dumary, Pacualoes [sic], Jumalpore, Singimari and Goalpara. The third via Sylhet, Cherra, Mophlung, Nung-khlow, Ranigodown, Canneeymookh and Gauhati . . . [5]

Internal communication within Assam was maintained through an excellent network of roads built by Ahom kings as well as the Koch kings. As M'Cosh writes:

> Very few provinces in India have been provided with such a splendid system of public roads as in Assam and from the great highways, which were carried uninterruptedly through the whole country to the great crossroads, between the principal towns and their minute ramification, which connected the villages.[6]

5. M'Cosh, *Topography of Assam*, pp. 8–9.
6. The brother of the great Koch King Nara-Narayan, after whom the road was named, constructed the *Gosain Kamal Ali*. It extended from Sadiya

However, these roads had been sadly neglected for over half a century. Most of them being over-grown with jungles became useless. They were primarily road-cum-embankments, constructed through the collective effort of the huge militia of freemen or *paiks*. Of the roads constructed in the medieval period, special mention may be made of the *Gosain Kamal Ali*, *Dhodar Ali*, *Dhai Ali* and the *Bar-Baruah Ali*.[7]

Public Works — Genesis

There was no separate Department of Public Works in India till 1854. There was a Military Board in each Presidency for constructing and maintaining public works, which functioned as a supervisory body. This sufficed, because the bulk of the expenditure — though insignificant in volume — was on account of military works. A separate Public Works Department was set up during Lord Dalhousie's administration in 1854.[8] With the removal of public works from the control of the Military Board, more attention was paid to 'Civil Works' — civil buildings, roads, establishments, canals and irrigation works. The funds available for public works development were a mere 60 lakh rupees in 1849–50, which rose to nearly Rs 2.25 crores in 1856–57.[9] Thus the East India Company, which had neglected public works for almost the entire period of its tenure in India, suddenly showed a spurt of activity in the last three to four years of its existence. They practically treated India like

---

to Koch Behar, a distance of 350 miles. The *Bangal Ali* stretched from North-East Darrang to North Gauhati. The *Dhodar Ali* was in the southern portion of the Sibsagar district and the *Dhai Ali* was from Rangpur to Jaipore.

7. Sabyasachi Bhattacharjee, *Financial Foundations of the British Raj* (Shimla, 1971), p. 114.

8. Ibid.

9. Ibid.

an oriental despot, as an area to be exploited and not to be developed.

In Assam too, road building was initially vested with the Military Board. In 1835, by an order of the Supreme Government, all public works in Assam were assigned to an Executive Officer operating from Dacca. Captain Jenkins was concerned about the delays and difficulties of operating with the officer stationed outside Assam. He suggested the employment of a European overseer in Assam.[10]

Accordingly, in 1836, the Military Board appointed J.N. Martin of the Iron Bridge Department as a Supervisor of Public Works in Assam.[11] The administration in Assam pressurized the Military Board to appoint Martin as an Executive Officer of Lower Assam. The Military Board had their reservations in appointing him, as he was not professionally qualified. Finally, in 1840, a Division of Public Works was created with Lieutenant Spilta as the Executive Engineer for Upper Assam, under the Chief Engineer, Lower Provinces, stationed in Bengal. J.N. Martin was appointed as an Executive Officer, Lower Assam, subordinated to the Executive Engineer.[12] It was from this period that road building received proper attention.

Working

The major problem encountered by the authorities in maintaining the roads was the rapid growth of jungles that often obliterated them. To tackle this situation in 1848, the Military Board ordered:

That all *Kutcha* roads should be in charge of and repaired by

10. Bengal Judicial Consultations (Criminal), 1836, 14 June, nos. 46–47; 12 July, nos. 58–59.
11. Ibid.
12. Bengal Judicial Consultations (Criminal), 1838, 7 August, no. 106.

the local authorities . . . that where assistance was required to mark out any particular line of road or report, upon the efficiency of any work executed, a requisition might be made on the Executive Officer who should be instructed to attend it.[13]

This order resulted in a certain degree of decentralization in the matter of public works. Decentralization was prompted not only for reasons of difficulty in maintenance of roads but also by the lack of a regular outlay of funds for the purpose. The measure of transferring all *kutcha* (unmetalled) roads to local authorities, was on the consideration that they were better informed about local needs and were also in a position to acquire local assistance in the form of land grants, labour and revenue. Decentralization in management continued even after the formation of the Public Works Department (PWD) for the country. In 1859, by an order, the Governor General in Council, declared that:

> in Assam the Public Works Department has the charge of the Trunk and Military roads . . . that all the other roads are local roads to be kept up by the local civil officers, not as a temporary measure, but as a permanent arrangement approved by the Government of India.[14]

Finance

A study of the working of public works in Assam would be incomplete without understanding the dynamics of its financial management. In Assam, the government was not in a position to utilize the revenue of the province for local improvements.

13. Letters received from Government, vol. no. 37, no. 8902 of 28 March 1848.
    14. Letters received from Government, vol. no. 44, 1859–1864, no. 931 of 3 March 1862.

Therefore, civil authorities in each district were authorized to utilize the money from the 'Ferry Funds' of their respective districts. The ferries in each district were managed by the government, and were farmed out to the highest bidder.

The annual revenue yield from the ferry funds varied between Rs 5 and Rs 70. These funds were managed by the magistrate who had to submit his proposal for expenditure to the government through the Deputy Commissioner.[15] The demands on the public revenue for works of imperial interest were so heavy and the means of meeting these demands from revenues so limited, that the government insisted that 'the wants of the smaller sections of the society should as far as possible be provided from local sources'.[16]

The government as a measure of raising funds encouraged public subscriptions. It was generally found that works undertaken by public money were not thoroughly executed by the government officers. The public too, after having paid the money, showed no interest in its execution, which resulted in misuse of funds. Strictures were therefore issued to treat such subscriptions as 'grant in-aid' and used only in case of non-availability of funds. In Upper Assam, many old and minor roads were cleared of jungles and repaired with the help of tea planters in the immediate vicinity of their gardens. W.O.A. Beckett, the Deputy Commissioner of Sibsagar aptly describes the role of the planters:

> I cannot conclude without bearing testimony to the very efficient aid, I have received from the Tea planters of the district in the repair of roads in their vicinity, they have cheerfully given their time and trouble to the work which has

15. Mills, *Report on the Province of Assam*, Goalpara, para 49, p. 13.
16. Letters received from Government, vol. 42, 1857, circular no. 3858 of 7 August 1857.

been done by them much better than I could have possibly hoped to do it, without their valuable assistance.[17]

Paucity of funds was a constant hindrance for local improvements. Attempts were made to meet the resource crunch by tapping other sources. Henry Hopkinson, the Commissioner of Assam, proposed doubling the land tax in 1861, so as to devote the excess so obtained, for works of public utility. The Board of Revenue did not consider it expedient to double the land tax.[18] Earlier Jenkins had made a similar proposal for a reasonable raise in land tax and 'to provide out of the local revenue for the general construction and periodical repair of Roads and Bridges of the Province'.[19] He emphasized the necessity of a 'good road through the Province' to promote general progress and attributed the failure in achieving the goal to:

> the extension of new works of absolute necessity is protracted while they are probably owing, in some measure to the absence of proper superintendence, are doubtless, in a great degree, attributable to the absence of independent funds of sufficient amount to cover the outlay which such works require.[20]

The Revenue Board extended the provisions of the Government Order No. 1847, of 28 July 1859, sanctioning 'the appropriation of 3 per cent on the collections to purposes of local improvements'.[21] In 1862, by an order of the Secretary of

17. Cooch Bihar Commissioner's Office, 1862, file no. 421, no. 166 of 19 May 1862.
18. Bengal Government Papers, 1861, file no. 388, nos. 1–6, no. 494, dated 6 July 1861.
19. Bengal Government Papers, 1861, file no. 388, nos. 1–6, dated 16 July, 1861.
20. Ibid.
21. Bengal Government Papers, 1861, file no. 388, nos. 1–6, no. 494, dated 6 July 1861.

Bengal, the government permitted the use of 'the surplus proceeds of 1 per cent on the Income Tax Collection'.[22] The creation of a full-fledged Public Works Department for Assam in 1868 ensured financial stability and streamlined its working. Further, Act X of 1877 levied a District Road Cess on all immovable property within the district, for raising funds for construction and maintenance of roads. It also provided for the constitution of Local District Committees' for the assessment and management of the road cess.[23] The Act was extended to all the plains districts of Kamrup, Darrang, Sibsagar, Nowgong and Lakhimpur. The funds for the Trunk roads and Military Roads were drawn from the imperial funds.

Construction

The basic criterion for choosing road alignments during the early years of British rule was military feasibility, for providing speedy troop movement, in the case of resumed Burmese attacks as well as in the case of incursions of the frontier tribes. The initial thrust therefore was on restoring 'portions of the great roads of Upper Assam'.[24] In 1840, alarming reports of Burmese attempts to open a road through the Naga Hills from the Kyendween [*sic*] river, made it essential to improve the line of communication between the Muttock country and the troops reserve at Sibsagar.[25] Repairs were undertaken on the *Bar-Baruah Ali*, the high road from Sibsagar towards Dibrugarh through Chokey Hat on the Buri Dehing. A portion of

22. Letters received from Government, vol. no. 44 (d), January 1859–1864, no. 931, 3 March 1862.
23. Bengal Government Papers, file no. 42/50 of 1873.
24. Letters issued to Government, vol. no. 9, January–September 1840, no. 23, 28 January 1840.
25. Letters issued to Government, vol. no. 9, January–September 1840, no. 85, 4 May 1840.

the high roads between Jaipore and Sibsagar was opened. This
road was to be:

> of great political importance, as affording the means of
> moving troops and of controlling the Nagas as well as highly
> valuable as one of the roads of internal communication on a
> line, by which much traffic in salt is conveyed.[26]

Repairs were undertaken on the road from Dibrugarh to
Saikwah [*sic*] and Jaipore to 'facilitate movement of the Assam
Light Infantry which has to guard the extensive frontier'.[27] The
Bund road from Sibsagar to Dikhu-mookh, according to
Jenkins, was of 'highest utility in a military and political view'.[28]
Captain Butler, the Principal Assistant of Nowgong, in a letter
to Jenkins urged the opening of two separate roads along the
frontier of the district in view of the operations against the
Nagas. The first alignment was to be from Nowgong via Samu-
guting to Dimapur, the other from Golaghat to Dimapur.[29] To
complete the line of communication along the frontier posts, a
road was constructed between Dum-duma [*sic*] and Makoom
[*sic*].[30] A small stretch of road between Golaghat and Nagorah
was opened, as it was 'much frequented by the Angami Nagas
and our traders and troops'.[31]

These military roads were unmetalled in most cases, which
were cleared, and repaired, just enough to enable the passage

26. Letters issued to Government, vol. no. 9, January–September 1840,
no. 147, 28 August 1840.

27. Letters issued to Government, vol. no. 10, no. 131, 9 March 1852.

28. Bengal Judicial Consultations (Criminal), no. 40, 19 September
1842.

29. Letters issued to Government, vol. no. 15, no. 112, 21 September
1850.

30. Letters issued to Government, vol. no. 15, no. 152, 28 November
1850.

31. Ibid.

of troops and elephants. These roads, because of their temporary nature, had to be constantly repaired. As the political situation gradually stabilized, roads for purely military purposes were rarely constructed.

The tea industry around which all the later developmental activities in Assam centred, played a crucial role in the growth and development of roadways:

> As early as 1845, the Assam Company claimed with some exaggeration, that it had opened or repaired some 1,280 kilometres of public road, had erected 266 bridges and established several ferries across the rivers.[32]

It is claimed that during the first two to three decades of its existence, the tea industry solely depended on its own efforts for improvements of roads. The condition of roads in Cachar hampered the growth of the tea industry, therefore the owners of the tea gardens contributed liberally towards road building both with men and material.[33] The roads mostly linked the gardens to landing places on the Brahmaputra, as well as to the steamers, wherefrom country boats to Calcutta shipped their produce. Roads linking the gardens with their neighbouring villages, 'materially improves [*sic*] the condition of imported labourers and affords [*sic*] the cultivators increased facilities for disposing off the produce of their lands'.[34]

The government too put in its effort to open branch roads from the main line of the tea gardens to the landing places (*ghats*) on the Brahmaputra. In the district of Sibsagar, portions of the *Dhai Ali* between Sibsagar to Buri Dihing Mookh;

32. Guha, 'The Geography Behind the History', p. 160.
33. *Report of the Commissioners appointed to Enquire into the State and Prospects of Tea Cultivation in Assam, Cachar and Sylhet: 1868*, p. 100.
34. *Report of the Commissioners . . . : 1868*, p. 101.

Barpatra Gohain Ali from Sibsagar to Disang, and the *Sologuri Ali* from Disang to Buri-Dehing were constructed.[35]

The government emphasized the need for road building in the hills, to establish markets and develop them, as 'roads and markets ought very speedily to create a social revolution in the hills'.[36] A road was constructed between Udalguri in the Kureaparah Doar [sic] and Mangaldoi [sic] on the banks of the Brahmaputra, with the object of 'inducing the Bhutias to come down to Mangaldoi [sic] for the annual fair'.[37] A road was opened from Goalpara to the eastern *hats* of Jirah, Damrah and Nibari. It was of great importance to the merchants of Goalpara as there was a large trade in cotton.[38]

As early as 1835, apart from repairing portions of the old *bund* roads for purely military purposes, restoration work to complete the old roads to the fullest extent was to facilitate the passage for carriages and ' . . . to reclaim wastes along their route and thus are long [sic] to repay largely the money expended'.[39] The principal roads in the well-populated parts of Kamroop [sic] were repaired. The repair of the great western road, connecting Gauhati to Goalpara and from there to Bengal was taken up. The *Gosain Kamal Ali* was restored between Manas and Bur-Nadi. The high *bund* road extending from Gauhati through East Dimarua to Raha, across the Kullung along its right bank crossing Nowgong, continuing

35. Mills, *Report on the Province of Assam*, Appendix F-1–23, 'List of Principal Roads in Sibsagar District'.

36. Bengal Government Papers, no. 1–3, file no. 15/18 (1873), cf. S.B. Medhi, *Transport System and Economic Development in Assam* (Guwahati, 1975), p. 42.

37. Letters issued to Government, vol. no. 16, no. 320, 10 August 1852.

38. Goalpara Papers 1873, file no. 981, serial no. 122, 28 February 1873.

39. Bengal Judicial Consultations (Criminal), no. 3, 13 October 1835.

upto Jorhat and Sibsagar was restored.[40] A major portion of the repair was undertaken with the help of the local populace, with the government providing funds for the restoration of bridges. However, the restoration was of a temporary nature, and thus the whole effort failed.

Apart from the necessity of improving the internal lines of communication, Jenkins in his scheme of colonization emphasized on the opening up of roads to the neighbouring populous districts of Rangpore [sic], Mymensingh and Sylhet. These roads were supposed to facilitate trade and ensure that 'some of the overflowing population of three neighbouring Bengal *Zillahs* would find their way into the wastelands of Assam'.[41]

The first road, conceived for external communication was the one connecting Gauhati with Sylhet. Its importance as a military road, in case of fresh Burmese incursions was undeniable. As early as 1826, David Scott did the groundwork for construction of the aforementioned road. He was instrumental in persuading the Khasi Chiefs of Khyrim and Mylliem to agree on the construction of a road through their territory.[42] Work commenced on the route in 1829, but had to be stalled because of the murders of Lieutenant Burlton and Beddingfield, who were in charge of the construction. Interest was renewed on the project following the annexation of Khasi Hills in 1832. Early correspondence, between 1833–36, highlights the military feasibility of the route.

The view, that this road was suitable for purely military purposes, changed in 1840 when Jenkins insisted on the road being aligned through the Khasi Hills, as it was perceived that,

40. Bengal Judicial Consultations (Criminal), no. 4, 13 October 1835.
41. Letters issued to Government, vol. no. 9, no. 139, 10 August 1840.
42. For details of David Scotts' policy in the Khasi Hills, refer to Nirode K. Barooah, *David Scott in North-East India*.

'the road was of highest importance to the bordering countries in a commercial point of view . . . also equally good with any other if not the best for military operations of any unforeseen exigencies'.[43]

The road offered viable commercial prospects as well. The rent-free Khasi land could be offered for settlement and cultivation along the route, thus ensuring British coffers a steady source of revenue. The Khasis were important traders too. They frequented the frontier *hats* as far as Nowgong to barter their merchandise, mainly iron implements, for cattle, goats, rice, salt, tobacco, cloth, etc.[44]

Colonel Hopkinson in 1862, in a letter to the District Officers on the issue of opening up of trunk lines through the province favoured an early construction of the Gauhati–Sylhet road, as he perceived that:

> communication with Bengal will be sooner established by it, because with the railway to Dacca, it will probably be the quickest route of the Presidency, as for mails to reach as from Calcutta, because it at once renders accessible large tract of country perfectly suited to European colonization and because of the community of interest between Cachar and Assam which a road also uniting the two provinces together will so well serve.[45]

The alignment was finally decided upon and sanctioned in 1863. The route selected was between Gauhati in Assam via Shillong to Chattak on the river Soormah [*sic*], a distance of 104 miles.

To complete the line of communication across the province

43. Letters issued to Government, vol. no. 9, no. 139, 10 August 1840.
44. Mills, *Report on the Province of Assam*, Letter from Jenkins to Mills no. 309, 4 June 1853.
45. Letters issued to District Officers, vol. no. 9 (a), 1861–1864, no. 32, 31 January 1862.

of Assam and to connect Lower Assam with Upper Assam, the authorities were in favour of opening a road between Gauhati and Goalpara as they felt, ' . . . the construction of [the] great western road connecting Gauhati with Goalpara and thence to Bengal . . . would be highly advantageous to the Province'.[46]

Apart from opening up the wastelands, it was intended to extend the route by a junction road at Rangpore [*sic*]. In 1854–55, to complete the line of communication with Bengal, the authorities contemplated opening up a high road to Assam via Rangpore. The line recommended was from Rangpore to Dhubri and was for 'better conveyance of the mail from Maldah [*sic*] as it would deliver mails about 18 hours less than the time required'.[47]

In 1866, a grand project for a 'Trunk Road' running through all the districts of Assam was conceived. The project was formulated on a much larger scale than funds could permit.

> The Assam Trunk road was begun with the design of making it a first class metalled and embanked highway, twenty feet wide and aligned in that manner that should render it possible to convert it into a railway. The first result of this conception was that more attention was paid to altering and trimming the existing roads to suit the railway alignments, than to extending on their old bases. Many old roads which if they had been maintained and improved would have answered all practical purposes to the present day were abandoned, and new roads were started on the model of railways.[48]

After assessing the financial implications of the project and

46. Bengal Judicial Consultations (Criminal), no. 3, 13 October 1835.
47. Letters issued to Government, vol. no. 23, 1860, no. 6, 14 January 1860.
48. W.W. Hunter, *A Statistical Account of Assam*, vol. i (London, 1879, reprint, Delhi, 1975), p. 55.

taking stock of the available funds, the idea of a 'railway formation for the Trunk Road was given up and orders were issued to continue work on a smaller scale of a sixteen feet top width'.[49] The financial restriction placed on PWD expenditure in 1870 was the primary reason for abandoning the idea of a trunk road with future provision of a railway formation. The trunk route had to be reduced to 'connect the fragmentary portions of made road situated on the through route into a continuous trunk road and extend it towards the Bengal frontier'.[50]

Labour

A major hurdle confronting the British in constructing roads was the dearth of local labour. The reason ascribed by the British was the indolence of people, and attributed this to their habit of consuming opium. Explaining this anomaly, Campbell, the Assistant Commissioner of Kamroop [sic] remarked:

> it is most difficult to get labour for local roads . . . that somehow people have [come] to look on all Government workmen as impressed labourers. It matters not if they are offered double the rates obtainable elsewhere, they are disinclined to take service, as it lowers their social position.[51]

A self-subsisting economy and their limited wants did not provide any inducement to the peasants to work for wages. High rates of revenue were fixed with the view to flushing out peasants from their landholdings to work on roads. Though enhanced tax rates put pressure on the peasants, they did not venture out on construction work, to supplement their income.

49. Hunter, *A Statistical Account of Assam*, pp. 47–8.
50. Ibid.
51. Ibid.

In 1864, free labour that worked for the PWD received a wage of Rs 7 per month.[52]

Protracted civil wars during the first half of the eighteenth century followed by the ravages of the Burmese invasion, natural calamities like earthquakes, *kala-azar* and other malarial epidemics had drastically decimated the population, which in turn contributed to the dearth of local labour.

Left with few options, the government insisted that the local *Zamindars* or Rajas furnish labour, for work on the routes traversing their territory. Convicts were also used as labour on the roads. The Raja of Jaintia furnished a 'gang of labourers' for constructing the road between Assam and Sylhet, through the Jaintia hills. The *tehsildars* of Nowgong provided a gang of 500 Assamese *paiks*, besides a large number of *teklahs* or peons, for constructing the road between Nowgong and Bishenath [*sic*]. The *tehsildars* were offered certain remissions for supplying *paiks*.[53] For constructing the road from Gauhati to Kurreahghat, the Choudhury of Ramsah was called upon to provide assistance for completing the road.[54] Captain Mathews drew upon a plan for 'giving subsistence of rice and salt to all *ryots* employed, with occasional money presents.'[55] In spite of securing local pockets of assistance, through the *Zamindars*, a permanent workforce for the purpose could not be created.

Tarasankar Banerjee while reflecting on the importance of roads remarks that, 'roads are a vital factor in the national

52. Mills, *Report on the Province of Assam*, see Dhekial Phukan, Appendix 'E', p. xxxvii.

53. Letters Received from Government, vol. 6, Letter no. 47, 17 May 1837.

54. Letters issued to Miscellaneous Quarters, vol. 7, 1840, no. 801, 16 November 1840.

55. Bengal Judicial Consultations (Criminal), no. 28, 1842.

economy. They link industry with agriculture, producer with consumers, and the external market with the internal one.'[56]

Road building commenced all over the country in the 1830s. The commercial aspect of the problem was completely overlooked. An agricultural country like India required roads that could connect the fields of the cultivators with the markets, for the speedy disposal of their produce. The initial thrust was on military roads and it was only in the middle of the nineteenth century that progress in road construction became steady and methodical, which was further intensified in 1870–1880 when the emphasis was on 'cotton roads'.

Conclusion

The real reform in the area of public road construction in British India was initiated by Lord Bentinck between 1828–35. Road building in Assam too was initiated during the same period, under the aegis of the Military Board. In 1835, public works in Assam were entrusted to an Executive Officer stationed at Dacca. The distance between the working headquarters and the place of work proved to be a major disadvantage in the working of the administrative unit. In 1840, the situation was rectified by the creation of a Division of Public Works, with an Executive Engineer of Upper Assam, which worked under the Chief Engineer, PWD, Lower Provinces, stationed at Bengal.

The bulk of the PWD expenditure, as that over the rest of the country was because of military works. The East India Company for almost the entire period of its existence in India neglected public works. It was under Dalhousie's administration, that a separate Public Works Department was set up in

56. Tarasankar Banerjee, *Internal Market of India: 1838–1900* (Calcutta, 1966), p. 60.

1854, removing public works from the control of the Military Board. It marked a turning point and there was a sudden spate of activity in road building after that.

In Assam, the thrust was primarily on the construction of military roads, with only a small proportion of funds assigned for constructing roads from the agricultural production centres to the centres of trade at the foothills. For military purposes, portions of the medieval road-cum-embankments were restored. A massive plan for constructing a trunk road through the province was conceived in 1866. The project was stalled due to the paucity of funds. Fragmentary portions of the old roads throughout the province were constructed to form a continuous trunk road, and finally extended towards Bengal.

It is imperative to assess the role of roadways in the development of the economy of Assam. With the abolition of the *Hadira Chowkeys* in 1836, the volume and extent of the external trade of Assam could not be ascertained. Internal trade, primarily barter-oriented, with the hill tribes was carried on, on both sides of the valley from Sadiya to Goalpara. To systematically tap this trade, the British set up permanent market sites in the foothills, where weekly markets as well as annual trading fairs were held. Most of these markets were connected with the trunk route, by a network of feeder routes. This facilitated an expansion of the trade, as hill produce like stick lac, cotton, *munjeet* and rubber, featured increasingly amongst the exports from Assam. Even during the years of bad communication, trade with the hills amounting to about Rs 13 lakhs was registered.[57]

Feeder roads were constructed to help tea gardens to transport their produce to the rivers. The conditions of most of the

57. Hunter, *A Statistical Account of Assam*, p. 48.

roads, which were unmetalled, were deplorable. In spite of
efforts to improve the condition of the roads, complaints on
the bad state of roads featured regularly in the deliberations of
the India Tea Association till the end of the nineteenth century.

Till about 1870 there was hardly any wheeled traffic on
the roads in Assam, with people travelling on foot and mail
carried by runners. As Hunter writes, the roads in Assam,
'were used by cattle dealers, elephant catchers, coolies for tea
gardens, pilgrims, etc.' The proportion of metalled roads to
unmetalled roads was very small. The role of roads for economic development in Assam was limited to internal trade,
the external trade of the province, being carried out mainly
through native boats.

Waterways

Pre-Colonial Period

Assam's trade with the neighbouring provinces, from ancient
times, was predominantly conducted through its river routes.
The Brahmaputra and the Ganges were the arterial routes of
communication with Bengal, Bihar and Orissa, with the
Brahmaputra being regarded as the 'highway of Assam' with
the outside world. Its numerous tributaries as well as a number
of navigable streams that criss-crossed Assam in every direction
— especially during the rainy season facilitated limited internal
trade. A major bottleneck in the communication network was
the slow movement of country boats up the Brahmaputra.

The Vaishnava saints also travelled in country boats to
Navadeep [*sic*] and other places of pilgrimage down the
Brahmaputra/Ganges river system.[58] In the ninth century AD,

58. Guha, 'Medieval Economy of Assam', p. 488.

the builder of the city of Haruppeshwara, on the banks of the Brahmaputra, mentioned that he possessed a large fleet of boats. So numerous were the boats that a naval regulation was necessary to prevent collision of the royal boats and those belonging to the fishermen.[59] According to M'Cosh, the journey from Calcutta to Gauhati by a large boat took six to seven weeks. It took a month from Gauhati to Dibrugarh, and in the rainy season, against the current, it took a much longer time.[60]

Colonial Period

David Scott who was instrumental in occupying Assam, immediately started investigating the economic advantages offered by the province. He considered the state of commerce in the province as unsatisfactory. The self-subsisting nature of the economy failed to meet the requirements of the expanding population, both indigenous and immigrant. He attributed the unsatisfactory state of commerce as:

> owing [*sic*] to the want of boats and navigational difficulties of the Brahmaputra, no relief of the evils could be expected from the exportation of so cheap and bulky a commodity as grain.[61]

An exponent of the mercantilist school, Scott believed in the policy of developing the economy by exploiting its natural resources. Encouraged by the prospects of the province, he directed efforts to gather concrete information on sites yielding coal. He awaited confirmed reports of the mineral resources so that it would be feasible to introduce steam navigation on the Brahmaputra.

59. Cf., N.N. Goswami, 'History of Communication Development: North East Region of the Country' (unpublished, 1989), p. 1.
60. Ibid.
61. M'Cosh, *Topography of Assam*, p. 66.

By the end of 1827, confirmed reports on the availability of coal were received. The sites identified were the north-eastern face of the Naga Hills at Teeragong, and twenty miles east of Rangpore in Upper Assam.[62] Scott endeavoured to convince the government to introduce steam vessels on the Brahmaputra. Finally, in May 1831, the government yielded to Scott's persistence and agreed to despatch a steamer to Assam on a trial run.[63] After his death in August the same year, the issue of the steamers was stalled, as the administration did not consider it economically viable.[64] His successors were more keen on formulating a viable land revenue policy.

The growth of the tea industry enhanced the importance of waterways as a reliable and efficient means of transportation. Road transportation, as discussed earlier, was unreliable as a form of internal communication. The Assam Company, formed in 1839, faced immense hardships in transporting tea to the port of Calcutta for export. The company started its own fleet of country boats, on which they annually spent a sum of Rs 20,000.[65] In 1842, a steamer was purchased at a cost of £ 13,000. It could not be successfully plied on the Brahmaputra, and was laid off for several years, till it was finally sold off in 1847.[66] Attempts, both by the government and the tea industry, failed to fully develop waterways within the province.

Pressure Groups

The issue of introduction of an efficient fleet of steamers, for the purposes of trade and conveyance of troops, picked up

62. Barooah, *David Scott in North-East India*, p. 115.
63. Barooah, *David Scott in North-East India*, p. 111.
64. Barooah, *David Scott in North-East India*, p. 113.
65. Guha, 'Medieval Economy of Assam', p. 160.
66. Ibid.

momentum during the 1840s. The use of steam ships in India had developed with the ascendancy of the interests of the industrial capitalists of Lancashire, who wanted to extract the maximum amount of raw material — cotton for their mills — and simultaneously convert India into a market for finished textile goods. Though the real value of trade with India had not reached exceptional dimensions, British businessmen campaigned for the introduction of steam ships into India, which was essentially an achievement of the Industrial Revolution.[67] In Assam too, certain pressure groups worked for the development of steamer communication in Assam.

Assam held the claim of being the lone province in British India to produce indigenous tea. The tea industry played a pivotal role in the economic development of the province. In the aftermath of the experimental stage, a steady growth was visible in the acreage as well as in the production of tea. The total acreage under tea production increased, from 2,311 acres in 1841 to 8,000 acres in 1852, with a corresponding increase in the output from 29,267 lbs to over 1,200,000 lbs.[68] A slump in production followed due to reckless speculation and mismanagement between 1863 and 1868, when the tea industry was threatened with virtual extinction. From 1869 onwards, the industry stabilized, with a subsequent steady rise in acreage and production of tea.

Very little of the tea produced remained in Assam for domestic use. Almost all of it was sent to Calcutta for transhipment to England and the world tea market. The tea companies virtually clamoured for the introduction of steam communication

67. Daniel Thorner, *Investment in Empire: British Railway and Steam Shipping Enterprise In India, 1825–1849* (Philadelphia, 1950), p. 3.
68. Hunter, *A Statistical Account of Assam*, p. 263.

in Assam, primarily in the tea producing districts of Sibsagar,
Lakhimpur and Cachar.

Jenkins encouraged production of cash crops with the
purpose of making agriculture commercially viable. The results
of this endeavour were an increase in the production of mustard, silk and lac. For speedy transit of goods from the hinterland to the trading centres, improved communication was
required. In 1851, Jenkins urged the Marine Department to
occasionally extend a steamer service to Upper Assam — the
centre of British investments in minerals and the plantation
industry. He pointed out, that apart from the bulk of the cargo
in tea, sugar produced in two new factories, a certain amount
of *caoutchouc* (India rubber) and opium produced in Sibsagar
and Lakhimpur, and the *moongah* silks and *munjeet* from
Lakhimpur, would form important items of merchandise. Coal
mines, if worked on scientific lines, with an insistence on
economy, would facilitate steam navigation within the province.[69] The indigo planters of Dacca appealed to the Government of India for deployment of government steamers between
Calcutta and Gauhati, via Dacca.[70]

The primary requirement of the tea industry was a large
labour force. The supply of local labour was very limited and
the plantations had to be worked on by coolies imported from
other parts of India. Many of the planters and some District
Officers in Assam thought that, ' . . . it was the duty of Government to stimulate the slothful Assamese and drive them to
work on plantations by enhancing the land revenue assessment'.[71] In spite of the high prices offered, local labour was not

69. Bengal Government Papers, file no. 285/614, 1854, letter no. 236,
10 May 1851.
70. Bengal Marine Proceedings 1854, letter no. 9, 8 June 1854.
71. A system of exchange of labour for the tea exported was adopted,
similar to the exchange of salt and piece-goods for rubber and oil seeds.

obtainable in sufficient numbers, and *coolies* had to be brought from Calcutta. For importing labour, a regular steamer service was imperative.

The first government steamer plied on the Brahmaputra in the year 1847. The service was very irregular, so the bulk of the cargo, consisting of tea had to wait for a long time at Gauhati for export. The irregularity was primarily because there was more than full employment for the diminished numbers of Inland Steamers belonging to the government in conveying troops and stores on the Ganges.[72] The war with Afghanistan in the 1840s, and the necessity to convey troops to the North-West Provinces, was the primary responsibility of government steamers, which made them unavailable for other purposes. In order to press the urgency of introducing regular steamer services, the Government of Assam furnished a statement of receipts and expenditure between 1847–48 and 1853–54.[73]

The post-Mutiny period of 1858 witnessed a total cessation of steamboat communication with Assam, with strategic issues being accorded priority. The total suspension of steamboat communication with Assam caused hardships to the tea planters in the vicinity of Dibrugarh. Spares for factories and particularly 'Tea Lead' used for lining tea boxes prior to shipping them out of the country to England, became scarce.[74] Apart from the planters, agricultural ventures, which involved capital and required markets for disposing their produce, suffered immensely.

The insufficiency of the available flat-bottomed boats and

72. Bengal Marine Proceedings 1854, letter no. 9, 8 June 1854.
73. In the 65 trips of the steamers to Assam, during this period, the receipts had exceeded the expenses by Rs 11,424. The receipts per trip stood at Rs 5,617.
74. Bengal Government Papers, file no. 254/601, 31 August 1858.

steamers made the trade heavily dependent on country boats. The Assam Company had to procure 'iron boats' to send down its cargo of tea. Boats monopolized a large proportion of the trade between Assam and Bengal. They carried the bulk of the lime, rice, gram, salt, sugar, tobacco, oranges and potatoes. The more expensive merchandise such as tea, piece-goods, metals, coal and mustard were carried by steamers.[75]

The government was in no position to restore its steamer services on the Assam line. The Indian Steam Navigation Company, a joint stock company, had to face stiff competition from the East Indian Railways in the area parallel to the Ganges route. It sought to minimize its losses by diversifying its area of operation. In 1860, the company sent a proposal to the government for running their steamers on the Dacca and Assam line every six weeks. The government accepted the offer and allowed the company to use coal in the same manner as used by the government vessels. They were permitted to use Pilots and were asked to maintain a Pilot Establishment, as long as their boats were run on the line. The government in return received preference in the rates charged, similar to the rates charged earlier by the government for private freight on the Assam line.[76]

The River Steam Navigation Company — an ally of the Indian General Steam Navigation Company — launched its fleet of three steamers along with flat-bottomed boats in 1863.[77] The entry of the two private steam navigation companies brought in a relative degree of efficiency in the communication

75. *Physical and Political Geography of the Province of Assam 1892–1893*, p. 43.

76. Bengal Government Papers, nos. 1–11, file no. 247/586, letter no. 6319, 31 May 1860.

77. In 1863, the Indian General Steam Navigation Company extended its area of operations to Cachar.

network. In spite of efforts by private enterprise, travel continued to be slow. The steamers generally failed to run on schedule, as the time taken for loading and unloading cargo at larger ports, was considerable.[78]

In the next phase of the development of waterways, attempts were made to coordinate the steamers with the nearest railway alignment. In 1864, the River Steam Navigation Company entered into agreement with the Eastern Bengal Railway for transporting goods to Assam by rail to Khustia and thence by steamer to Assam and vice-versa.[79] The Indian General Steam Navigation Company also entered into a similar contract with the Eastern Bengal Railway. However, in 1871, the river-rail coordination agreements signed by the River Steam Navigation Company and Indian General Steam Navigation Company were discontinued and direct steamer links between Assam and Calcutta were restored.[80]

As the volume of trade increased, both the steamer companies faced stiff competition from the Eastern Bengal Railway, which had introduced both passenger and goods traffic between its various stations on 'through railway tickets and documents'.[81] In order to regain a reasonable proportion of trade from the railways, the Indian General Steam Navigation Company in 1879, negotiated with the Eastern Bengal Railway for carriage between certain river-cum-railway junctions by the vessels of the Indian General Steam Navigation Company under 'through railway documents'.[82]

78. Allen, *Assam District Gazetteers*, vol. VIII, Lakhimpur, p. 226.
79. Medhi, *Transport System and Economic Development in Assam*, p. 21.
80. Ibid.
81. Allen, *Assam District Gazetteers*, vol. VIII, Lakhimpur, p. 226.
82. Medhi, *Transport System and Economic Development in Assam*, p. 21.

The situation considerably improved in 1882 when the River Steam Navigation Company entered into an agreement with the Assam Government, for running a daily steamer service between Dhubri and Dibrugarh. Furthermore, Dhubri was connected in the direction of Bengal to Jatrapur, from where a traveller could take a train to Calcutta.[83]

The introduction of a daily steamer service was an enormous step towards improving the communication network between Assam and the outside world. The daily service effectively combined the advantages of speed with regularity, which in comparison to that attained by the large boats was commendable.[84] A network of fast steamers also plied between Dibrugarh and Calcutta via the Sunderbans, 'through which goods could be directly sent to Calcutta without any necessity for handling.'[85]

In Cachar, communications with the outside world was maintained through steamers. During the rainy season, big steamers came up the Barak river to Silchar. In the cold weather however, with barely three feet of water in the channel, the journey from Calcutta to Silchar was slow and irksome, taking five days, and had to be terminated at Fenchuganj. In 1887, a daily steamer service was introduced on the river Surma, between Goalundo and Silchar in the rainy season, and Fenchuganj in the cold weather.[86] Boat traffic was an important component of river communication in the Surma Valley, as big steamers lacked all-weather navigability.

Apart from the arterial routes, a number of feeder steamers

83. Allen, *Assam District Gazetteers*, vol. VIII, Lakhimpur, p. 226.
84. In the aftermath of the introduction of steamers, even during the rainy season, the upward journey to Dibrugarh took five days and the downward journey took three days.
85. Allen, *Assam District Gazetteers*, vol. I, Cachar, 1905, p. 108.
86. Allen, *Assam District Gazetteers*, pp. 107–8.

operated in all the districts. In the district of Lakhimpur during the rainy season feeder steamers went up occasionally to Jaipur, carrying tea as an important item of merchandise from the tea gardens in its vicinity. Some traffic also went up the Noa-Dehing and Tengapani rivers during winter. Small feeder steamers plied twice a week to Badati in the cold weather. The river Subansiri was navigable by large boats up to the frontier of the province in all seasons. Feeder steamers plied regularly between Dibrugarh and Sadiya.[87]

In the district of Cachar, feeder steamers went up the Barak from Silchar to Lakhipur; up the Madhura to Chandighat; up the Ghagra to the Hatia rocks; and up the Katakhal to Kukicherra.[88]

Trade

Very few statistics are available regarding the amount of external trade of Assam upto the 1870s. After Assam was constituted into a Chief Commissionership in 1874, regular registration of traffic by native boats was commenced. This was followed by introducing a system of registration from September 1875, for all districts of Assam. From 1881 onwards, annual compilation of the steamer and boat traffic in Assam took place. The registering stations were, (a) Dhubri — for boat and steamer traffic — on the Brahmaputra, and (b) Sylhet and Bhairab Bazar in Mymensingh for boat traffic in the Surma Valley.[89]

The second half of the nineteenth century witnessed a steady expansion of foreign trade in India. The colonizers projected the expansion in foreign trade as an indicator of economic

87. Allen, *Assam District Gazetteers*, pp. 107–8.
88. Allen, *Assam District Gazetteers*, vol. VIII, Lakhimpur, p. 234.
89. Allen, *Assam District Gazetteers*, vol. I, Cachar, p. 108.

growth and development. Increasing exports were taken as an indicator of increase in productivity, while expansion of imports signified an improvement in the purchasing power of the Indian buyer. An immediate follow-up of the increase in imports was large-scale commercialization of agriculture, with a remarkable trend towards diversification. Indian agriculture had thus abandoned the 'stationary stage'. D.R. Gadgil assigns the reasons for growth of commercial agriculture to:

> ... the ease of communications which made the exportation of agricultural produce out of the village possible, together with the introduction of money economy, brought about this movement towards a commercialization of Indian agriculture.[90]

Commercialization of agriculture had not occurred on a wide scale in Assam, like in other provinces, such as Bengal. More often than not, commercialization was not a natural process but was imposed. Cash crops were produced for acquiring enough cash to enable the cultivator to pay land revenue, rent, buy opium, and certain other necessities like salt, sugar, oil, etc., which were not locally produced.[91] The average percentage of cropped area in 1875–76 in the five districts (Kamroop, [sic] Nowgong, Lakhimpur, Sibsagar and Darrang) were as follows: rice (70 per cent), mustard (7.2 per cent), sugar cane (1.4 per cent), cotton (0.7 per cent) and other food grains (8.3 per cent) — this heading of other food grains excludes the total cropped area under rice cultivation.[92] In the

90. D.R. Gadgil, *The Industrial Evolution of India in Recent Times: 1860–1939* (Delhi, 5th ed., 1971), p. 159.

91. The cash crops produced in Assam in the 1880s were mustard, pulses, sugar cane and some jute.

92. Hunter, *A Statistical Account of Assam*, vol. I, pp. 46, 128, 192, 254 and 373.

1890s the average cropped area increased to 74 per cent for rice, 9.9 per cent for mustard, 3.5 per cent for pulses, 1.6 per cent for sugar cane and another 9 per cent for orchard and garden produce.[93]

The bulk of the trade from Assam was carried on with different trade blocks of Bengal, but primarily with Calcutta, a gateway for the products of North-East India. The traffic was primarily river-borne. The most valuable imports to the Brahmaputra valley were rice (husked), salt, mustard oil, gram, pulses, sugar, tobacco, coal, coke, cotton (twists and yarn), European piece-goods, drugs and liquors. The principal exports were tea, rice (unhusked) mustard seeds and rape-seeds, timber and raw jute, while the Surma Valley mainly exported lime, potatoes and oranges.

The goods imported by steamers were piece-goods, liquor and opium, while the exports were tea, tea-seeds and silk. A small proportion of the import in salt and the export in oil-seeds was carried on by steamers, which transported commodities, which were more valuable in proportion than their bulk. Salt, oils and tobacco were mostly carried into the province by boats, while jute and timber were chiefly sent out in them. In terms of weight, boats monopolized a large proportion of the export traffic. In 1881–82, steamers imported 89 per cent of the piece-goods, all the opium, and 67 per cent of the brass, copper and iron, and the entire exports of tea.[94] In 1885, exports by steamers increased by 10 per cent, with a slight fall in the exports by boat. Imports also rose in value by

93. Aditya Mukherjee, 'Agrarian Conditions in Assam, 1880–1890: A Case Study of Five Districts of the Brahmaputra Valley', *IESHR*, vol. xvi, no. 2, 1979, p. 214.

94. *Report on the River Borne Trade of the Province of Assam: 1881–1882*, p. 7.

5 per cent, there being a slight increase in the steamer and a decrease in the boat traffic.[95]

The increase in the export of cash crops was on an account of improved communication through waterways. A very peculiar feature of the trade in mustard was that a sizeable quantity of it was exported outside the province, principally to the Northern-Bengal Trade Block. This was because the local oil-extracting technology was primitive, as it did not make use of cattle-powered mills. Attempts to set up oil presses at Barpeta met with limited success.[96]

The consumption of mill-made goods began to increase rapidly after the 1880s, which is evident from the data available on the rail and river-borne trade of Assam. The inflow of cotton (twists and yarn) almost doubled between 1881 and 1882, from 5,013 maunds (184.15 tons) to 12,579 maunds (462.09 tons) in 1884–85.[97] Increased imports of piece-goods bore testimony to the growth of an extensive demand in the interior of the province. The influx of piece-goods to a certain degree affected the indigenous handloom industry.

Effects of Trade on the Peasantry

Marwari traders from Rajputana, who were locally known as *Kyahs*, carried on almost all the trade in the Brahmaputra Valley. They monopolized the banking and wholesale business of the valley. Their shops were found not only in the business centres, but also in 'every tea garden, and on the paths by which hill men bring [sic] down their cotton, rubber, lac and other

95. *Report on the River Borne Trade of the Province of Assam: 1881–1882*, pp. 16–18.
96. *Report on the River Borne Trade of the Province of Assam: 1884–85*, p. 3.
97. *Report on the River Borne Trade of the Province of Assam: 1884–85*, p. 6.

products'.[98] In addition, a few Bengali Muhammadan traders in larger towns sold furniture, haberdashery and oil-man's stores. The natives of Kamrup handled a negligible share of trade, mostly oil-seeds. In the Surma Valley, a powerful trading community of natives existed along with a handful of *Kyahs*. Amongst the hillmen, the Khasis and Nagas were keen and energetic traders and sometimes went as far afield as Calcutta in search of goods.

It is imperative to assess the gains in real terms by the Assamese peasantry. Increase in the percentage of cropped area was regarded as a touchstone in determining the economic prosperity of a cultivator. Rice formed an important staple in almost all the districts of Assam. Production however remained at a subsistence level, leaving very little to feed the immigrant population. Whatever surplus rice was available was sold to the garden coolies in the village or at the local market or to intermediaries like the *Kyahs*. The 1880s witnessed a reasonable increase in the exports of paddy from the Brahmaputra Valley.[99] The prices of paddy and other cash crops registered a rising trend, but not at rates more than what could be obtained in Bengal. The gains of the Assamese peasantry from the price rise remained modest. The increasing demand from the expanding tea industry and the concomitant overall rise in population, both natural and immigrant, failed to boost agricultural production in Assam to a desirable limit.

The gains of the Assamese peasantry from expanding commerce were negligible. The cultivator was satisfied with

98. *Imperial Gazetteer of India*, vol. vi (Argaon to Burdwan), p. 76.
99. From a mere 227 maunds (8.34 tons) in 1880–81, the export of unhusked rice from the Brahmaputra Valley rose to 160,557 maunds (5,898 tons) in 1884–1885. During the corresponding period the exports from the Surma Valley rose from 163,260 maunds (5,997.32 tons) to 1,918,115 maunds (70,461.61 tons).

tilling his fields, and matters like wholesale trade, craft and industry concerned him very little, allowing the *Kyahs* to conduct all the trade, and appropriate and remit the surplus out of the province. More often, the peasant in order to clear his revenue dues turned to the *Kyah*, in his role as a money-lender, who usually offered loans on the condition that a particular crop would be cultivated, preferably mustard seeds. The cultivator had little choice but to sell it to the *Kyahs* at a price lower than that obtainable in the market. To cite an instance, the *Kyahs* bought mustard seeds for one rupee per maund, while the prevailing market price was between Rs 3 and 4.[100] The peasant in the long run became indebted to the merchant-moneylender, for paying the ever-increasing revenue demand. This prevented any accumulation of capital in their hands.

As the peasant sector lacked internal dynamism, no development of productive forces as a natural outcome of improved communication took place. To the colonizers an increase in imports represented an advance in the purchasing power of the peasants or an improvement in their material conditions. However, evidence on the contrary revealed that a heavy increase in .land revenue diminished the purchasing power of the peasants. Amongst the imports, the bulk of the rice, piece-goods and liquors were consumed by the immigrant coolie population.[101]

The tea industry, largely dependent on the immigrant labour population, derived immense benefits from the opening of the daily steamer service in 1881. In the immediate aftermath of opening up steamer routes between Dhubri and

100. *Census of India*, 1891, vol. i, para 405.
101. *Report on the River Borne Trade of the Province of Assam: 1884–85*, p. 3.

Dibrugarh and finally Bengal, the Superintendent of Emigration [*sic*] in Bengal reported that:

> While the Dhubri route has [*sic*] drawn away many emigrants into Assam Valley districts, the direct route to Goalundo seems to have increased in favour of immigrants proceeding to Cachar and Sylhet.[102]

In 1882, it was reported that 10,902 immigrants and their dependents of all classes were registered and sent through Calcutta and Goalundo, against 8,794 in 1818. Steamers played an important role in transporting migrant labourers into the province.

Overall Impact

Waterways played a pivotal role in transforming the self-subsisting economy of Assam, to set it on the path of capitalistic development, and through which imperial investments in Assam were rendered financially viable. Calcutta, a major port of the East, through which all the products of this province reached the world markets, was linked with Assam. The economy of the province was integrated with the external markets. Internally, the process of monetization of the economy was achieved with forces of the world markets operating in the province, which in turn was achieved by the extraction of cheap raw materials. Commercialization of agriculture led to a diversification of the raw materials, thus changing the nature of the economy. The plantation industry that was firmly entrenched in Assam, witnessed a steady growth. It constituted seven per cent of the total exports of the country in 1871. The period between 1860 and 1870 — when the waterways

102. *Report on the Labour Immigration into Assam: 1882*, p. 10.

developed in Assam — broadly corresponded with the phase of the expansion of foreign trade of India.

Limitations

In spite of the major role of water communications in the all-round development of the province, there was ample scope for improving the existing network of communications. What the province lacked was 'feeder roads' between the river ghats — the centres for external trade — and the tea-producing hinterland. The plantation industry had to depend on roads for transporting their cargo from the gardens to the steamer ghats. The planters had to use unmetalled roads for all their transportation needs. Having to take the burden of increased cart traffic, most of the roads were rendered absolutely and hopelessly impassable during the rains. W.R. Gawthropp describes the road between Dibrugarh and the steamer ghat, during the rainy season as, 'a perfect slough of despond, strewn with broken carts, burst rice bags and damaged tea boxes'.[103] In the face of such disadvantages, the planters mooted the idea of a light railway, connecting Sadiya in the extreme east to the steamer ghat at Dibrugarh.

The idea of initiating a trunk line of the railway and connecting it through the shortest route to either the ports of Calcutta or Chittagong, received an impetus in the 1880s. The trade returns of the corresponding period indicated that a railway line through the province would be feasible to meet the growing needs of trade. Statements show that there was great room for equalization of prices if a railway line was constructed, linking up Sylhet and Tipperah [sic] to Sibsagar and Lakhimpur. The latter were the rice exporting districts of

103. W.R. Gawthropp, *The Story of Assam Railways and Trading Company Limited, 1881–1951* (London, 1951), p. 10.

Assam which imported grain used 'by Europeans and wealthy natives and to feed the tea coolies'.[104] Such an equalization of prices was expected to initiate the rapid progress of colonization of the wastelands in the north-eastern districts, which were hitherto retarded by the high cost of food.[105] This intra-valley commercial project encouraged the colonial government to undertake surveys for a railway to connect Bengal with Assam.

The coalfields of Upper Assam, situated on the Northern face of the Naga Hills — from the Dehing, east of Makum, and west of the Desoi — could be developed with a railway connecting them to the nearest port. The prospect of extracting coal from the Khasi and Jaintia Hills, the North Cachar Hills and the fine coalfield existing on the Someswari river, in the heart of the Garo Hills, drove the railway project.

A general survey of the trade of the province in the context of a railway connection with Bengal revealed that inward traffic would consist principally of piece-goods, rice, lime and tea-garden supplies. The outward trade would comprise tea, coal and a few articles of high value and small bulk. The expected passenger traffic would generally be small as the railway lines would pass through uninhabited areas, with only certain portions expected to get heavy passenger traffic. To the colonizers the future of Assam was inextricably linked with the extension of immigration that would boost up the railway receipts, compensating for the lack of general passenger traffic.

104. *Report on the River Borne Trade of the Province of Assam: 1881–1882*, p. 9.
105. Another article found in abundance in Sylhet, but lacking in the Assam Valley was lime. *Ghi* [sic] another product of Sylhet was extremely dear and in great demand in Assam. In exchange, the Assam Valley could offer tea, coal and small quantities of the more valuable articles of little bulk, such as lac, rubber and silk.

All these factors combined to improve the means of communication connecting the province with the ports of either Chittagong or Calcutta, through the shortest route. In this backdrop, surveys were conducted on a route that would connect the central range of Assam, through either Sylhet or Mymensingh, with Bengal.

However, even after the introduction of the railways in Assam by 1895–96, steamers continued to dominate the entire trade with the Calcutta Trade Block. Apart from the necessary consumer goods, locomotive engines, steel rails, fishplates and other railway materials were imported by steamers.

Table II gives an account of the river-borne traffic and the rail-borne traffic in the last quarter of the nineteenth century.

TABLE II: Rail and River-borne Imports
and Exports of Assam[106]

Years	Imports into Assam				Exports from Assam			
	By rail		By river		By rail		By river	
	Qty	Value	Qty	Value	Qty	Value	Qty	Value
1896–1897	1.03	8.34	55.98	428.32	0.14	4.78	101.86	648.05
1897–1898	2.86	19.66	51.91	384.60	1.05	33.21	85.83	449.62
1898–1899	6.84	33.00	47.71	383.25	1.64	45.05	92.16	608.35
1899–1900	4.54	22.76	41.86	298.48	2.37	42.06	92.44	550.18
Average	3.82	21.57	49.37	363.66	1.30	42.06	93.07	550.18

All quantities in maunds, and values in rupees lakhs.

106. *Rail and River Borne Trade of Assam*, (for various years), 1896, 1897, 1898 and 1899.

As the table shows river-borne trade averaged over 14,200,000 maunds (521,634.46 tons), worth Rs 914 lakhs, in contrast to rail-borne trade of 500,000 maunds (18,367.41 tons), worth less than Rs 64 lakhs.

3

Introduction of
Railways in Assam
Preparatory Stage

The coming of the 'Iron Horse'[*] to India, had the effect of strengthening the political and economic control of the British in India. The first stage of economic and political control was exercised through a mercantile company, the East India Company, formed by grant of a royal charter on 31 December 1600, for carrying out trade with the East Indies. The Seven Years' War (1765–1773) in Europe transformed the East India Company into a military and territorial power, when it laid the foundations of the British Empire in India.

> The East India Company as a modern capitalist corporation of an advanced bourgeois nation entrenched itself like a parasite in the agrarian state dominated by a decaying feudal

[*] Horses were the main mode of transportation during much of American history. Railway engine's were at first called the 'Iron Horse', in an attempt to describe new technology in terms of an old familiar one.

regime. The parasite adjusted to the system of its host and benefited from it without changing it very much.[1]

The East India Company operated primarily as traders and did not make any effort to introduce major changes in the Indian economy. They remained content in their role as revenue collectors.

The Industrial Revolution in England brought with it the supremacy of a new capitalist class, comprising the textile manufacturers of Lancashire and Manchester. This necessitated a revolution in the economic system, from the principles of merchant-capitalism to free-trade capitalism. This in turn brought about a corresponding change in the operation of the colonial system. The new system required the creation of a free market in India, replacing the previous monopoly. It meant, a complete changeover from the system operating under the East India Company.

The first step towards transforming India into a raw-material adjunct was to curb the special prerogatives of the East India Company, whose monopoly in importing Indian cotton and silk, for selling them in the European continent, was proving ruinous to the British manufacturers. In 1813, largely owing to the pressure of merchants and industrialists, the British parliament ended the Company's monopoly of trade with India. Twenty years later the British parliament finally forbade the East India Company to trade at all, thus terminating its commercial character and privileges.

Between 1814 and 1835 British manufactured cotton clothes exported to India rose from less than one million to fifty-one million yards. Correspondingly, Indian cotton piece-goods imported into Britain fell from 1,250,000 pieces to

1. Dietmar Rothermund, *An Economic History of India: From Pre-Colonial Times to 1986* (New Delhi, 1988), p. 16.

306,000 pieces.[2] In real terms, the value of British trade with India was far from impressive and failed to attain the dimensions expected of it. To put this trade on a firm footing, British businessmen campaigned for the application in India of two principal achievements of the Industrial Revolution — the steamship and the steam railway. Systematic efforts to obtain government support for steamship lines from Britain to India's chief ports began in the 1830s. The steamship brought India closer to England. However, it did not guarantee British manufactured goods access to the interior of the country nor did it meet the requirements of securing both raw materials as well as that of finding a market for its finished products. To achieve this objective the next logical step was the introduction of a network of railways.

EARLY ATTEMPTS

The earliest efforts to construct railways in India may be traced back to as early as 1832, when a railway line was mooted between Madras and Bangalore.[3] A decade later Rowland Macdonald Stephenson launched an unrelenting campaign for the introduction of railways in India.[4] Shipping lines and railways were all part of his plan for a vast communication scheme, which would eventually link Britain not only with its

2. Palme Dutt, *India Today*, p. 119.
3. M.N. Das, *Studies in the Economic and Social Development of Modern India: 1848–1856* (Calcutta, 1959), p. 26.
4. Rowland Macdonald Stephenson, a civil engineer, became interested in India in 1830. In 1836, he became the Secretary to the London Steam Committee. In 1840, he was Secretary of the short-lived rival of the Peninsular and Oriental East India Steam Navigation Company. After Peninsular and Oriental's victory over its rival companies, Stephenson turned his attention to preparing the way for introducing railways in India.

great Eastern Empire, India, but also with the other immense market, China.

As a pioneer, he began by disseminating the idea of railways and its effects through native as well as English journals. He systematically collected data and documents on the resources and trade potential of the important trading centres all over India, and published a comprehensive report. In response to this report, the East Indian Railway Company (subsequently known as East Indian Railway) was formed in England, with Stephenson as the Managing Director, for constructing a line from Calcutta to the North-West Provinces.[5] Simultaneously, the Great Indian Peninsula Railway Company was formed with a view to construct a railway 'from Bombay to the Eastern-Ghats to terminate on the eastern coast or near the harbour at Coringa'.[6] A Provisional Committee of the railway companies submitted their proposals to the Court of Directors for approval. The Court of Directors appointed F.W. Simms to conduct an enquiry into the feasibility of railways in India. His observations were not encouraging. Discussions then ensued between the companies, the Court of Directors, and the Board of Control on various aspects like the guarantee on capital, duration of the contract and the railway lines to be constructed. 'Correspondences' to thrash out the various issues continued for three years before the first contract was signed in 1849.[7] Lord Dalhousie was instrumental in securing governmental approval of the projects, which were taken up as experimental railway lines.

5. Das, *Studies in the Economic and Social Development of Modern India*, p. 33.

6. Das, *Studies in the Economic and Social Development of Modern India*, p. 34.

7. Thorner, *Investment in Empire*, p. 48.

PHILOSOPHY OF THE RAILWAYS

At this point an insight into the basic considerations working behind the introduction of railways is essential. Railways served as an instrument of colonial exploitation and conformed with the contemporary view of making the economy of the colonies subservient to the economy of the mother country. The dominance of Industrial Capitalism was characterized by a quest to exploit the natural resources of India. The colonial government wanted foreign investment, and the railways were a major area where it could be utilized in India.

According to Stephenson, the choice of the railway alignment was to be guided by the following considerations:

> The first consideration is a military measure for the better security with less outlay, of the entire territory, the second commercial point of view, in which the chief object is to provide the means of conveyance from the interior to the nearest shipping ports, of the rich and varied productions of the country and to transmit back the manufactured goods of Great Britain, salt, etc., in exchange.[8]

Stephenson, a true exponent of the Manchester School of Thought, sought to introduce railways to effectively market British goods as well as to ensure a steady supply of raw materials from the vast Indian hinterland. There was no consideration for the welfare of the teeming Indian masses, for whom advanced technological innovations in agriculture, with a provision for irrigation would have represented real development.

Lord Dalhousie in his famous 'Minute' outlined the underlying motives for introducing railways from a purely economic standpoint:

> the commercial and social advantages which India would

8. Thorner, *Investment in Empire*, pp. 48–9.

derive from their establishment are, I truly believe, beyond all present calculations. Great tracts are teeming with produce they cannot dispose off . . . England is calling aloud for cotton which India does produce in some degree and would provide sufficient[ly] . . . if they were provided the fitting means of conveyance for it from the distant plains to the several ports adopted for shipment.[9]

Political and military considerations were also outlined in the 'Minute'. Lord Dalhousie inherited an indistinct and disconnected empire, which he brought together through a policy of conquest and annexation. He conquered almost all of the economically more attractive regions of India, transforming it into an extensive territorial empire. He was of the view that effective administrative control over the vast empire could be maintained through a network of railways. In the event of an internal political crisis, the railways would provide greater mobility to military forces. Affording rapid movement of food grains to the affected areas could also minimize the evils of famine. Another factor of importance was surplus British capital that was seeking employment abroad, and Lord Dalhousie saw in the railways of India the best opportunity for investing it.

EVOLUTION OF THE POLICY FOR CONSTRUCTION AND MANAGEMENT OF RAILWAYS

Lord Dalhousie was a representative of an era of economic individualism, commonly referred to as free-trade capitalism. A significant feature of the era was the formation of Joint Stock Companies wherever there was an import of foreign

9. N.B. Mehta, *Indian Railways: Rates and Regulations* (London, 1927), p. 11.

capital. Dalhousie favoured joint stock companies to act as instruments for the construction and management of railways. His 'Minute' runs thus:

> I hold the creation of great public works which although serve the important purposes of the state are mainly intended to be used in those multifarious operations, which that enterprise, the trade and the interests of the community, for ever in motion, is in no part of the proper business of the Government.[10]

He was of the opinion that unless private companies were encouraged, money could not be easily raised through governmental agencies.

Private companies were not willing to undertake construction, unless the government offered a guarantee on the capital. Initially the demand was for a guarantee of 3 per cent. Four years elapsed in settling the issue of the guarantee; the guarantee finally decided upon for signing the first contracts was 5 per cent. The issue of the guarantee was so vital that it dominated the proceedings of railway construction for over four decades. Three distinct phases of development of railways can be identified: (a) The Old Guarantee System (1853 to 1869), (b) State Construction and Management (1869 to 1882), and (c) Revival of Companies or Modified Guarantee (1882 to 1903).

The acceptance of Dalhousie's recommendation by the Court of Directors, led to the sanction for the construction of 5,000 miles of railways by eight companies under terms of the 'Old Guarantee System'. The contracts were signed for 99 years at the end of which the railway would become the property of the government. The company guaranteed an interest of 5 per cent per annum on all paid up capital to the

10. Mehta, *Indian Railways*, p. 13.

government for a period of 99 years. This guarantee was to be repaid from the profits above the guaranteed minimum, with a part of it being accredited to the company and the other half to the government towards the repayment of the debt. Government was to provide land free of cost, and it was to control and supervise the working of the railways. The government retained the power of purchasing the railway lines on a six months notice at the end of the twenty-fifth or fiftieth year. The sum to be paid was to be calculated at the mean market value of shares in London, during the preceding three years.

It was easy to elicit capital by offering a guarantee, as there was no limit on the capital to be guaranteed. The greater the capital, the greater was the amount to be paid as guarantee. The shareholders were relieved of all risks and therefore made no effort to economize. It promoted recklessness, which involved the country 'in liabilities which people could bear or the needs of time could justify'.[11] Government control proved ineffective with the inexperience of the consulting engineers and an imperfect audit system.[12] The shareholders were too far removed in England and did not care to know about the details of construction, maintenance or the operating expenses, as long as they received their dividends.

The guarantee system operated at a loss to the state exchequer. The original estimate per mile for double lines was £ 15,000 and for single lines, it was £ 9,000. The actual expense averaged at more than £ 20,000 per mile. For the first five years (including 1854) the average outlay was £ 3.5 million

11. Nalinaksha Sanyal, *Development of Indian Railways* (Calcutta, 1930), p. 17.
12. Government engineers were not experienced in railway construction and in the fear of causing delay in construction, they overlooked the negligence of the companies.

and in the subsequent years, it averaged £ 5 million annually. The total capital outlay till 1868 stood at £ 78 million. The aggregate receipts towards interest was £ 13 million. In the year 1863, more than a £ 1.5 million had to be paid towards revenue. To top it all the government incurred a loss on the acquisition of land, on supervision, and on loss of exchange because of the rise in exchange rates. The total loss on this account stood at £ 3.6 million in 1868–69.[13] The rapid depreciation of the rupee occurred because the 'Home Charges' were fixed in gold, while Indian revenue was collected in silver. The guarantee system stood discredited on account of all these factors, and the search for an alternative began.

In 1858, Lord Canning expressed alarm at the reckless management of finances by the companies and objected to the guarantee system. He pressed to limit the capital amount on which the guarantee was issued. In the British parliament, a strong opinion grew in favour of state management of railways. Simultaneously attempts were made at forming unguaranteed railway companies.[14] Lord Lawrence made the first move to induce the Secretary of State to sanction State Railways. In 1869, Lord Mayo succeeded in securing the approval of the Secretary of State for India, to raise capital and to undertake state construction of railway lines.

13. All statistics have been compiled from Nalinaksha Sanyal, *Development of Indian Railways*, pp. 43–4.
    14. The two unguaranteed railways were the Indian Branch Railway Company that constructed a line on four feet gauge between Naihati and Azimganj, and in 1867 constructed a forty mile track from Kanpur to Lucknow. The other railway was the Indian Tramway Company, which constructed a short section of a line between Arconum and Coonjeveeram [sic]. The companies could not manage to survive on their own finances and later had to be guaranteed. The first was merged into the Oudh and Rohilkand Railway Company and the second into the Carnatic Railway Company.

A new epoch dawned in the history of Indian Railways, when the state took upon itself the responsibility for future construction and for raising the necessary money for that purpose. The goal laid before it — to achieve a target of a tolerably complete network of main lines traversing all parts of the country, which would ultimately prove profitable. The government was permitted to raise a loan, which, after the reckless guarantee system, was in itself a great measure of economy. It was stipulated that henceforth the State was to confine its activities to constructing only 'political' lines, leaving the 'commercial' or profitable lines to railway companies. In an effort to induce economy, it was decided that the lines would be extended on:

> a narrow gauge track laid on a substantial road and subway, with rails proportioned to the limited wheel loads of the improved engines now obtainable and to the moderate speed required by the circumstances of the country.[15]

This pronouncement was regarded as the parent of the metre gauge railway system. The railways came to be divided into two classes, the primary broad gauge trunk lines, and the secondary narrow gauge lines to open out the less productive areas. After much debate, the metre gauge was adopted for State Railways.

The money, which the Government was allowed to raise for construction, was fixed at £ 2 million and that for extraordinary works were to be undertaken from borrowings on the surplus balances. The annual allocation was found inadequate for the purpose and increased to £ 4 million in 1875.[16]

The policy of state management enthusiastically initiated

15. Mehta, *Indian Railways*, p. 35.
16. Ibid.

by the government, was energetically pursued for a period of ten years. Private enterprise in any form was not encouraged during this period. The greater proportion of extensions was on the metre gauge, which being mostly feeders to the trunk lines, did not serve the commercial aspirations of either the capitalists or the peasantry. This fact is borne out by the average returns on the capital raised: company managed lines yielded a return of 6.2 per cent, the return on state managed lines was 2.15 per cent.[17]

It was under compelling circumstances that the government reverted to construction by private companies. The reversal was on account of two important factors. In its bid for colonial expansion beyond the frontiers, the British embroiled themselves in a war with Afghanistan. To secure its North-Western Frontier against further incursions and to gear up to meet a future war-like exigency, a series of broad gauge lines, strategic and military, were constructed. They were constructed regardless of cost and commercial prospects. Furthermore, certain lines which had proved expensive, were reconverted to metre gauge. Working expenses being very high with very little commensurate returns, the state was left heavily burdened with a series of unproductive lines. Meanwhile between 1874 and 1879 the country was ravaged by a scourge of famines, leaving behind a trail of destruction and desolation, paralyzing the economic life of the people. A commission was instituted to investigate into the cause of the often-recurring phenomenon and to suggest means of tackling famines constructively. In 1880, the Famine Commission in its report urged the government to immediately construct 5,000 miles of famine protection lines, with an additional provision of 20,000 miles of

17. Sanyal, *Development of Indian Railways*, p. 119.

railways. The government was eager to follow the recommendations, but could not raise the requisite capital. This was owing to a large-scale diversion of funds for the Afghan War and a consequent depletion of the government's finances. An additional problem was the limit assigned by the Secretary of State for India on the borrowing power of the government for railway construction, as a measure of financial stringency.

Financial constraints underlay the new policy, which once more heralded the reintroduction of private enterprise in the railways, alongside the state. In 1878–79, the railways were responsible for a burden of Rs 236 million on the state.[18] This did not permit satisfactory progress in railway extension and the delay had an adverse effect on the trade of the country — both internal and external.

The ultimate pressure to revert to private enterprise for railway construction came from the powerful lobby of British manufacturers. Throughout the 1840s the lobby urged for, 'a rapid construction of railways in India for developing cotton cultivation and trade'.[19] In the 1880s, they pressed for a greater mileage in the interest of wheat trade, for which they saw prosperous potentialities. The existing trade in wheat according to them languished under the handicap of slow, risky and costly means of transportation. America being a leading producer of wheat held a sway over trade in wheat. To counter this monopoly, the British capitalist lobby envisaged an alternative by extracting wheat from India. This could be achieved by a rapid construction of railways into the wheat growing regions of the country.[20]

18. Mehta, *Indian Railways*, pp. 38–9.
19. Ibid.
20. There was also a growing demand for export of iron from India in the 1880s.

Thus, the 1880s witnessed the re-emergence of the 'guar-antee companies' under modified conditions. The new terms were framed with a view of ensuring greater governmental control and simultaneously ensuring greater participation of the capitalists. Capital required for the purpose was to be raised in India as far as possible, and further construction of railways should not involve any additional taxation. The Parliamentary Select Committee appointed in 1883 gave a final shape to the new policy. Its report highlighted the reasons for rapid construction of railways as follows: (a) protection against famines; (b) for providing stimulus to external and internal trade; (c) growth of more remunerative crops in the tracts reached by the railways; (d) opening up of the coalfields, and the (e) improvement of the general condition of the people.[21]

The railways under the new system of guarantee were to be regarded as a property of the state, with the companies to act as agents for construction. A clear distinction was made be-tween 'productive' and 'protective' lines. It was stipulated that as a rule the state was to undertake the construction of 'pro-tective' lines (commercially unprofitable lines), while the com-mercially viable or 'productive' lines were made the exclusive domain of the private companies. A permanent guarantee of 3.5 per cent was made. The government retained a large share amounting to three-fifths of the surplus profits. Finally, the government retained the right to terminate the contracts at the end of the twenty-fifth year, and at subsequent intervals of ten years on the repayment of the money at par, as paid by the companies. The stipulation was aimed at inducing economy as well as efficiency in construction.

21. Sanyal, *Development of Indian Railways*, p. 80.

BEGINNINGS OF RAILWAYS IN ASSAM

It was within this broad framework of the 'modified guarantee system' that railways were introduced in Assam. The economy of the province had not reached the 'take-off' stage, to provide the fillip for bringing in railways. Though it had a predominantly agriculture based economy, there was no surplus production, nor was the level of trade and commerce substantial enough to act as an impetus. Primarily an importing economy, it singularly lacked the vital pre-requisite for any capitalistic enterprises, labour. The population of the province — depleted by natural and political factors — was widely scattered as well as sparse in proportion to the total land area. In spite of such major disadvantages, the tea industry was firmly entrenched in Assam. It thrived on imported labour from the neighbouring provinces of Bengal and Bihar, which brought about an influx of population into the province. The concentration of population was only in certain pockets, since large portions of the province were wastelands.

In most parts of India where railways were constructed, it connected the teeming agricultural hinterland to various ports for export of produce to England. The scenario in Assam was entirely different; except for the plantation industry there was no other initiating factor. Here the railway was more or less introduced on the American model. America in the pre-railway era was vastly unexplored. They adopted a policy of building railways over desolate prairies with the presumption that, 'an influx of population would follow in their wake'.[22] In America, as anticipated, the enterprising population took advantage of the developed communication network and railways became

22. Financial 'A', January 1920, no. 173, F-19/1–16, 'Extract from the Proceedings of the Council Meeting', 5 April 1919, p. 6.

the largest initiator of economic growth. In Assam the introduction of railways followed the same thought process, for here too, efficient land communication of any sort did not exist, while large tracts of land were still unproductive.

INITIAL CORRESPONDENCE

From 1868 to 1873, there was a fair amount of correspondence between the Government of Assam and the Government of Bengal (PWD Railway Branch) relating to introduction of railways in Assam. During this period, the Commissioner of Assam did not favour the opening of a railway into the province, as it was not considered economically viable:

> It is obvious too that all the tea we can produce in Assam for many a year would go very little towards providing traffic for railroad. Nor do I know of any merchandise or produce whereby traffic could be maintained between Assam and the Presidency that would cover the cost of working expense of railway, much less repay the guarantee.[23]

Henry Hopkinson, in spite of being aware of the benefits that would accrue to the plantations was unwilling to allow that, '... all India should be mulcted [sic] of three or five millions of its revenue, for the sake of mainly the English tea grower and the English tea consumer.'[24] To him the only reason which could make a railway viable, was the extraction of coal in Upper Assam, to supply mineral fuel for steam navigation and railroads in Bengal. Till the 1860s a proper

23. Letters issued to Government, letter no. 18, 22 January 1868, from H. Hopkinson, Chief Commissioner to the Officiating Joint Secretary to Government of Bengal, PWD (Railway Department).

24. Letters issued to Government, letter no. G.T. 373, Government of Bengal, General Department Industry and Science, 18-10-1873, vol. 50, 1873.

assessment of the coalfields and the economic viability of having a railway to draw out the coal reserves had not been made. It was not before 1874 that the authorities responded positively and favoured a railway project for Assam.

H. Luttman Johnson, Secretary to the Chief Commissioner, in a letter to the Secretary Agriculture, and Commerce, for the first time expressed the desire to:

> make it apparent to the Chief Commissioner that if it is desired that the trade in Assam should prosper, the first step is to make a light railway connecting the coal deposits with the Brahmaputra.[25]

The reason ascribed by him was that it would foster overall development of Assam in the long run. It would in a great way help to develop steamer communication, which was heavily dependent on the coal brought 620 miles from Burdwan (approximately 800 miles from Dibrugarh). For enhancing production, the tea industry was slowly substituting 'hot air for charcoal leaf drying', and it was imperative to replace manual labour in leaf rolling and other processes by steam power.

Enquiry into the mineral potential of Assam began in right earnest with its annexation in 1826. Evidence of the existence of coal dated back to as early as 1774. David Scott deputed Lieutenant Wilcox to report on the various coal bearing areas in Assam. Preliminary investigations revealed the existence of coal in the Suffrai Valley.[26] In 1828, Scott informed the government of coal deposits in the Someswari Valley in the Garo hills. The next move in this direction was the constitution of a Coal Committee in Calcutta, to report on the issue of opening out the coalfields.

25. Revenue Department Proceedings, May 1874, no. 129, 15 May 1874, p. 6.
26. Barooah, *David Scott in North-East India*, p. 111.

J.G. Medlicott of the Geological Survey of India surveyed the prospective localities summarily in 1865. He conducted his survey on the river Dehing. In view of the low ash content of Assam coal, he considered it superior to the coal from the rest of India.[27] F.R. Mallet of the Geological Survey India, conducted two other summary surveys in 1874–75 and 1876–77.[28] A careful inspection was made on the outcrops from the rivers Tirap to the Desoi. The five coalfields identified were Makum and Jaipur in Lakhimpur and Nazira, Jhanzi and Desoi in Sibsagar district.

PRESSURE GROUPS

The opening up of the coalfields was undoubtedly an important factor in the introduction of railways in Assam, but it did not minimize the role of the tea industry as a pressure group. Access to the Brahmaputra, Assam's great natural highway, was of vital importance to the tea industry in Upper Assam. Lack of a network of feeder roads leading from the gardens to the river mouth, was a major hurdle in transporting their produce. The state of the road between Sadiya to the steamer ghat at Dibrugarh was in a hopeless state rendering it practically unusable during the rains.

FEEDER RAILWAYS AND TRAMWAYS

During the rainy season of 1878, Dr Berry White, a planter, represented to the Chief Commissioner of Assam, the shocking state to which the roads between the tea factories and

27. *Physical and Political Geography of the Province of Assam: 1892–1893*, p. 53.
28. Ibid.

Dibrugarh had been reduced to by heavy traffic and lack of timely repairs. He expressed that the planters feared that if such a state of affairs continued, the communication between tea factories and the steamer ghat at Dibrugarh would cease altogether. It would render both import of labour as well as export of produce impossible for the planters.[29]

The Government of Assam sympathized with the plight of the planters. They perceived that a remedy to this ill was the introduction of light railways on the Sadiya Road. The view of the government was endorsed in a letter from the Public Works Department, to the Finance Department of the Government of India:

> during the last few years there has been an extraordinary development of the tea industry in this part of the district, there being no less than 60 gardens along this line of the road, employing 20,000 imported coolies, for whom 15,000 maunds [551 tons] of rice had to be annually imported, while the weight of tea exported is 60,000 maunds [2,204 tons] . . . The recent opening out of numerous gardens has been accompanied by a large development of cart traffic, and the unmetalled road under the burden of this traffic become hopelessly and absolutely impassable during the rains.[30]

The Government of Assam was favourably inclined towards the scheme as a joint venture with the planters. It was visualized that the scheme if successful, would be parent to similar such projects. The government would be relieved of the onerous burden of providing the means of communication in the district of Lakhimpur.

A large number of tea gardens in the vicinity of Jorhat, in the Sibsagar district, experienced great difficulty in carting their

29. Gawthropp, *Story of Assam Railways*, p. 10.
30. Ibid.

produce between the trunk route and the bank of the Brahmaputra. The distance between Jorhat and the Kokilamukh on the riverbank was just over 12.5 miles.[31] This portion of the road was subjected to inundation even at normal times reducing it to a hopeless state. The cost of metalling this portion of the road was estimated at approximately Rs 80,000, as stones for this purpose had to be carted or brought by boat over a long distance. The government therefore considered it viable to lay a light tramway from the banks of the river Brahmaputra to Jorhat. This would save the fund-strapped PWD of the burden of an enormous outlay on the roads.

Detailed surveys were taken up to ascertain the alignment for a two feet gauge tramway, which would ensure connectivity to most of the tea gardens in the area. The alignment was decided to be from Jorhat along the *Garh Ali* to Titabar, and a branch line of 7.25 miles along the *Hatigarh Ali* to Mariani. The name of the tramway was named the Jorhat–Kokilamukh Tramway, the construction of which was taken up by the government from the provincial revenues.[32]

The interests of the planters in the district of Darrang — which contained some of the finest gardens in Assam — suffered on account of the bad state of communication. A stretch of twenty miles between Tezpur ghat and Balipara contained seventeen of the twenty-one gardens in the district and ran close to the three large weekly markets. The increased traffic from these gardens could not be carted over the existing road, which was in a deplorable condition. To resolve the communication issue, an obvious alternative was to consider the scheme of a tramway. The Chief Commissioner was approached for a

31. PWD (Railway Construction) Proceedings, February 1884, letter no. 1135, dated 23 June 1883.
32. Ibid.

subsidy from the provincial revenues. The government allowed the Local Board to subsidize the line, 'so far as it can afford to do so with the means at its disposal'.[33] However, no special grant was made to the local board to enable them to make this subsidy. The tea gardens however, contributed in proportion to their production of tea, a sum of Rs 1,75,000, in ordinary shares, to form a corpus of the capital.[34] It was the genesis of the Tezpur–Balipara Tramway on the 2 feet 6 inches gauge.

Apart from coal and tea, petroleum was an important mineral found in Assam in the neighbourhood of the coal-bearing areas. Initial surveys for petroleum as well as its extraction was inextricably linked with the first railways in Assam. Maiden attempts were made in 1866 by F. Goodenough of McKillop, Stewart and Company to extract oil from the area, on both sides of the Dehing, from Jaipur to the Noa-Dehing.[35] The attempt was a failure. In 1878, an application was made by Balmer Lawrie and Company as the Managing Agents of the Assam Mineral Company to extract petroleum in certain sites in Upper Assam. They were granted concessions by an order of 30 April 1880, to extract petroleum in specific localities in the Jaipur sub-division. The term of the concession was for a period of fifty years on payment of a rental of Rs 50 per square mile.[36] In 1881, it was discovered that the area specified in the lease, overlapped with the Makum Coal Licence granted to the Assam Railways and Trading Company.[37]

33. Railway Construction 'A', February 1894, nos. 236–249, letter no. 241, 3 May 1893.

34. Traffic 'A', June 1915, nos. 167–171, letter no. 167.

35. Gawthropp, *Story of Assam Railways*, p. 44.

36. Railway Construction 'A', December 1881, despatch no. 120 R, dated 15 October 1881.

37. The petroleum concession was added to the original railway contract by an order of 16 December 1882.

TRUNK ROUTES

A careful perusal of the trade reports in the 1880s indicated that a very negligible proportion of the trade was carried out through the overland routes with Bengal. Trade was conducted through steamers and boats both in the Brahmaputra and Surma Valley. For the colonizers the levels of trade had attained a 'take-off' stage. As the bulk of the trade was with various blocks of Bengal; therefore, a railway connecting the two provinces became a necessity under the 'modified guarantee system'. A survey to identify trunk routes, on three independent routes, was undertaken. In 1881, J.W. Buyers, the Engineer-in-Chief, was deputed to conduct a survey on the Garo Hills railway. The survey was to consider the extension of the Dacca–Mymensingh Railway, across the Garo hills into Gauhati in Assam. A second alignment on the same route was surveyed along the western spurs of the Garo hills. The first line surveyed totalled a length of 181 miles, of which 85 miles was through extremely hilly terrain.[38] The second route, which traversed around the western end of the Garo hills, skirted the *chars* of the Brahmaputra, covering a distance of 220 miles.

The hill route, apart from having its self-evident advantages, also served as a direct route to tap the coalfields in the Someswari Valley. It was proposed that a light tramway be constructed from the trunk line to the coalfields. The route identified was from the left bank of the Brahmaputra, opposite Mymensingh, along the existing district road to a point opposite Shusung Durgapur. A railway from the Assam Valley either through the Garo hills or the western spurs would have

38. Railway Construction 'A', October 1882, nos. 87–108, no. 1797, September 1882.

communication with the port of either Calcutta or Chittagong broken by just one ferry.[39]

> The crying want of Assam apparently being labour, it is obviously desirable to put it in the most direct communication with those districts from which the supply is drawn.[40]

The Government of Assam as well as the Government of India voiced this opinion. A line along the western spurs of the Garo Hills would have the advantage of being placed in communication with the Northern Bengal State Railway, either by a line from the mouth of the Durla to Kaunia or the alternative route proposed through Dhubri. The projected line along the western spurs failed to attract the attention of the government, as it could not tap the coalfields. The Garo Hills, served as the shortest line of communication between Mymensingh and Gauhati, but the conjectured costs were extremely prohibitive. The estimate for the 85 miles of the Hill Section of the line stood at approximately Rs 1,10,100 per mile.[41] The work on the hill section was expected to be heavy and would require approximately £ 230,000 more than the other line. The advantages of connecting the Brahmaputra Valley with Eastern Bengal was so strong that it struck a death blow to the project for continuing the Dacca–Mymensingh Railway to the valley of the Brahmaputra near Gauhati.

In 1882–83 the Chief Commissioner of Assam (Sir Charles Elliot) urged the taking up of a survey on a route connecting it to either of the ports of Bengal with Upper Assam. Attention was drawn to the populous districts 'of the country lying East

39. Railway Construction 'A'. Report by J.W. Buyers, Engineer-in-Chief, Garo Hills Railway Survey, season 1881–1882.

40. Railway Construction 'A', October 1882, nos. 87–108, no. 1797, September 1882.

41. See Note 40.

of the Meghna' — Sylhet and Chittagong, which did not have a single line of railway.[42] Towards the close of 1882, the Government of India, recognizing the urgency of the claims of these districts, coupled with the urgency of settling the issue of the best route to the Brahmaputra Valley, sanctioned a re-connaissance survey. The railway route conceived was aimed at connecting the port of Chittagong through the important districts of Sylhet and Cachar to Makum junction in Upper Assam, with a branch line to Gauhati.

River-borne trade returns of the corresponding period had an important bearing on the issue of a railroad with Eastern Bengal. A railway linking Sylhet and Tipperah [*sic*], with Lakhimpur and Sibsagar, offered ample scope for equalization of prices. While the former two were rice-exporting districts the latter two were the main rice importing districts. Rice was required to feed their native population, Europeans, as well as imported coolies. Sylhet could not only meet the demand for rice in the Assam Valley, but could also find a market for its abundant lime and *ghi*.[43] It was perceived that the scope for equalization of prices would result in a rapid progress of colonization of wastelands, which was hitherto retarded due to high food prices.

The chief imports from the Eastern Bengal Trade Block to the Brahmaputra Valley was rice for the tea gardens of Upper Assam, and tea-seed and drained sugar for the Surma Valley. The exports were mainly uncleaned cotton, lac and oranges. Cotton and lac was exported through boats from the Brahma-putra Valley, and the oranges went from Sylhet. This block

42. Railway Construction 'A' December 1887, nos. 224–269, enclosure no. 868 RC of 1887, 'Final Report' of J.W. Buyers.

43. *Report on the River Borne Trade of the Province of Assam: 1881–1882*, p. 9.

received 69 per cent of the total amount of raw cotton exported from the province.[44]

The great bulk of the trade from the Chittagong division was with Sylhet and Cachar. The main staples imported were sheep and goats, bricks and tiles, turmeric, coconuts, wheat (65 per cent of the total imports) and tobacco. Amongst the exports, canes, rattans, oranges, rice and paddy, mats and bamboos (mainly from the Surma Valley). Of the rice and paddy sent to Chittagong, almost the whole of it was from the Surma Valley.[45] A railway alignment connecting Assam, through the North Cachar Hills and the Surma Valley, to Chittagong was perceived to be practicable from the point of view of its trade potential.

While deciding upon this alignment, the planters of Cachar acted as an important pressure group. The trade of Cachar suffered immensely during the dry season, as steamers could not ply beyond Fenchuganj, a distance of seventy miles off Silchar. It was during this season that the bulk of the tea garden labourers were transported. The existing communication network put the planting community to a considerable expense towards procurement of labour. It also impeded free immigration. In view of these facts, William Ward strongly pressed upon the Government of India, the urgent need for a railway to connect Cachar with Bengal, in view of the depressing condition of the tea industry.

Two important resolutions were passed on the issue of a railway connecting Cachar with Bengal. The resolution proposed by E. Livermore, highlighted the issue.

What is required by us is an ample supply of labour, and this

44. *Report on the River Borne Trade of the Province of Assam: 1884–85*, p. 4.
45. Ibid.

labour must be secure and unfailing. At present the labour is not nearly sufficient for our wants and so our operations are hampered and enterprise is prevented from expanding at the same rate, as it would otherwise do . . . [46]

Another resolution that was put forth by Adam White on this issue revealed:

To cure this a railway is what we need. This was clearly recognized in a recent speech by Sir Rivers Thompson about the Behar [sic] and Assam railway, and it was further emphasized by what he said about the Chittagong projected Railway. By a railway alone our labour wants could be adequately met. [47]

William Ward, who succeeded Sir Charles Elliot as Chief Commissioner of Assam, differed on the issue of having a single railway connecting Assam and Eastern Bengal to the port of Chittagong. He was opposed to the route across the North Cachar Hills and instead favoured two independent systems of railways on both the valleys. One line was proposed between Chittagong and Cachar, and the other line was to be confined to the Brahmaputra Valley, with an extension from Gauhati to Fakirganj. He was for an Assam Valley line and opposed 'the North Cachar Connection Scheme' as he perceived that it 'will bring no additional traffic to the Assam Valley line that a disconnected Assam Valley line from Dibrugarh to Gauhati and Dhubri would also bring'. [48]

Ward projected that the route through Fakirganj was the shortest to Calcutta, the existing natural export outlet for the tea from Assam. The Chittagong route from Upper Assam, he felt would not serve the purpose of importing labour from

46. Railway Construction 'A' (PWD), December 1887, no. 241, 3rd Resolution.
47. Ibid.
48. Railway Construction 'A', December 1887, enclosure no. 7 to PWD Resolution no. 868 RC of 1887, p. 9.

North Bihar and Bengal — an urgent requirement of the tea industry. He found that the existing port facilities at Chittagong were inadequate for handling the growing tea trade. The opposition of Ward did not hold ground in the face of the pressure from the planters of Upper Assam.

The planters of Upper Assam were united in their support for a railway connecting the two river valleys to Chittagong. Phillips, Superintendent of the Assam Tea Company at Nazira, opined that, 'the planter would gain little by carrying his tea to Fakirganj by rail and shipping it there'.[49] The gardens that sent their tea directly to London had no objection to the Chandpur route, as it would enable them to ship their goods without a break in transportation. The planters were concerned about securing the cheapest and most expeditious means of conveyance.

Another important lobby comprised capitalists who were keen on developing Chittagong as a natural port for the districts of Eastern Bengal and Assam. Sir Rivers Thompson maintained an unchanged opinion that the Chittagong Railway would be the best in Bengal and held prospects of being remunerative in every respect. The extraordinary development of trade through the port of Chittagong over a period of ten years, commencing from 1876, afforded him ample scope to justify his claim. He viewed the development as 'extraordinary' as it occurred in spite of adverse circumstances. The means of communication between the port and the interior, as well the port and the sea was unsatisfactory. The total traffic in the decade between 1876–77 and 1885–86 rose in value from Rs 40,68,429 to Rs 2,03,87,811.[50] A railway connecting the

49. Railway Construction 'A', no. 255, 15 September 1887.
50. Railway Construction 'A', December 1887, enclosure no. 14 to PWD Resolution no. 868 RC of 1887, no. 463 R of 2 March 1887.

port to Upper Assam could ensure a steady supply of coal to the sea going steamers. It was assumed that this would enable the 'shipping business to be dealt with there at a cost with which Calcutta with its dangerous river approach cannot compete.'[51]

The administrative gains from this route were also highlighted. The only overland route connecting the two provinces was the road from Gauhati to Sylhet via Shillong and Cherrapunji. The railway, if constructed, would reduce the tedious journey by this road and serve as an alternative route.

The strategic importance of this route according to J.W. Buyers, the Engineer-in-Chief, was that it would help the passage of troops into positions 'which command the whole mountainous districts which separates the Province of Assam from Upper Burmah [*sic*] and which is inhabited by savage and unruly tribes'.[52] The route would enable troops stationed in Upper Assam and Cachar to render mutual support to each other. The line was projected in the light of the future prospects of connecting Assam with the Burma Railways system, both on strategic and economic considerations.

By the 1880s, immigration of plantation labourers took place on an extensive scale. There was no corresponding expansion in food grains production to meet the growing demand. Consequently, rice was imported from other provinces and Burma. The market mechanism operating in India in the post-1870 period was geared towards export of a considerable amount of food grains. During the post-famine period in the 1880s a search for alternative areas, capable of food grain production — especially rice — was sought. Assam, with its

51. Railway Construction 'A', December 1887, enclosure no. 11 to PWD Resolution no. 868 RC of 1887.

52. Railway Construction 'A', December 1887, enclosure no. 14 to PWD Resolution no. 868 RC of 1887, no. 463 R of 2 March 1887.

millions of acres of cultivable wastelands, offered immense potential for rice cultivation. Lack of initiative amongst the local peasantry — despite encouragement and punitive revenue enhancement — acted as a deterrent to surplus production. The situation it was felt could be redeemed by inviting cultivating classes from Bengal to settle on the wastelands of Assam. The policy-makers visualized that the success of a scheme of large-scale immigration was largely dependent on a speedier means of communication. Railways on the American model, made with the purpose of opening up unknown tracts, rather than on the model of the Indian commercial railways, were required. The various pressure groups and their common interests contributed, in deciding about the construction of the Assam–Bengal Railway, the trunk railway route for Assam.

By the beginning of the twentieth century, though a trunk route ran through the province, it could not ensure large-scale immigration into the wastelands. The existing route was found inadequate for the purpose. In the second decade of the twentieth century, the issue of connecting Assam with Calcutta gained momentum. The principle factor for desiring this connection was to foster large-scale immigration into the wastelands of Assam. The annual trade reports revealed that Calcutta continued to command a major share of the trade, which was to the tune of 67 per cent.

In the decade between 1870 and 1880, it was impressed upon the local governments' to take up railway extensions on their own initiative. This was because in the 'Schedule' of the Railway Department, the construction of railways to meet local needs, did not receive priority. Private entrepreneurs initiated short lines of light railways without state assistance, to develop local resources like coal, etc. Notable among the light railways constructed, were the Port Commissioners'

Railway and the District Board Railways. The Madras Board took a lead in constructing a District Board Railway, a parent of similar other ventures. With a view to encourage railway projects outside the 'Railway Programme' the provincial governments in 1898 issued orders authorizing the local boards to levy cesses for railway construction, or to provide interest on capital. Apart from the direct form of assistance by the boards, indirect subsidies in the form of cash subsidies for a certain number of years after construction was given, for which a limit was specified. In order to supplement the net earnings a minimum dividend was fixed on the capital outlay. The Tezpur–Balipara Tramway, also known as the Tezpur–Balipara Light Railway, was constructed in Assam under this scheme. Tramways served to minimize expenses hitherto incurred in construction and maintenance of district roads.

CONCLUSION

The 'March of the Iron Horse' into Assam was an extension of a larger scheme of railroad expansion in India. The 1880s witnessed the re-introduction of private enterprise in railway construction under the modified guarantee system. A systematic, well-defined and uniform policy was not adopted after 1881. The schemes were sanctioned on the basis of 'circumstance of each case'.

Initial correspondence on the issue of introduction of railway into Assam between 1868–1873 was very discouraging. Assam was considered a *cul-de-sac* offering limited traffic for the railways. The provincial authorities were apprehensive of its economic viability and felt that the existing traffic would neither cover the working expenses of the railway, nor repay the guarantee.

Interests of the tea planters in both the Brahmaputra and Surma Valley provided a fillip for introducing railways in Assam. Subsequently, confirmed reports of the existence of extensive reserves of coal and petroleum provided an added incentive. Feeder railways were initiated, connecting the tea producing and mineral bearing areas to the river mouths.

Multiple factors operated in deciding on the trunk route. An important criterion was to link the tea producing areas to the nearest port, without a break in transportation. Prospects of inter-district equalization of prices acted as an impetus. The railways had to fulfil the colonial desire of ensuring a steady labour supply to the plantations. It had to fulfil the strategic needs of the province. An added criterion was the feasibility of the railroad in connecting Assam to the Burma Railways system on both strategic and economic counts. The desire to develop the populous districts of Eastern Bengal and developing Chittagong as a natural port for the region, worked in favour of the selection of the route for the Assam–Bengal Railway. The introduction of railways and tramways in Assam was in conformity with the policy followed over the rest of the country, excepting that certain special concessions like timber and mineral grants formed an integral part of the agreement with the railway companies. Without such extra incentives, it would have been difficult to attract capital for railway construction in Assam.

4
Railways in Assam
Transitional Phase

An exhaustive account has been given in the preceding chapter on the pressure groups, which worked for the introduction of railways into Assam. Construction was taken up by various agencies ranging from private enterprise to state agencies. Agreements between the Government of India and the companies evolved out a series of discussions, on matters vital to the contracts — rate of interest, mineral and timber concessions. This chapter provides an overview of the railway projects taken up in Assam.

DIBRU–SADIYA RAILWAY CONTRACT

The maiden railway venture in Assam was the Dibru–Sadiya Railway. The formation of a company for the construction and working of the line, evolved out of a series of interactions. The Chief Commissioner of Assam, Sir Stuart Bailey was apprised by the planters of the shocking state of roads in Upper Assam.

Sympathizing with the plight of the planters, he drew up a scheme for a light railway, and initiated consultations with a firm at Calcutta, Shaw Finlayson and Company. After a series of discussions, a provisional agreement was drawn up on 22 October 1879, for constructing a metre-gauge railway. The proposed railway comprised a trunk route from the steamer ghat near Dibrugarh to the fifty-first mile on the road towards Sadiya with three branch lines. The first line was from Dibrugarh to Nagogolie [*sic*], a distance of eight miles. The second was from Panitola to Hopewell on the Rangagora road. The branch line from Makum to Doomdooma on the Dehing bridge was the lifeline of the project.[1]

The government on its part offered a guarantee to the company. On the date of the completion of the trunk line as well as the first two branch lines, the company would receive a guarantee in the form of a subsidy of Rs 80,000 for a term of five years. A separate subsidy of Rs 20,000 annually, for a period of five years, was offered for the Makum branch.[2]

In February 1880, Shaw Finlayson informed their London office of their inability to float a company. This was because the capitalists were unwilling to invest on the terms offered by the government and desired further concessions. The provincial government was eager to launch the project, and were willing to extend the period of guarantee from five to twenty years. The government recommended the omission of the two branch lines incorporated in the agreement. The subsidy payable was to be applicable on those portions of the line, as and when they would be opened to traffic. The Secretary of State for India, found the terms offered too liberal in contrast to the

1. *Dibru–Sadiya Railway: Contracts, Prospectus, Etc.* (Government of India, PWD), (Shillong 1914), agreement dated 22 October 1879 with Shaw Finlayson and Company, para 1.

2. *Dibru–Sadiya Railway*, para 13.

agreements drawn up for the railways for the rest of India. He however accepted that an extension of the term of guarantee was vital for attracting necessary capital for the project. To ensure that projects with similar concessions were not granted in future, a clause was inserted making it binding on the Government of India to consult the Secretary of State prior to making similar commitments. He justified granting of the liberal concessions.

> A guarantee for this length of time is very different for a period during which this undertaking is passing through its first stage of development. Trusting however that such a scheme in question had in it elements of success which will keep the demand of the Provincial Treasury and probably relieve it altogether of the subsidy and feeling the importance of making a beginning with railway enterprise in the Province.[3]

The rate of interest, which had been guaranteed, was 5 per cent on an estimated capital of 16 lakh rupees. The rate was high as compared to that granted for the rest of India, where it varied between 3.5 to 4.5 per cent. Since the project was of a pioneering nature, it was sanctioned on the 'merit of the case'.

The construction of a branch line to Makum coalfields played a vital role in giving final shape to the project. The Government of India had approved an additional guarantee of Rs 20,000 for this branch line. Shaw Finlayson and Company could not raise the requisite capital for this line. In 1881, the company sold out its rights to another London syndicate, the Assam Railways and Trading Company. The promoters of the company desired a guarantee of 5 per cent for the line, or

3. Railway Construction 'A', January 1881, no. 9 R of 26 August 1880, para 5.

'a monopoly of the coalfields for a short term or a part of the coalfield for a long term of years'.[4]

The Assam Railways and Trading Company was desirous of taking up the entire project. However, they insisted on the inclusion of certain clauses, granting them rights over the Makum coalfields, and also timber and petroleum rights over an area of thirty miles around the proposed railway. The Chief Commissioner was of the view that granting these concessions were:

> indispensable for the successful development of the enterprise . . . very desirable even at the cost of some exceptional concessions to secure commencement for the further development of a much neglected Province and he [felt] sure that once it is obtained there will be a steady progress in future.[5]

The Government of India strongly recommended the acceptance of the scheme and urged the Secretary of State to sanction the project for furthering colonial interests in Assam. The Assam Railways and Trading Company issued a prospectus for raising capital through shares. It contained conjectural estimates on the returns expected from the proposed line.

Estimates for annual freight charges were — tea factory supplies, Rs 1,20,489; coal, Rs 1,50,000, (the coalfield was expected to produce 18 million tons); timber to be tapped by the projected line, Rs 2,73,437; passenger traffic, Rs 56,873 calculated at 4 per cent of the population; minor forwarding agency revenue of Rs 20,000; making the gross revenue Rs 6,20,801. Subtracting the working expenses of about 50 per cent, the approximate yield on the capital was expected to be

4. Railway Construction 'A', November 1879, nos. 71–74, letter no. 292 of 16 July 1879.
5. Railway Construction 'A', May 1881, nos. 34–44, letter no. 21 T of 7 February 1881.

10.3 per cent.[6] Armed with these estimates, the local government pursued the scheme vigorously with the Government of India, in spite of the low revenue potential of the province.

The colonial policy of upholding commercial interests above all other factors was largely responsible for the initiation of such a project. The Secretary of State signed a contract in July 1881, with the Assam Railways and Trading Company:

> for constructing and working the railways under the guarantee by the Secretary and also for working the coal, petroleum etc; in Assam for establishing a service of steamers on the Brahmaputra river and for other purposes.[7]

The first indenture designated as the 'Makum Timber Licence' allowed the Company, exclusive rights to 'fell, use and export the timber lying within a distance of 1½ miles on either side of the Makum Branch for a period of 20 years'.[8] The company on its part had to pay a half-yearly royalty at specified rates for each tree they felled. It practically gave the company exclusive rights over all the available timber in the vicinity of the line.

The second indenture inextricably linked with the railway, was designated as the 'Makum Coal and Iron Licence'. The company was granted exclusive rights for mining coal and iron, within an area of thirty square miles, which covered the Makum and Jaipur coalfields. Rights for exploring mineral oil in the vicinity of the Makum coalfields was first granted to Balmer Lawrie and Company in 1878. As the agents of the Assam Mineral Oil Company, they were allowed, 'to extract petroleum at certain localities in the Jaipur sub-division for a

6. *Dibru–Sadiya Railway*, agreement dated 15 July 1880.
7. *Dibru–Sadiya Railway*, agreement dated 2 August 1881.
8. *Dibru–Sadiya Railway*, agreement of 26 July 1881.

term of 50 years, at a rent of Rs 50 per square mile'.[9] In 1881, it was found that the area assigned to the company coincided with the coalfields granted to the Assam Railways and Trading Company. Hence, in order to remove the problem of the overlapping of areas granted for operation to the two companies, the Assam Railways and Trading Company was granted petroleum concessions in 1882. These two indentures formed the core of the agreements with the Assam Railways and Trading Company.

Construction

Construction on the Dibru–Sadiya Railway commenced in January 1882. The collieries were developed as a part of the agreement. The Ledo Colliery commenced production in 1882. In early 1883, the miners and railway engineers estimated the production at over 10,000 maunds (367.35 tons).[10] Tikak Colliery became operational in 1884 and in October the same year, the weekly output stood at 1,200 tons.[11] The necessity at that point was the completion of a railway, connecting the coalfields to the main line.

A distance of 8.5 miles between the Dehing bridge at Margherita on the main line had to be connected by a colliery line. In 1883, the Assam Railways and Trading Company commenced the construction of the Ledo–Tikak–Margherita Colliery line. The government leased out land for the railway and mining premises on a fixed rental, and granted a royalty on the output of coal. It reserved the right to purchase the line in 1931.[12] This was the first instance of an 'unassisted railway'.

9. *Dibru–Sadiya Railway*, agreement dated 30 July 1881.
10. Gawthropp, *Story of Assam Railways*, pp. 28–30.
11. Ibid.
12. Sanyal, *Development of Indian Railways*, p. 162.

The entire length of the railway including the colliery line was opened in 1884. Completion of the Dehing bridge connected the colliery line with the main line. In 1896, the colliery line was worked as a part of the Dibru–Sadiya Railway on the following terms:

i) That all the maintenance charges of the Colliery Branch line with sidings, etc, be kept separate and are borne by the colliery company.

ii) That all other charges for working the system be divided between the Railway and Colliery in proportion to the gross earnings of the Railway to the gross earnings of the Colliery branch.

iii) That the Colliery pay the Railway 5 per cent on the gross earnings of the Colliery Branch line for the use of rolling stock.[13]

The original alignment planned for the Dibru–Sadiya Railway was to terminate at Saikhowaghat. This was with the view of meeting the military requirements of the frontiers beyond Sadiya. During its construction, it was felt that the threat from the trans-frontier tribes had ceased. The line was therefore terminated at Talap, the furthest tea garden on the line.

To understand the strategic implications of the area it is imperative to understand the prevalent political situation of the tract, between Dibrugarh and Sadiya. These tracts were inhabited by the Adis (Abors) who, until 1848, had been amicably disposed towards the British administration. Subsequently, in the decade between 1848 and 1858, they carried out a series of attacks on British frontier outposts. In 1859, after a series of expeditions, the government managed to

13. Railway Traffic 'A', June 1897, nos. 81–95, no. 3325 G of 17 November 1896.

subdue the recalcitrant tribes. It consolidated its position by constructing a road along the frontier and setting up a series of military outposts along the road. An agreement was signed, following which there was a reasonable period of respite from the attacks. This minimized the necessity of extending the railway to Saikhowaghat.

The border attacks were resumed once again in 1889, which culminated in a major offensive in 1893. The government faced considerable resistance, and it was not until 1913 that a general submission was enforced on the Abors (Adis). The fluid political situation in the frontiers made it imperative to reconsider the issue of the extension of the railway beyond Saikhowaghat.

A railway line between Talap and Saikhowaghat, a distance of 8.5 miles, would facilitate rapid military movement in the event of future attacks. An extension of the railway to Saikhowaghat was sanctioned in 1907, at an approximate cost of Rs 4,95,816.[14] The main clauses of the contract were similar to that envisaged in the original agreement of 1880, containing free land grants and timber grants. A subsidy of Rs 600 per mile or Rs 5,100 per annum was fixed for ten years.[15] A proposal was mooted for constructing a branch line of the Dibru–Sadiya Railway, between Tinsukia and Rangagora in 1913, which however did not materialize.

Technical Aspects

The main line of the Dibru–Sadiya Railway was laid with 50 lb flatfooted steel rails, on *uriam* (*Bischolia javanica*) sleepers and

14. Railway Construction 'A', February 1908, nos. 51–58, no. 147 RC, dated 16 January 1908.
15. Railway Projects 'A', nos. 19–23, enclosure no. 1 to despatch no. 22 of Railway of 1905.

cast-iron plates of Denham Olpherts.[16] The Talap branch was laid on 41.25 lb flatfooted steel rails on *uriam* sleepers. The colliery branch was laid on *uriam* sleepers with 50 lb flatfooted rails.[17] The lines were partly ballasted with stone chips, as local ballasting material was not available. The sleepers were extracted from the local forests on both sides of the railway line. The daily output was about 1,000 sleepers. The number of sleepers laid per mile was 2,400. All the lines on this railway were of metre gauge.

Locomotives and wagons, as well as rails and fishplates were all imported from the United Kingdom. In 1899, the Assam Railways and Trading Company imported locomotives from the Baldwin Locomotive Works (USA).[18]

The subsidy offered on the paid-up capital for the construction of the Dibru–Sadiya Railway was charged to the provincial revenues of Assam. Such a charge on the state's revenues was unexpected in view of the opinion expressed by the Chief Commissioner in 1879 that the existing state of finances could not offer such a guarantee. The annual subsidy stood at Rs 1 lakh for a period of twenty years. In addition, the grants of monopoly over the coal, timber and petroleum to the railway company were exceptional concessions, with no parallel in the rest of India. The pioneering nature of the project resulted in the incorporation of clauses for the development of natural resources as well.

The Secretary of State for India while sanctioning the project, stressed on its role in opening out the resources of Assam, a province that he felt had been hitherto deficient in

16. Gawthropp, *Story of Assam Railways*, pp. 16–24.
17. Ibid.
18. Frederick Lehmann, 'Great Britain and the Supply of Railway Locomotives in India: A Case Study of Economic Imperialism', *IESHR*, vol. ii, no. 4, October 1965.

adequate communication links. The guiding factor in sanctioning a railway in a vastly unexplored area was to expand the ambit of British investments in the province, as well as to allow the existing ones to flourish. Import of capital into the region, which had a vast mineral potential, was hampered largely for the want of proper communication. The British sought to unleash the dual forces of colonialism, which aimed at promoting an influx of capital into Assam, as well as to integrate the expanding economy of Assam with world markets. The project was taken up as a 'commercial line' under private enterprise, as stipulated by the Parliamentary Select Committee of 1884.

JORHAT PROVINCIAL RAILWAY

Several tea gardens near Jorhat languished under conditions of insufficient communication. The condition of the existing roads was extremely deplorable which hampered marketing of their produce as well as import of essential commodities. The planters experienced great difficulties in carting goods between gardens on the trunk road and the banks of the Brahmaputra at Kokilamukh, where commercial steamers called on their way up and down the river. Six miles of the road between Jorhat and Kokilamukh was subjected to heavy inundation, rendering it almost impassable during the rainy season.

The estimated cost of metalling the road was Rs 80,000, a burden on the finances of PWD, which was faced with a resource crunch. The idea of a tramway was mooted under such circumstances, on the existing *Dhodar Ali* — an ancient embankment-cum-road. The use of the *Ali* was stressed upon, as it would provide for a cart road alongside the tramway. A tramway also had the advantage of reducing expenses on earthwork and cuttings, as well as on ballasting, for which stone had to be carted over a great distance.

A detailed survey was taken up to fix the alignment, which would ensure tapping the maximum number of tea gardens *en route*. The alignment finally settled for, was between Jorhat — along the cart road — to Kokilamukh on the riverbank, a distance of four miles. A provision was made for allowing future extensions on the line over a distance of approximately twelve miles southward and twenty miles eastward 'to tap the Headquarters of the old Assam Tea Company to tap the whole of this tract, which is the chief tea producing area in Assam'.[19] The line of the tramway was for all practical purposes a short lead to the steamer ghat.

As the line was a short lead to the river, it was conceived on a smaller gauge, of 2 feet 6 inches. Sir John Wolfe-Barry addressing the Institution of Civil Engineers in 1897, on the advantages of the narrow gauge, relative to the conditions in Assam, said:

> Every river Steamer ghat in Assam is virtually a port and there can be little doubt that in case of such feeders the narrower gauge can be constructed much more cheaply than the metre gauge . . . Provided there is no probability of such a feeder connecting later with the main line . . . The narrower gauge having an undoubted advantage where long ghat sidings have to be taken up and relaid every year.[20]

Along with the state construction of railways, private enterprise was also re-introduced. Both were simultaneously

19. Railway Construction 'A', January 1883, nos. 1–3, enclosure no. 2 of despatch no. 168 of Railway, 1882, para 14.
20. Railway Projects 'A', April 1916, no. 256-P/1-6, Appendix 'A', 'Note on the Question of Suitable Gauge for Branch Lines in Assam', p. ii.

continued, with an insistence on encouraging 'productive railways' — railways, which were self-supporting. The project commenced in 1882 with a sanction from the Chief Commissioner of Assam, pending the approval of the Government of India as well as the Secretary of State in London. It was presumed that the line would 'soon pay its cost' as well as serve the tea industry. Initially named the Kokilamukh Tramway, and operated under the provisions of the 'Tramways Act', it was later on classified as a railway, and named the Kokilamukh State Railway.[21]

Financial projections of the railway were furnished by the existing steamer companies at Kokilamukh to emphasize its commercial viability. The estimated cost of the tramway was projected at approximately Rs 1,11,230 and the returns, expected on the outward traffic, was Rs 21,125 annually, just enough to meet the working expenses.[22]

In 1884, the Chief Commissioner submitted a scheme for the extension of the railway along the *Garh Ali*, and from Jorhat to Titabor on the *Dhodar Ali*. A branch line was proposed to be constructed along the *Hatigarh Ali* to Mariani, a distance of 7.25 miles. These extensions on the parent gauge were to run through the Noa–Cachari tea gardens; and the one between Jhanzi and Nazira, was to cover all the plantations of the Assam Tea Company.[23] These extensions were suggested not only to serve the tea gardens but with a far-sighted political end in view:

> if the project of a valley railway [was] delayed, it may prove desirable to continue the line to Golaghat and even to Dimapur,

21. Railway Construction 'A', February 1884, nos. 202–206, letter no. 1135, dated 23 June 1883.
22. Railway Construction 'A', nos. 1–3, enclosure no. 2 to despatch no. 168 of Railway 1882, para ii.
23. See note 21.

so as to facilitate the supply of provision to the troops in the Naga Hills.[24]

The Government of India while finally sanctioning the project objected to any further extensions of this narrow gauge line for strategic purposes. They perceived that such an extension to Dimapur might 'seriously interfere in the extension of the metre gauge line already made in Upper Assam'.[25] The extensions were sanctioned at a cost of Rs 4,00,000. The gross receipts were anticipated to be Rs 67,916. After calculating the total working expenses of Rs 44,110, a balance of Rs 8,140 was projected to be the profit.[26]

The self-supporting nature of the line inspired the local government to forego a major share of the provincial revenue. The line was constructed and maintained from the provincial revenues. The railway was laid on 28 lb rails with local timber sleepers. However, one mile of the railway line between Jorhat and Cinnamara was laid on 25 lb per yard rails.[27]

CHERRA–COMPANYGANJ MOUNTAIN TRAMWAY

In the immediate aftermath of the annexation of Assam, the British directed their attention to developing military routes. In course of the Burmese war, the importance of a western route to Bengal, for supplying troops and provisions was realized. Details of the western road-link connecting the town of Sylhet, via Cherrapunji to Gauhati have been discussed in detail in Chapter 2.

24. Railway Construction 'A', nos. 1–3, enclosure no. 2 to despatch no. 168 of Railway 1882, para iv.

25. Railway Construction 'A', no. 105 RC of 13 September 1883.

26. Railway Construction 'A', no. 1135 of 23 June 1883, paras 10, 11, and 12.

27. *Administrative Report of the Railways: 1910.*

In 1874, an excellent cart road existed between Shillong and Cherrapunji. Below the steep slopes of Cherrapunji, excellent water communication existed with Sylhet over the river Piyian. There was a break in communication between 'the carts and the boats' because of the precipitous descent below Cherrapunji to the river. The most practicable means of tiding over this break could be achieved by constructing a series of wire tramways.[28]

The tramway was planned on purely commercial considerations. A significant amount of trade was already carried on by this route, which would be further augmented by a tramway. Its development was expected to facilitate a steady supply of military stores and rice to the commissariat stationed at Shillong.[29]

The hill populations were directly dependent on the plains, partly for their supply of rice and entirely for that of fish, tobacco and oil. These articles were transported up to the hills, through various routes.[30] Shillong too received all its stores in a roundabout way from the direction of Gauhati. All the goods coming from Sylhet had to be carried by coolies up the slopes of Cherrapunji.

By 1881–82, traffic through coolie-carriage had been considerably reduced because of two important factors. Firstly, during the corresponding period a large number of coolies were involved in the construction of the Shillong–Cherrapunji Road and hence they were unavailable for carrying merchandise from

28. Railway Construction 'A', February 1883, nos. 1–5, no. 162 T of 9 January 1883.

29. Railway Construction 'A', August 1883, nos. 60–68, no. 1146 of 26 June 1883.

30. Railway Construction 'A', January 1884, nos. 77–79, 'Cherrapunji Mountain Tramway', T.J. Willans, Executive Engineer Khasi and Jaintia Hills.

Sylhet. In addition, on several occasions the outbreak of cholera along the Sylhet–Shillong route caused fear amongst the coolies, resulting in a cessation of coolie-carriage.

The downward traffic comprised primarily potatoes and such minor products like hides, rubber, cinnamon and local liquor. It was anticipated that coal from Cherrapunji would form an important item of downward traffic. A tramway on this route would not only provide cheap carriage, but also ensure steady trade in the face of epidemics and other natural calamities.

The quantum of trade estimated from the existing coolie-traffic was calculated at approximately 140,000 maunds (5,142.88 tons) for upward traffic, and 80,000 (2,938.79 tons) maunds for downward traffic. The projected cost of a wire-tramway was estimated to be Rs 20,00,000.[31] If charged at an average rate of three annas per maund for the upward traffic and two annas for the downward traffic, the carriage costs would be reduced by one-third. The tramway at the projected estimates was expected to yield an annual return of Rs 34,000. With the working expenses estimated at Rs 24,284, a profit margin of Rs 10,000 per annum was anticipated, giving a return of 5 per cent on the total outlay.[32]

Technical Aspects

The proposed mountain tramway was a unique project in its technical aspects. The idea for such a tramway was mooted as early as 1842, by Colonel Yule, a Bengal Government engineer, for extracting and carrying coal from the mines at Cherra. His ideas were followed up by Major T.J. Willans, the

31. Railway Construction 'A', January 1884, nos. 77–79, 'Cherrapunji Mountain Tramway', T.J. Willans, Executive Engineer Khasi and Jaintia Hills.
32. Ibid.

Executive Engineer Khasi and Jaintia Hills Division, who visited several such successfully worked tramways in Europe and America, before implementing this project.[33]

Major Willans submitted a preliminary scheme, for working the inclines of Cherrapunji by a wire-rope tramway, to the Chief Commissioner of Assam and the Consulting Engineer, State Railway. The tramway was to comprise seven inclines covering a distance of 3.25 miles, ascending a height of 3,470 feet on a 2 feet gauge.[34] The lines were to be worked on the balance system, with trucks used on both the ascending and descending wire-lines. The weight of the descending truck would haul the ascending truck. The descending truck was to be loaded with water to render it heavy enough to haul up the ascending truck loaded with goods. For an element of safety, the trucks were to be attached to a drum with self-acting brakes. Sir Guildford Molesworth, the Consulting Engineer for State Railways, put forth his objections to the existing plan.[35] Accordingly, Major Willans submitted a modified plan to the Government.

Overhead pulleys were proposed to prevent the ropes from surging, and that of grooved rollers to prevent the swaying of

33. There are several well-known wire tramways all over the world. The passenger inclines at Pittsburgh in America, which ascended a height of 400 feet over a length of 793 feet, worked on the balance system. A line up Mount Vesuvius, over a height of 5,000 feet and gradients of 1 in 1 was worked on the Fell System. At Buda in Europe a passenger incline connected the town with a fortress at a slope of 30° ascending a height of 160 feet. The Sao Paulo Railway ascended 2,000 feet of the slope of the Sierra de Mar, in a series of 4 inclines, by wire ropes and stationary engines.

34. For details refer to Railway Construction 'A', August 1883. Note by G.L. Molesworth, Consulting Engineer to the Government of India for State Railways, 'On the Wire Tramway between Cherrapunji and Therriaghat', dated 2 August 1883.

35. Railway Construction 'A', January 1884, nos. 77–79, 'Cherrapunji Mountain Tramway', T.J. Willans, Executive Engineer Khasi and Jaintia Hills.

ropes. For balancing the water in the descending truck with that of the gross weight of the ascending truck, the truck carrying water was to be divided into three compartments. To draw up a truck filled with goods, all the compartments were to be filled with water. However, for sending down an empty truck the central compartment was not filled with water.

The provincial government approved the plan, overlooking the reservations of Molesworth. The tramway, apart from its apparent benefits, was expected to carry limestone from the foot of the proposed tramway to the river Piyian and thence to Sylhet. The importance of this line of tramway was:

> that ultimately it is probable [that] the line will be continued
> to Sylhet forming a link in the communication between
> South-Sylhet and the Assam Valley, through the Khasi Hills
> and also a feeder to the proposed South-Sylhet Railway, as
> Sylhet will be connected by a branch line with Hingajiya, a
> station on the Chittagong–Cachar line.[36]

With a view to tapping the coal reserves at Cherrapunji, a proposal was made by the Government of Assam for connecting the line from the top of the mountain tramway incline to Cherra. The wire-tramway project was sanctioned in 1885. The portion of the tramway on the top of the mountain incline was sanctioned for construction in 1887.

The mountain inclines of the Cherra–Companyganj State Railway were completed in November 1887. They were then subjected to a series of tests throughout 1888 and 1889, to determine their workability by Molesworth. The results were very discouraging. The question as to whether the project was to be continued or abandoned, depended largely on a proper

---

36. Cherra–Companyganj State Railway, 'General History of the Scheme', with Chief Engineer's Proposals, Shillong, dated 19 September 1888.

assessment of the Cherra coalfields and the figuring out of its traffic prospects. The issue was debated upon extensively between the Secretary of State for India, the Government of India, and the provincial administration from 1888 to 1890. Finally, in 1890 it was declared that the 'Hill Section' of the tramway should be abandoned as:

> it would not be desirable in the interests of this Province to incur further expenditure, either upon maintenance or extension of the Cherra Companyganj State Railway, as investigations into the financial prospects of this line proved conclusively that it cannot be worked otherwise than at a very serious loss to the State.[37]

The abandonment of the 'plains section' of the tramway was deferred in order to honour certain agreements, contracted by the provincial administration, for carriage of limestone. In 1891, after a careful perusal of its earnings, which showed a reasonable increase over the year, the Chief Commissioner declared that the plains section should be kept open in perpetuity. This was because 'closure of a railway after construction and opening for traffic is clearly a measure to be avoided if possible'.[38]

The earthquake of 1897 caused considerable damage to the tramway. The rains, which followed the earthquake, loosened the mass of debris, which practically washed away the railway line. Once again, the question as to whether it was practicable to keep the plains section of the line open to traffic was re-opened. Though maintaining the line was proving expensive, the Chief Commissioner was keen on keeping the line open, as

37. Railway Traffic 'A', November 1898, nos. 49–50, no. 1185 RT of 25 October 1898.
38. Railway Construction 'A', August 1895, nos. 400–405, Office Note, no. 2844 of 4 July 1895.

its closure would deal a death blow to the quarrying industry. He expressed his concern on the issue:

the Sylhet limestone will be unworked, the royalty to government and to different Khasia [*sic*] communities will be lost and the persons engaged in working the limestone and in the limestone trade must turn their attention to other pursuits . . . [39]

He thought it desirable to retain the line, not only for carrying limestone but also for its role 'as a link in the chain of communication between Shillong and Sylhet'.[40] Abandoning the line would reduce its value in the event of G.L. Garth's Syndicate taking over the line in future. The plains section was restored to traffic after repairs in 1899. It was finally abandoned in 1900 due to a change in Garth's projected railway alignment, which did not include this section of the Cherra–Companyganj State Railway.

The project, which had been taken up so over-enthusiastically, did not take into account the natural difficulties of the terrain as well as the effects of excessive rainfall in that area. It was an instance of sheer recklessness and extreme shortsightedness of the provincial administration. This colonial misadventure was aimed at safeguarding the interests of a handful of European investors who held monopoly rights over the limestone quarries and the coal tracts. A major share of the financial burden of this disastrous project was borne out of the provincial revenues, which was indirectly a burden on the taxpayer of Assam.

The financial results of the Cherra–Companyganj State Railway, in the period between 1886 and 1898 were very

39. Railway Traffic 'A', March 1899, nos. 156–158, from Chief Commissioner to Secretary PWD, dated 10 January 1899.
40. Ibid.

discouraging. During this period the gross earnings of the railway fell short of the working expenses by Rs 1,68,407. The total loss to the state exchequer from the commencement of operations on 1 June 1886 to 30 June 1898, including the interest on the cost of the 'open' section, amounted to a whopping Rs 4,63,376. After adding the interest on the cost of the 'abandoned' section, the total loss to the state came to Rs 5,65,685.[41]

In the decade between 1870 to 1880, the Government of India encouraged railway extensions to be taken up entirely at the initiative of local administration. Mention has been made in the preceding chapter about railways being initiated in other parts of the country by district boards.

Tezpur–Balipara Tramway

The Government of Assam, burdened with the failure of the Cherra–Companyganj State Railway, was not in a position to extend financial grants to similar railway ventures in its immediate aftermath. The provincial government was very categorical about its inability to offer financial aid in the form of a guarantee to any railway venture.

The stretch of twenty miles between Tezpur ghat and Balipara contained some of the finest tea gardens in Assam. It contained seventeen of the twenty-one gardens in the districts and three large weekly markets. The increasing traffic from these tea gardens could not be carted along the existing road, which was in a deplorable state. An obvious alternative was to consider the scheme of a tramway along the existing road, a cart road.

41. Railway Traffic 'A', November 1898, nos. 49–50, from Government of India, Railway Traffic to Chief Commissioner Assam, dated 25 October 1898.

As the government was not forthcoming with financial assistance, the onus of raising the capital for a tramway fell on the district authorities. A series of deliberations ensued to decide on the issue of raising the capital. The District Board of Tezpur with authorization from the provincial government offered a subsidy. Accordingly, in 1892 W. Skinner floated the Tezpur–Balipara Tramway Company. Seventeen gardens contributed a sum of Rs 1,75,000 to form a nucleus of the capital, in the form of ordinary shares. In addition, McLeod and Company raised Rs 3,05,000 for the tramway.[42]

The Government of Assam granted the following concessions:

i) The use of Government wasteland for the construction of the line, free of charge.

ii) The right to obtain free of cost, timber for [the lines] first construction from Government forests.

iii) The use of the land taken from tea-estates, free of cost, subject only to payment for [the area under the cultivation of] tea, that may have to be taken up [for the tramway].

iv) The use of the Provincial Roads [that would be] convenient and necessary for laying the line.

v) The permission to the Local Board authorities to grant an annual subsidy to the tramway for five years of Rs 5,000.[43]

The Chief Commissioner of Assam authorized the commencement of work on the tramway, pending approval of the Government of India, as the project would in no way be a

42. The capital of Rs 4,00,000 was divided into 1,750 ordinary shares of Rs 100 each, and 2,250 preference shares of Rs 100 each.
43. Traffic 'A', June 1915, nos. 167–171, no. 167, B.

burden on the imperial or provincial revenues. The Government of India considered 'the project is prima facie one deserving encouragement' and sanctioned the project.[44] The desire of the promoters, for preferential rights for constructing a tramway in Darrang district was disallowed. Construction of the tramway commenced in December 1893, and was opened to public traffic over its entire length on 1 September 1895.

The gauge of the line was 2 feet 6 inches, with rails of 30 lb to a yard, and the number of sleepers used per mile on the line was 2,200. The line was principally unballasted, with ballast used only in moist places and wherever essential. The owners of the Borjuli Tea Company in Darrang constructed two miles of tramway between Rangapara and Borjuli in 1895. In 1896, the owners leased the siding to the Tezpur–Balipara Tramway and jointly applied for the extension of the provision of the Indian Tramways Act to the siding.

The tramway was to exclusively cater to the tea industry and primarily act as a feeder for steamers. Downward traffic mainly comprised tea, while the imports were coal, tea-lead, tea-shooks and other stores for the gardens. It was self-supporting and therefore a successful project from the colonial standpoint.

TRUNK ROUTE

Constructing small stretches of railway lines as feeders for the steamers, catering primarily to industries like tea, coal and mineral oil, introduced railways in Assam. A trunk route, running through the entire province was necessary for the overall development of resources as well as opening up the province.

44. Railway Construction 'A', February 1894, nos. 236–249, letter no. 246.

It was imperative to link Upper Assam, the centre of European investment, to Calcutta, the natural outlet for the trade of Eastern India. Henry Hopkinson first discussed the issue of a trunk railway connecting Assam with Bengal, as early as 1867–68. In his view, Assam was a dead-end, which obviated the necessity of having a trunk railway. A low population ratio, low revenue yield and the self-subsisting nature of the economy made the province unpromising 'customers for a railway'.[45] In his scheme of administration, real development of Assam could be achieved by increasing its agricultural production. For the success of such a scheme, permanent settlement of cultivating classes from neighbouring Bengal should be encouraged.

He was not keen on promoting the tea industry at the cost of agricultural development, and refused to agree to the desire of the planters in Assam of construction of a trunk route:

> it'd give a considerable impetus to tea cultivation and independently of this impetus, would largely augment the value of plantation properties, but the question is whether all India should be divested of 3–5 million of its revenue for the sake mainly of the English tea-grower and the English tea consumer . . .[46]

The winds of change in the form of the return of private enterprise in railway construction did not take long to change the stance of the local government, on the issue of a trunk railway traversing the entire length of Assam. The success of the Dibru–Sadiya Railway and the development of ancillary industries alongside, led to a concentration of British capital in Upper Assam. The major exports from Upper Assam were tea, coal and petroleum, while it received machinery for the

---

45. Letters issued to Government, no. 18 of 22 January 1868.
46. Letters issued to Government, vol. 50, 1873, no. G 373T, Government of Bengal, General Department of Industry and Science, of 18 October 1873.

tea gardens and rice for feeding large bodies of imported tea garden labourers. To facilitate the growing trade of the area, it was imperative to link Upper Assam with either the port of Calcutta or Chittagong.

In fixing the alignment of the railway line, certain criteria had to be fulfilled which subscribed to the demands of the colonialists. The primary stipulation was that it should be instrumental in fostering the growth of the tea industry, by providing the shortest route to the port. It was necessary that the districts which it traversed, should offer scope for equalization of trade. The line should afford easier and quicker facilities for transporting tea garden labourers from their recruiting districts. Its role in fostering immigration of cultivating classes into the vast wastelands of Assam, from the congested districts of Bengal, was considered. The alignment had to be decided largely on its capability for meeting the future military exigencies of the North-East Frontier. Apart from the above-mentioned considerations, the line had to be cheap to construct and had to be a dividend earning or productive line.

To ascertain the shortest route to Bengal, surveys were conducted on three independent alignments, which has been discussed at length in the preceding chapter. Recognizing the advantages of connecting the Brahmaputra Valley with the province of Eastern Bengal and making Chittagong into a natural port of Assam, all efforts were directed to conduct detailed surveys on the routes facilitating the plan. J.W. Buyers was appointed for the purpose, and he completed the survey for the Bengal–Assam line in the working season between 1882 and 1886.[47]

47. For details, refer to Railway Construction 'A', October 1887, nos. 224–229.

ASSAM–BENGAL RAILWAY

The railway route was to comprise a main line of 575.93 miles, from the sea-port of Chittagong to Makum junction. There were to be three branch lines: (a) from Laksham, 80 miles from Chittagong, on the Meghna river of 31.895 miles; (b) from Badarpur, 254 miles from Chittagong, to Silchar of 17.842 miles; and (c) from Lumding, 370 miles from Chittagong, on the main line to Gauhati of 110.503 miles. The total length of the main line along with the branch lines, stood at 736.143 miles.[48]

Guildforth Molesworth carefully examined the final survey reports. His opinion entirely confirmed the reports on the route obtainable through the hills which he described as a good 'loco-motive line, with gradients of about 1 in 70'. On the question of its general importance, he said:

> It is difficult to overrate the importance of this line to Assam in a strategical, political [and] administrative point of view. The whole line between Silchar and Golaghat is, however, virgin forest and the population practically nil. But there are rich tracts of land suitable for tea along the line of railway, which, would be eagerly taken up if a railway were con-structed especially in the Dimapur Valley, and such a line would undoubtedly revolutionize Upper Assam. As a direct route to Calcutta, such a line would possess many advantages compared with the route via Dhubri.[49]

Colonel F.S. Station, Director-General of Railways, ap-proved of the route decided upon by Buyers. On its importance he remarked:

48. Railway Construction 'A', December 1887, nos. 224–269, enclosure no. 7 to PWD Resolution no. 868 RC of 1887, 'Final Report' by J.W. Buyers on the Surveys.

49. Railway Construction 'A', no. 868 RC, no. 250 RC, 25 August 1887.

In regard to the great question of route to Assam via the Cachar Hills or via the Valley of the Brahmaputra, it certainly seems to be that the former possess enormous advantages over the latter, as a means of developing this backward region . . . Chittagong should obviously be the port for Assam and Cachar and this railway by supplying the one great want, good coal for sea going steamer, would enable shipping business to be dealt with there at a cost with which Calcutta with its dangerous river approach cannot compete.[50]

Under the conditions of the modified guarantee system, lines which were financially viable, were taken up by private enterprise. The data secured from the river-borne reports of the preceding few years, indicated that in the section of railway between Chandpur and Chittagong, the lowest net return expected was approximately 9 per cent. In the section between Commilla [*sic*] and Silchar, a net return of 6 per cent was anticipated. Over the rest of the Brahmaputra Valley from Badarpur to Dibrugarh and Gauhati, a net return of 2.75 per cent was expected. Therefore, on the completed system of the railway, it was conjectured that the yield would be 5 per cent, which was an indication of it being a self-paying line.[51]

In 1885 when the survey on the line was halfway through, William Ward, the Chief Commissioner of Assam, expressed serious objections to the alignment proposed by Buyers. The premise of his argument was that a separate Surma Valley line or Cachar–Commilla–Chandpur line would pay a fair share of interest to the government or any private company seeking to take up its construction. On the other hand, an Assam

50. Railway Construction 'A', enclosure no. 11 to PWD Resolution no. 868 RC of 1887.

51. Railway Construction 'A', December 1887, nos. 224–269, enclosure no. 7 to PWD Resolution no. 868 RC of 1887, 'Final Report' by J.W. Buyers on the Surveys.

Valley line from Dibrugarh to Gauhati or Dhubri would be unremunerative, unless it was linked with Bengal. He was of the opinion that:

> it would be unwise to hamper these two lines by an unprof-
> itable and expensive connection between Lumding and Bad-
> arpur, a distance of about 114 miles, passing through a barren
> country and no population.[52]

The Assam Valley line could be completed by an extension to Fakiragram. He refuted Buyer's opinion that the North Cachar Hills connection was indispensable for the planters, as he had personally discussed the issue with the planters. He states ' . . . it is perfectly immaterial to them whether they ship their tea for Calcutta at Fakirganj or at Chandpur. All [that] the planter, cares about is the cheapest and most expeditious means of conveyance'.[53]

The political developments in the region had an important bearing on the route finally selected for the Bengal–Assam railway. With the annexation of Upper Burma in 1885, Lord Dufferin conceived the grand idea of connecting Bengal via Assam to the new possession.[54] Sir Theodore Hope, then Public Works Member of Council, backed him in this premature and fantastic idea. Hope left India in 1887. In course of the survey Molesworth recommended:

> if a feasible route can be found through the hills which sep-
> arate Cachar from Burma, this branch from Badarpur . . .
> may eventually form a portion of a connection between Assam
> and the Burma Railway Systems.[55]

52. Railway Construction 'A', enclosure no. 4 to PWD Resolution no. 868 RC of 1887.
53. Ibid.
54. Railway Construction 'A', December 1903, nos. 79–87; Remarks made on the despatch to the Secretary of State from the Viceroy (Lord Elgin).
55. Railway Construction 'A', December 1887, nos. 224–269, enclosure

During the course of the surveys, several concessionaires put forward terms on which they desired to float private companies to take up the railway. General Dickens had applied on behalf of the Bengal Central Railway. Earlier in 1881, the Bengal Central Railway Company had been granted:

> a preferential right to construction of all line of railway east of the Ganges and the Meghna, in traffic connection with the primary undertaking by river steamers, including railway communication with Dacca and Mymensingh.[56]

Based on this concession they put forth their claim on constructing the section of railway between Chittagong and Cachar, on the proposed Bengal–Assam railway. Simultaneously Colonel R.H. Keatinge, (later Chief Commissioner of Assam) submitted a proposal to form a company in England to undertake the construction of two separate metre gauge railway lines. One of the lines proposed was from Chittagong to the river Meghna at Daudkandi or Chandpore, or any other point at a convenient steamer terminus. The second one was proposed between Laksham through Comilla to Silchar, with the company seeking powers for future extension of the line in the direction of Lumding to Dibrugarh and Gauhati.[57]

The proposals were turned down, as they did not cover the entire length of the proposed project. An additional reason given by the Government of India, in its despatch to the Secretary of State for India, stated their inability to undertake the financial liability of a guarantee. The project had been placed in Schedule B 1883–1884 as, 'not indispensable for protective

no. 7 to PWD Resolution no. 868 RC of 1887, 'Final Report' by J.W. Buyers on the Surveys.

56. Railway Construction 'A', January 1885, nos. 93–106, no. 93 of 18 September 1884.

57. Railway Construction 'A', no. 95 of 1 March 1884.

or other urgent purposes'.[58] It was all schemes under Schedule A, 'all productive and protective lines', which received precedence over purely commercial projects.

In 1889 Hope, now a concessionaire, submitted a proposal on behalf of an English syndicate and desired, that apart from the usual concessions the:

> grant of wasteland and timber, and the monopoly of coal and petroleum, in lieu of a Government guarantee on the capital to be raised for the construction of the projected line from Chittagong to Assam.[59]

The proposal submitted was entirely at variance from the existing railway policy in India. It was unacceptable to the Government of India, as determining the value of the concessions was problematic, since most of the areas desired had not been explored.

In 1890 Matheson and Company of London, proposed undertaking construction of a railway on the following terms. The term of the contract was to be for a period of twenty-five to thirty years, with the government retaining the right to terminate the contract, every tenth year by returning the share capital at par. Land was to be supplied free of cost. On the share capital a guarantee of 3 per cent in sterling from the date of receipt of the money in the Home Treasury, was to be given by the government. In the event of further assistance, an additional guarantee not exceeding 0.5 per cent was desired for a period of four years. On the opening of the line, after

58. In 1882 the Select Committee, with a view to regulate the fluctuating financial policies and the supply of funds for railway projects, drew a forecast for a number of years, by adopting an annual scale of expenditure. Thus evolved the system of providing capital, under the 'Programme'.

59. Railway Construction 'A', July 1889, nos. 26–32, no. 81 Railway of 1889, Government of India to Secretary of State, 14 June 1889.

deducting the interest paid on the debentures and the guarantee of 3 per cent the government was to receive an interest at 3 per cent on the capital raised.[60]

The Secretary of State for India, proposed minor modifications in the terms sought by the promoters and was agreeable in allowing the formation of a sterling company. The promoters were unable to obtain capital on the terms agreed upon by the government, because of the abnormal state of the money market.

An overview of the financial administration of railways in India will throw light on the financial constraints, and its bearing on railway construction in Assam. Within a few years of the re-introduction of private enterprise in railway construction, financial stress due to an imbalance in the exchange rate became a cause for alarm for the Government of India. A massive increase in sterling liabilities was a major cause for concern. A major share of the burden in form of a guarantee, fell on the Indian taxpayer, who had to foot the bill for the sterling debt to Britain, because of railway construction.

In view of the financial embarrassment caused by the fall in the value of rupee and increasing difficulty in obtaining a sterling guarantee, the government was forced to stop assistance to private capital.[61] The Government of India issued

60. Railway Construction 'A', October 1891, nos. 32–54, 'Chittagong–Assam Railway', terms to form the basis of negotiations.

61. The Indian economy in the post-1858 period had an unlimited capacity to absorb silver, which helped to support the silver price in the world market, and also facilitated the collection of land revenue. The initial depreciation of the rupee was accepted with equanimity as it represented a bonus for India's raw produce and also shielded India's home market against the fall in gold prices in the world agricultural market. But it created serious repercussions in the payment of the 'Public Debt' or 'Home Charges', which were fixed in gold, and revenue receipts were fixed in silver. Land revenue could not be enhanced to keep pace with the depreciation of silver. Between 1873 to 1893, the sterling debt mounted from £ 13.5 million to £ 15.8 million,

orders, that henceforth sterling guarantees were to be discouraged in favour of a rupee guarantee. The fall in the value of sterling exchange had brought railway extension between 1889 and 1892 practically to a standstill. In 1892 however:

> to the astonishment of the public and still more the Government of India, the Assam–Bengal Railway Company was formed as a sterling company against the declared policy of the Government of India, in favour of rupee guarantee.[62]

A sterling guarantee for a line 'which was not urgently wanted and which for two-thirds of its length was of no practical value to the provinces it was to serve',[63] was a clear case of repudiation of the stand taken up by the Government of India. Indian public opinion was alarmed at the knowledge, that the line was constructed to please the English planters who had invested capital in the Assam tea estates and who wanted railway facilities for export of tea.

Matheson and Company could not raise the money till as late as November 1891. In the normal course, negotiations would have fallen through. The Secretary of State not only granted an extension of the period for raising money, but also urged upon immediate commencement of construction on the northern section of the proposed railway, between Gauhati and Dimapur, immediately. He stated:

> In the present state of the money market, it does not appear probable that the concessionaires will be able to obtain capital on the terms granted at an early date. In order to avoid the delay which would occur if the company is not formed

---

bringing the British Indian Government to the verge of bankruptcy. In 1893, Indian mints were closed to the public to prevent further devaluation.

62. Sanyal, *Development of Indian Railways*, p. 157.

63. Amba Prasad, *Indian Railways: A Study in Public Utility Administration* (London and Bombay, 1960), p. 86.

before the end of the year, it seems to me desirable that your
Government should take such measure as may be necessary
for commencing operations at the earliest practicable period.[64]

Underlying this tone of urgency was a serious strategic
concern. The Manipur outbreak was perceived as a 'serious
threat to the North-Eastern Frontier and hence a menace to
the Empire'.

It is imperative to have an overview of Anglo-Manipur
relations and their bearing on the political situation in the
North-East. Manipur had maintained a British levy, under two
British officers at their expense since 1834. The levy was withdrawn in 1835 to be replaced by a Political Agent. The British
troops stationed there, monitored the political situation and
helped to quell uprisings against the native Raja.

Ever since the death of Maharaja Chandra Kirti Singh in
1886, a series of attempts were made to oust his son and legal
successor, Sur Chandra Singh. In 1890 the *Senapati* attacked
the palace forcing the Maharaja to abdicate in favour of the
Jubraj (Crown Prince), next in order of succession, who was
placed on the throne as a puppet. The Maharaja sought refuge
with the Political Agent, repudiating his abdication and expressed his desire to be reinstated. The Government of India
found it politically expedient to recognize the *Jubraj*, rather
than restore the Maharaja. They sought to remove the *Senapati*, who was proving to be an unscrupulous intriguer.

The Chief Commissioner was ordered by the Government
of India to proceed in person to deal with the situation. The
Senapati was ordered to appear before the Chief Commissioner. On his refusal to oblige, British troops stormed the

64. Railway Construction 'A', October 1891, no. 57 Railway of 28 May
1891.

palace. They met with stiff resistance from the Manipuris. An armistice was agreed upon and the Chief Commissioner, along with four of his companions was induced to proceed to the Darbar [*sic*] unarmed, with a promise of safe conduct. Here they were treacherously murdered. 'A petty uprising in a quasi-Bengali village of peasants, was magnified into a menace to the empire, and the immediate construction of the Hill section was regarded as an Imperial necessity'.[65]

The Secretary of State allowed the construction of the northern section as a state railway, until a company was formed for the purpose. His orders to the effect were transmitted by telegram to avoid delay and stated:

> In consequence of transport difficulties in connection with the Manipur garrison . . . we propose to commence at once on Bengal–Assam Railway, Lumding Section and some 42 miles from Lumding northwards. This will connect with [the] road to Manipur via Kohima. This section will be worked on completion as a State Railway until the Company's [*sic*] line is connected with it from the north or south.[66]

Matheson and Company withdrew from the negotiations and another financial house in England, the Assam–Bengal Company submitted their proposals. The terms were accepted and the Assam–Bengal Railway Company was formed in 1892. The main features of the contract were as follows:

i) The Company was to subscribe £ 1,500,000 under the guarantee of the revenues of India of 3.5 per cent per annum till 30 June 1898 and thereafter at 3 per cent.

65. Lord Curzon expressed this view in 1903, when a revised estimate for the Hill Section of the Assam–Bengal Railway was sent to him for approval.
66. Railway Construction 'A', October 1891, nos. 32–54, no. C 117 of 26 August 1891; telegram from Viceroy to Secretary of State.

ii) The project was to be completed by 30 June 1898.

iii) If the project required further financing, the Secretary of State was to contribute or help in raising the required amount.

iv) Surplus profits were to be divided between the Company and the Secretary of State in ratio of their respective expenditure.

v) Land was to be provided free of cost to the Company.

vi) The Government was to exercise its power in matters of Police, Telegraphs, Rates and Fares, Audit and Control and in any other matter requiring arbitration.[67]

For convenience in construction, the main line was divided into three sections. The portion of the railway between Chittagong and Badarpur was referred to as Section I. Section II was the portion between Badarpur and Lumding. Section III comprised the length of the line between Lumding and Makum junction. Of the three branch lines, the one between Laksham and Chandpur was included in Section I, that from Badarpur to Silchar in Section II, and the branch line from Lumding to Gauhati was included in Section III. Work commenced on all three sections simultaneously. Guildford Molesworth travelled over the entire route and reported favourably on them.

Within a short span of time however, flaws in the estimates submitted by Buyers on the hill section (Section II) became obvious, and they appeared inflated. As early as 1893 H.W. Warden, the Consulting Engineer, pointed out the difficulties of the hill section and urged its postponement. Alternately, he suggested that efforts should be concentrated on the Gauhati branch, which was arguably remunerative. He held similar

67. Railway Construction 'A', August 1892, nos. 18–40, no. 33 RC, 'Prospectus'.

views on the Chittagong–Badarpur section as well. His views were conveyed to the Secretary of State. The agents of the company in India and England expressed concern that massive liabilities had been incurred on the three sections. In the event of any scheme of its withdrawal, the government would have to bear all the expenses incurred thus far. Any revision of the contract had to have a stipulation to protect the interests of the shareholders.[68]

The Secretary of State in a telegram to the Viceroy opined on the issue that:

> After very careful consideration of your views, I have decided that it is in every respect disadvantageous to withdraw from [the] conditions of [the] Contract with [the] Bengal–Assam Railway Company. Financial obligations of [the] Government [towards the] scheme can be met by enabling you to provide funds exceptionally from cash balances beyond ordinary limits . . . [69]

With the prospects of opting out of the hill section having been ruled out, it was imperative that operations on this section be kept as economical as possible. A proper road cutting across the section was necessary, before undertaking the railway construction, as the area lacked the essential pre-requisite of labour and food. F.J.E. Spring the consulting engineer, inspected the section in 1894. He suggested that instead of adopting a policy of spreading labour all over the section, it should be worked forward telescopically, in short annual lengths of about twenty-five miles each working season. He

68. Railway Construction 'A', December 1903, nos. 79–87, from W. Chadwick, Officiating Consulting Engineer for Railways Assam to Director of Railway Construction.

69. Railway Construction 'A', July 1894, nos. 282–294; telegram from Secretary of State, London, to Viceroy, 1 May 1894.

also suggested that the river Barak could be used as a base for importing food and labour into the section.[70]

He was of the view, that since little progress had been made on the Gauhati–Lumding section and its military necessity had diminished, work on the section should be stopped. As most of the line was practically through a terrain full of 'forest and pampas grass', it would not even pay for its working expenses. He also pointed out that the hill section was of little value, as tea from Upper Assam would take the river route either to Chittagong or to Calcutta.

As construction progressed on the controversial hill section, the costly nature of the undertaking became very evident. The section traversed an exceedingly mountainous terrain through dense forests, devoid of population, excessively unhealthy and practically inaccessible. The other two sections of the railway though expensive, could be constructed within a reasonable capital expenditure. The middle section was a tremendous undertaking and thus no reliable estimate could be made for this section.

In 1895 J.R. Bell, the consulting engineer, reiterated the difficulties in construction and the unremunerative prospects of the hill section, and urged upon the government to reopen the issue of its postponement. Lord Elgin's [Viceroy] government made yet another attempt to opt out of continuing with its construction. Lord George Hamilton, the Secretary of State, expressed concern at the immense liabilities in the form of compensation, which the government would have to bear for opting out of this section.[71] The Government of India debated

70. Railway Construction 'A', July 1894, nos. 282–294, enclosure no. 1 to despatch no. 42 of Railway of 1894, no. 565 of 27 March 1894.
71. Railway Construction 'A', December 1903, nos. 79–87, demi-official from Consulting Engineer Railways Assam to Director Railway Construction.

the issue at length. It was ultimately declared that it was too late to stop work on the hill section. This was however the last opportunity for opting out of the hill section, which in the years to come was to prove to be an immense financial drain on the government.

Since 1896, the financial allocations for the Assam–Bengal Railway were marked by expenditure in excess of projected estimates, which had no parallel in the history of railway construction in India. The history of the Assam–Bengal Railway could well be used:

> as a practical object-lesson to emphasize the disastrous effect of the intervention of the India Office [in London] in railway matters, and of their habits of overruling the objections of our Local Technical Advisors.[72]

The preliminary assessment of the geological composition of the hill section was conducted in 1897. Results revealed that the proposed railway alignment ran through beds of the Upper Tertiary Age consisting of soft and friable sandstone, overlying a series of blue and black carbonaceous shale. The shale weathered into soft or reddish brown clay, which turned exceedingly plastic when wet and powdery when dry. The beds were intensely crushed and full of sheer planes, which acted as channels, through which water percolated in the rainy season. The sandstone beds turned soft, with a tendency to slide at the slightest disturbance.[73]

The treacherous nature of the shale, which disintegrated on exposure, caused cracks and slips, making it necessary to

72. Railway Construction 'A', December 1903, nos. 79–87; remarks on a despatch to the Secretary of State while under circulation, by E.F.G. Law of the Finance Department.

73. Railway Construction 'A', May 1897, nos. 256–264, Assam–Bengal Railway; Report by F.H. Smith of 13 March 1897.

convert many of the projected 'open cuttings' into tunnels. There were instances of tunnels being lined throughout their length, while in some, the lining had to be continued beyond the face of the hill to provide for external slips. The delay in completion of the hill section and the enormous expenditure incurred could be attributed to contingencies like, heavy slips during construction, provision for new cuts and covers, renovation in tunnelling techniques, and realignments. The earthquake of 1897 further retarded the progress of work on this section, and thus it could not be completed on schedule.

Tunnels were constructed under the supervision of European contractors, who charged very high rates. Workers from Cornwall were imported to work on the tunnels. Not only was construction expensive, but its subsequent maintenance and supervision proved expensive too. Constant renewals, restorations, replacements and substitution of original works had to be taken up. As the line was subjected to the vagaries of nature, an enormous sum of money was spent on repairing damages caused by earthquakes and floods. Restoration cost an additional Rs 21 lakhs.[74]

Section I of the Assam–Bengal Railway was opened to traffic in 1896. Section III was completed in a phased manner between 1896 and 1900. The controversial hill section was completed and opened to traffic on 16 February 1904.

In 1904, shortly after re-opening the section for traffic, it had to be closed again for a considerable length of time due to damages caused by heavy rainfall. The devastating floods of July 1915 caused extensive damage to the line, thus raising once again the question of its closure. The arguments in favour

74. Ways and Works 'A', W/1–64, June 1916, 'Report on Inspection of the Damages to the Hill Section, Assam–Bengal Railway due to Heavy Rain in July 1915', by Sir Robert Gales, Chief Engineer Railway Board.

of keeping the line open were so strong that a huge sum of Rs 28 lakhs was spent on its restoration.[75]

Technical Aspects

Considering the hostile conditions of the hill section, it stands as an eloquent testimony to the unique engineering skills of the railway engineers. The steepest grade was 1 in 37–40, for a distance of nine miles. From an altitude of 117 feet as it enters the hill section at Damcherra, it rises to an elevation of 1,800 feet between Jatinga and Mahur and gradually descends into the plains of Upper Assam.

The permanent way was laid on 50 lb flatfooted steel rails, partly on *sal* (*Shea robusta*) and *pyinkadu/pyngadu* (*Xylia xylocarpa*)[76] and partly on *nageswar* (*Mesua ferrea* L.), *Jarrah* wood (*Eucalyptus marginata*) and chipped stone ballasting.[77] The hill section was fully ballasted. Among the engineering marvels of the railways, were the tunnels across the section. The entire length of hill section had thirty-seven tunnels, aggregating 15,569 feet in length, the longest tunnel measuring 1,922 feet. In addition, there were 560 bridges, both major and minor. It is said that for every mile of sleeper laid on the hill section, a man laid down his life.

Until about 1914, the annual earnings of the Assam–Bengal Railway could not reach the 3 per cent mark, because of the losses it incurred on the hill section. To place the railway on a firm financial footing, the Chief Commissioner of Assam, suggested in August 1915 that the company be relieved of the

75. Ways and Works 'A', W/1–64, June 1916, 'Report on Inspection of the Damages to the Hill Section, Assam–Bengal Railway due to Heavy Rain in July 1915', by Sir Robert Gales, Chief Engineer Railway Board.

76. The *pyngadu* sleepers were imported from Burma.

77. Medhi, *Transport System and Economic Development in Assam*, p. 71.

Lumding–Badarpur section. Thereafter, the line was to be treated as a government managed line worked on favourable terms.[78] The Railway Board did not agree to the proposal and suggested that the profitable Dacca section of the Eastern Bengal Railway be transferred and worked as a part of Assam–Bengal Railway,[79] to enhance the revenue raising capacity of the railway.

The Secretary of State was unwilling to accommodate this proposal and alternately suggested improving the port of Chittagong and developing the country through which the railway line passed. This, he felt, could be achieved by encouraging construction of feeder lines.

FEEDER LINES

The strong disinclination of the Government of India to increase its sterling liabilities, which depreciated the value of the rupee, led to the introduction of a new policy of subsidies. In 1893, a policy of offering subsidies to encourage construction of branch or feeder lines was announced. The primary purpose of these lines was to augment the earnings of the main line. In many instances, these lines helped in opening up the trade in the areas away from the main line, which would have otherwise remained neglected.

The main features of the policy were:

  i) Free land grants;
 ii) The main line was to provide rolling stock and work the line for not more than 50 per cent of its earnings;
iii) A rebate on payment from the gross earnings of the

78. Financial 'A', February 1916, nos. 16/1–3; extract from Chief Commissioner Assam's Letter no. 5889, B-Railway of 1 November 1916.
    79. Ibid.

main line through interchanged traffic between the two lines, so that the total profit of the branch line yielded a dividend of 4 per cent. Thus, the subsidy in the form of rebate substituted for the onerous guarantee.[80]

These terms were not sufficient to attract capital, therefore in 1896 the branch line companies were offered an absolute guarantee of 3 per cent, with a share in the surplus profits. They were also offered a rebate to the full extent of the earnings, with the total not exceeding 3.5 per cent on the capital outlay.[81]

In 1897 the Chief Commissioner of Assam, in accordance with the terms offered to the branch line companies, proposed the construction of a branch line running from Kulaura or Tilagaon to Sylhet on the main line of the Assam–Bengal Railway. This line 'would tend to augment the receipts of the Assam–Bengal Railway and to develop the resources of one of the largest and wealthiest districts of Eastern India'.[82]

The Secretary of State sanctioned this line in 1905 on the parent gauge, a distance of thirty-one miles at an estimated cost of Rs 22 lakhs. In the same year, a short length of the Noakhali Railway (34.9 miles), managed by the state was merged with the Assam–Bengal Railway.[83]

In 1905, another branch line was taken up as a part of the Assam–Bengal Railway from Akhaura, a station on the main line of the railway, to Ashuganj on the river Meghna, opposite Bhairab Bazar, a distance of nineteen miles. The line was opened for traffic in 1910.

80. Mehta, *Indian Railways*, p. 43.
81. Ibid.
82. Assam Secretariat PWD nos. 1–14, file no. 4306 of 1896–97, from Secretary to Chief Commissioner Assam in PWD to Secretary PWD, Government of India.
83. *Report on the Administration of Assam: 1905–1906*, pp. 158–9.

The first section of the Kulaura–Sylhet branch line between Kulaura to Kushiyara [*sic*], a distance of thirteen miles, was opened to traffic on 16 April 1912.[84] The second section of the line was delayed because of the damage caused by the floods of 1915. Besides tapping the trade of the wealthy district of Sylhet, this branch if continued till Chattak, 'could form a valuable link with Shillong, rendering it more accessible to the districts of Eastern Bengal'.

Two other branch lines were taken up under the scheme. One was from Chaparmukh station on the main line of the Assam–Bengal Railway, and the other from Katakhal on the Assam–Bengal Railway. The Chaparmukh–Nowgong–Silghat railway was surveyed in 1908. It sought to link Nowgong with Chaparmukh on the Assam–Bengal Railway and further link it with the river Brahmaputra at Silghat. Besides tapping all the tea gardens *en route*, it could secure a fair amount of traffic of the local produce of the area. The line would serve as a feeder for both the railway and the steamers. There was a proposal for extending the line to Amguri, as a chord line. The chord line was expected to reduce the distance between Gauhati and Tinsukia by forty miles and run for a considerable distance through the tea gardens and tracts yielding greater traffic. However, the scheme did not materialize.

In 1915, the Katakhal–Hailakandi–Lalabazar branch line was sanctioned as a part of the Assam–Bengal Railway.[85] Work on the line commenced in 1916, but had to be stopped in 1917 due to the war in Europe. This was for the want of rails, which were generally imported from Europe. Construction of the line was resumed later and it was reopened to traffic in 1924. The Chaparmukh–Silghat Railway was completed in 1920.

84. *Report on the Administration of Assam: 1911–1912*, p. 34.
85. *Report on the Administration of Assam: 1915–1916*, p. 42.

EASTERN BENGAL RAILWAY

The Assam–Bengal Railway was constructed as the shortest route to the ports of Eastern Bengal, through which the tea from Upper Assam was shipped to Europe. Uncertainty of transportation over the hill section of the route, due to natural calamities, affected transportation of both goods and passengers. During the period when traffic over the rail route was disrupted, tea continued to be sent out of the province by steamers. This railway failed to cater to a strong desire of H. J. S. Cotton (Chief Commissioner) to induce cultivators to settle in the wastelands of Assam from the congested districts of Eastern Bengal.

The primary source of revenue for the British in India was land tax. They inherited the traditional system of land revenue from the Mughals, and transformed its basic character. In Assam too, they attempted to optimize returns by enhancing land revenue. The *Raiyatwari* settlement, under which each cultivator paid directly to the government, reduced the Assamese cultivators to the status of petty agriculturists. They cultivated enough for their sustenance and there was no orientation towards production of a surplus. The faulty land revenue system failed to attract native cultivators to extend their domain of cultivable land. This retarded the process of recovery in agriculture, which was aggravated by the system of collection. Until 1853, revenue collection was entrusted to a group of *Chaudhuris* who received 10 per cent as remuneration on individual collections, in addition to the income from any new cultivation.[86] Till 1866, the revenue amounted to Rs 10 lakhs and the cultivation extended over an area of 1,324,000 acres.[87]

86. Mills, *Report on the Province of Assam*, paras 20–21.
87. Revenue 'A', November 1898, nos. 128–138, proceedings no. 30; note by the Chief Commissioner of Assam, 'On the Extension of Cultivation in Assam and Colonisation of Wastelands in the Province', para 11.

Against this backdrop of declining agriculture, the government in 1868–69 doubled the land revenue. The percentages of increase on the *rupit* land was 66.66 per cent and *faringhati* land was 100 per cent.[88] Hopkinson justified this increase because he found the revenue rates 'ridiculously low'. The area under the plough declined considerably on account of the new revenue rates. In 1874–75, the revenue amounted to Rs 21,32,008, with only about a quarter million acres of land under the plough.[89] In the span of 33 years between 1866 and 1899, the revenue demand quadrupled, but land under ordinary cultivation increased by a mere 7 per cent, in spite of an infinite scope for its expansion.

About five million acres of cultivable land was estimated to await 'the axe and the plough' in 1896–97. The Assam–Bengal Railway, which was close to completion during the corresponding period, was expected to facilitate the colonization of wastelands, which also received attention in the Imperial Legislature.

Sir Patrick Playfair, a mercantile member of the Viceroy's Council, conveyed to Henry Cotton (Chief Commissioner), that the Government of India was 'eager to consider any well-thought out scheme for emigration of large bodies of agriculturists into Assam'.[90] Commenting on how little had been done to reclaim land in Assam, he wrote:

> Five million acres of culturable waste remain to be reclaimed
> ... The great tea industry had made Assam what it is, and it
> is good that land should be covered with tea bushes, but it is

88. Dharma Kumar and Meghnad Desai (eds), *The Cambridge Economic History of India: 1757–1970*, vol. II, p. 123.

89. Kumar *et al.*, *The Cambridge Economic History of India*, vol. II, p. 123.

90. Railway Projects 'A', from Sir Patrick Playfair to H.J.S. Cotton, dated 30 March 1897.

no less and even more desirable that land should be covered with food grain crops . . . The million of acres of culturable land now lying waste represent millions of rupees which might be dug out of the soil, but are now allowed to be useless like the talent wrapped in a napkin.[91]

It was generally accepted that the 'stout and fanatical Mohammedans of Eastern Bengal [to be] the most eligible for immigration, as they were hardworking and prolific cultivators'.[92] Alexander Porteous, while discussing on the scheme of colonization of the Dhansiri Valley opined that:

> the best hope for colonizing the Dhansiri Valley will be by colonization from Sylhet. The Muhammaden of Eastern Sylhet, who have opened out much land under Tipperah [sic] Hills . . . would make the very best stuff for imported colonists both industrious and habituated to the kind of climate that prevails in the Dhansiri Valley.[93]

The province of Assam was dependent on the import of food grains to support its large immigrant population, employed in the tea gardens. The import of rice was a huge burden on the financial resources of the planters. It was also a severe drain on the agricultural resources of Bengal. During the occurrence of a famine in Bengal, while large supplies of food grains into Bengal came from Burma, nearly a million maunds (36,735 tons) of rice were exported from Bengal to Assam. Yet, the area available for cultivation of rice was practically unlimited within Assam.

Meanwhile, a growing demand for jute worldwide necessitated the expansion of jute cultivation. The produce from

91. Mills, *Report on the Province of Assam*, para 32.
92. Nag, *Roots of Ethnic Conflict*, p. 90.
93. Revenue 'A', March 1904, nos. 132–157, no. 34–1625 R of 14 April 1903.

Bengal could not meet the increasing demands and there was little scope for further expansion of its production in that province. The jute traders turned their attention to areas where climatic conditions were suitable for jute cultivation. In 1898, F.J. Monohan compiled a report on the prospects of jute cultivation in Assam, based on the information obtained from the District Officers.[94]

Jute was already grown in small quantities in the districts of Sylhet and Goalpara as a natural extension of the jute growing areas of Bengal. The cultivation of jute in these two districts was confined to permanently settled tracts. The major producer of the crop in the Brahmaputra Valley was Goalpara. Small quantities of jute were produced in the Garo Hills, Kamrup and Nowgong. The extensive tracts of sandy alluvial soil on both banks of the Brahmaputra, was suitable for jute cultivation. Numerous water channels afforded an abundance of water for steeping, an indispensable requisite for the production of good quality jute. The Gauhati branch line of the Assam–Bengal Railway, which traversed large areas of wastelands in the districts of Nowgong and Kamrup, were identified as areas where jute could be cultivated with success.

The prospects for extension of jute cultivation were dependent on a number of conditions. To prepare the crop for the market, additional labour was involved. Assamese cultivators were averse to putting in additional labour inputs. Employing hired labour was an expensive proposition, as the production costs would go up. Cultivation of jute could not be paying unless it was linked with encouraging immigration and the reclamation of wastelands in general.

94. F.J. Monohan, *Report on Jute Cultivation in Assam*, Shillong, 7 February 1898.

The government was keen on encouraging immigration to enhance the revenue potential of the province. It was felt that this objective could be achieved with an improvement in the communication network. The gradual completion of the Assam–Bengal Railway undoubtedly afforded a scope for colonization but it failed to link Assam directly with the heavily populated districts of Bengal. Henry Cotton expressed his concern in this manner:

> What is necessary for the facilitation of immigration into Assam, is the connection of Gauhati with the Eastern Bengal Railway System, and until this is done a great majority of the immigrant coolies will undoubtedly follow the Goalundo steamer route as they do at present. It will be impossible to workout any large scheme of immigration into Assam and so as to supply the inextinguishable need of the province of which five-sixths of the culturable land is still uncultivated, unless this extension of the Assam–Bengal Railway is carried out . . . [95]

F.J.E. Spring the consulting engineer, was sanguine that before long the Eastern–Bengal Railway connection with Gauhati would prove remunerative. The traffic that it would attract would ultimately help in enhancing the revenue of the province.

Accordingly, in 1901 a rough project was sent to the Secretary of State for sanction. The consulting engineer proposed that the Dhubri–Gauhati Extension should be worked in phases at an expenditure of approximately Rs 10 lakhs, or a station length, annually. To ensure cheap construction, it was suggested that it should not be given to private enterprise. It

95. Assam Secretariat PWD, file no. 4339, nos. 1–21, 'Proposed Connection of the Eastern Bengal State Railway with Gauhati', no. 2285, Shillong, 10 May 1897.

was also suggested that the services of the agency involved in the construction of the Eastern Bengal State Railway be utilized.

By 1902, two important links for through communication with Bengal were completed. One was the Kosi bridge, connecting Bengal and the North-Western Railway system with the Eastern Bengal Railway system. The other, was the Dhubri extension, which had four important river crossings.[96] The completion of these links left a gap of 151 miles between Golakganj on the Dhubri extension and Gauhati, which was the western terminus of the Assam–Bengal Railway. The alignment decided upon for this Dhubri–Gauhati extension was the northern route from Golakganj via Bhabanipur and Rangiya to Gauhati. To connect it across the Brahmaputra to the town of Gauhati, it was decided to set up a wagon ferry at Pandu.

The northern route was decided upon for the collateral advantages it offered. The railway could tap the entire trade of Mangaldai. It also provided a ready outlet for the surplus rice of the area around Nalbari, which was one of the most fertile and densely populated tracts of the Assam Valley. It would help in opening up Goalpara and the Eastern Duars. The Cacharis and Meches of the Eastern Duars and those of northern Kamrup would get the opportunity to migrate to the tea gardens of Upper Assam for employment.

The project received the sanction of the Secretary of State in 1903. An allocation of Rs 10 lakhs annually was made for the Dhubri–Gauhati link.[97] This provision for annual grants was made, as the Government of India could not accommodate

96. Assam Secretariat PWD, file no. 4339, no. 73 Railway of 1902, Government of India, PWD Railway Construction to the Secretary of State for India, 11 September 1902.
97. Railway Construction 'A', February 1903, nos. 85–97.

the project in its 'Schedule' of railways. Construction of the Dhubri–Gauhati line was vested with the Eastern Bengal State Railway. To ensure minimum expenditure in construction, it was proposed to 'open a few miles at a time, to construct the line in the first instance, of the cheapest possible character with timber bridges, *kutcha* or bamboo buildings and without ballast at all'.[98]

However, during the initial phase of its construction it was found that the physiographical conditions prevailing in districts it traversed were not conducive. The nature of the soil, heavy floods and rains, necessitated a very heavy outlay on bridges, to ensure stability. For the same reasons the line had to be ballasted throughout its length. Thus, the programme for a 'primitive cheap line' was reluctantly abandoned and the task of constructing 'all the works of fully substantial character' had to be taken up. Under the provisions of the new scheme, the line was to be constructed on a metre gauge of the usual 50 lb rails. The line was partly ballasted. A wagon ferry with a capacity of 100 wagons per day had also been provided for at Pandu near Gauhati.[99] The strictest attention was paid to economical construction in every direction. The extension was completed in 1909.

In 1910, a branch line was sanctioned from Rangia, a station on the Eastern Bengal Railway, to Tangla, a distance of twenty-four miles, on the metre gauge.[100] This line was of great importance to the tea gardens and the area in general. The Mangaldai sub-division of the Darrang district, which was poorly provided for in respect of communications benefited immensely. The line was completed in 1912 and opened to

98. Railway Construction 'A', no. 1524 RC of 9 December 1902.
99. Railway Construction 'A', August 1903, nos. 342–357, no. 44 Railway of 23 July 1908.
100. *Report on the Administration of Assam: 1909–1910.*

traffic in 1913. The promoters proposed to extend the line to Tezpur. The owners of the Tezpur–Balipara Tramway were apprehensive that such an extension would encroach upon its traffic and thus threaten its very existence. The promoters of the Mangaldai–Tramway also opposed this extension.

In 1920, a resolution in the Legislative Council of Assam advocated the transfer of the Gauhati–Tinsukia Section of the Assam–Bengal Railway to the Eastern Bengal Railway. The mover of the resolution A.B. Hawkins, emphasized:

> that the best scheme for railway connection between Assam and Burma is by the Hukong Valley and the transfer of the Gauhati–Tinsukia Section to the Eastern Bengal Railway will facilitate the construction of the Hukong Valley connection.[101]

The proposal did not receive an approval as the Secretary of State, who retained the right to terminate the contract of the Assam–Bengal Railway in 1921, decided that no such proposal would be entertained till the termination of the contract.

PROJECTED TRAMWAYS

The enormous expenditure incurred on the hill section discouraged the prospect of further railway extensions in Assam. Both the capital and revenue expenditure for the Assam–Bengal Railway was borne by the government and so there was little incentive on working the line economically.[102] The

101. Financial 'A', January 1920, no. 173F-19/1–6, from Officiating Secretary to the Chief Commissioner of Assam in the PWD to Secretary Railway Board.

102. The 'Capital Account' of any railway closes, as the railway opens for public traffic. However, in the hill section of the Assam–Bengal Railway, no distinction was made between maintenance and new works. There was a tendency by the company to relegate works like clearing slips, widening cuttings, renewal of walls of tunnels that had collapsed, replacement of banks, bridges and retaining walls, etc., to the capital account. An increase

extraordinary feature of the line was that in spite of recognizing it as a 'huge mistake' and insistence of the consulting engineers at various stages of its construction to opt out of the scheme, it was continued as a 'wicked waste of the Indian taxpayers money'. Lines taken up by private enterprise had to find a place in Schedule A of the Railway Programme, where funds were allotted for maintenance of existing lines, lines under construction, etc., with any remaining funds being available for new lines. As a major portion of the funds allocated for Assam, were used for the upkeep of the Assam–Bengal Railway, the growth of any other railway projects for the development of Assam was severely retarded. An extension from Dhubri to Gauhati to link the North Assam Valley with Calcutta was essential. However, it was not possible to accommodate it in the Railway Programme, as funds were not forthcoming.

Henry Cotton, while discussing the future of railway projects in Assam, pressed for the inclusion of the Dhubri–Gauhati extension within the Railway Programme. He felt that for the rest of the province, it would suffice to develop a system of tramways:

> What appears to be needed for the development for the almost inexhaustible resources of the province is a well devised system of tramways on say, 2 feet 6 inches gauge, and varying in length from 15 to 30 miles, which would ordinarily constitute as feeders to the main line of the railway and occasionally where there is railway . . . to the river bank.[103]

---

in the capital account increased the liability of the government in the form of subsidy and interest charges. The government, in order to prevent liberal charges on capital, stipulated that the cost of clearing of slips and repairs of banks or cuttings should be charged on 'Revenue' and any special work requiring substantial improvement or addition to capital charge.

103. Assam Secretariat File no. 4339 of 1897, nos. 1–21, 'Proposed connection of the Eastern Bengal Railway with Gauhati'.

The subject was prominently brought to the notice of the Government of India by Sir William Ward (Chief Commissioner) in his letter to the Government of India, which included a 'Practical Note' on the tramways submitted by F.J.E. Spring, the consulting engineer for railways in Assam. While reporting on the success of the 2 feet lines — the Jorhat State Railway, the Cherra–Companyganj State Railway and the Tezpur–Balipara Tramway, he was of the view that it would be wise to introduce a definite policy of 'light railways' in Assam.[104]

Tramways were particularly suitable for a province like Assam where rainfall was exceptionally heavy. Metalled roads could not be maintained because of the enormous cost of metalling them. Existing earthen roads were incapable of bearing the load of regular wheeled traffic during the rainy season. The only means of keeping communication permanently open in a satisfactory manner was by constructing tramways. He hoped that before long there would be tramways stretching from either side of the main railway, in both the Brahmaputra and Surma Valleys. On the issue of spending money for the construction and maintenance of roads he said:

> I need scarcely point out what a very different thing it is to bury one's capital in the work from which, except clumsy toll bars, generally no longer used in advanced countries, it is impossible to recover anything from using one's credit to borrow money for works which may reasonably [be] expected to pay all working and maintenance charges and something over towards interest besides. Assam seems to me to be essentially the country for some sort of forced development of this sort.[105]

104. Financial 'A', file no. BT/114F, June 1912, no. 1483 of 12 August 1896. 'Note by the Consulting Engineer to the Government of India for Railways, on Light Railways on the Provincial Roads in Assam', Shillong, 31 July 1896.
105. Financial 'A', file no. BT/114F, June 1912, no. 1483 of 12 August 1896. 'Note by the Consulting Engineer to the Government of India for

These light railways were expected to pay not only for their upkeep, but also in most cases, yield a fair share of return on its capital, besides proving to be of infinite value to communication. Its value was not only viewed in the context of the railway balance sheet, but for its role in enhancing the land revenue component of the provincial balance sheet.

Henry Cotton insisted that extension of tramways should be taken up with the guarantee, charged from the provincial revenues. He was sanguine that the amount could be recovered, from the savings of the PWD on the maintenance of roads. It could ensure the tramways being cheaply constructed.

> . . . the object of the tramways in Assam is to open out the country, to establish communications in a province where, during the greater part of the year, roads are impassable, to assist the tea-industry, and above all provide feeders to the main railway. It will be sometime, before these branch lines are paying speculations, as they will not pay at all unless they are implicitly supported by tea interest.[106]

This is why Henry Cotton wholeheartedly favoured projects, exclusively run for the tea industry. Proposals for several tramway projects were subsequently sent to the Government of India for its approval. The first of these proposals was by Williamson Magor and Company, a well-known Calcutta agent and local planter. The project remained in abeyance for some time and was abandoned by the promoters. In 1899, Shaw Wallace and Company, while applying for constructing tramways in the district of Sylhet, desired that the undertaking

---

Railways, on Light Railways on the Provincial Roads in Assam', Shillong, 31 July 1896.

106. Railway Projects 'A', no. 5298, Shillong, 2 December 1897, from Secretary to the Chief Commissioner Assam in PWD to Secretary PWD, Government of India.

be transferred and sanctioned along with other proposals. However, as the concessions asked for were not accepted, the project was abandoned. The scheme was transferred to McLeod and Company, who desired that the government should replace the subsidy by a guarantee.[107]

Several other promoters submitted schemes for tramways in the Cachar and Sylhet districts of Assam between 1897 and 1899. The district of Cachar was intersected by the Barak from the east to the west. The proposed scheme contemplated one system of tramways to the north of the river and two separate systems to the south of it. The alignment in all these cases was so designed as to tap the principal tea gardens in the district and converge on the Assam–Bengal Railway extension between Badarpur and Silchar. The tramways planned on the north bank were to be between Silchar and Tikalpur, a distance of fourteen miles. The two tramways to the south of the river were to be between Silchar via Silkuri and Derby to Duarband, a distance of twenty-two miles. The other was from opposite Sealteck via Hailakandi to Lalabazar, a distance of twenty-four miles.[108]

In 1897 Octavious Steel and Company proposed a tramway scheme. It was designed to tap the important tea districts in the Longai and Chargola Valleys, and connecting them to Karimganj, a station on the Assam–Bengal Railway. The proposed alignment was between Karimganj and Chandkira in the Longai Valley, with a branch line from Patherkhandi to Maguracherra in the Chargola Valley. The length of the line

107. Railway Projects 'A', July 1899, nos. 42–56, no. 1546 from Secretary to Chief Commissioner Assam in PWD to the Secretary PWD, Government of India.

108. Railway Projects 'A', June 1898, nos. 40–57, from Jardine Skinner and Company to the Deputy Commissioner of Cachar, Calcutta, 21 July.

in the Longai Valley was 23.5 miles and that in the Chargola Valley was 19.5 miles, with the total length being 43 miles.[109]

Shaw Wallace and Company put forward tramway schemes for the rest of Sylhet district. The proposed tramways were designed to tap all the important tea tracts of South Sylhet as well as provide feeder lines to the Assam–Bengal Railway, from the most populous portions of the Sylhet district. Three distinct lines of tramways were planned: (a) from Kulaura on the Assam–Bengal Railway to the town of Sylhet; (b) from Srimangal on the Assam–Bengal Railway through Maulavi Bazar to Manumukh, a distance of twenty-two-and-a-half miles; and (c) from Ashuganj, to cross the Assam–Bengal Railway at Shaistaganj and continue southward to the river Sutnga, a distance of eighteen miles.[110]

The financial concessions sought by the promoters were varied, ranging from a fixed annual subsidy, a per mile subsidy, to a guarantee of 3 per cent. The proposals were submitted to the Government of India, with an insistence by Henry Cotton on a guarantee of 3 per cent on the capital, in lieu of a subsidy for the first ten years. He also proposed an equal sharing of the financial burden by the provincial government as well as the local boards concerned.

By an order on 4 July 1898, the Government of India broadly accepted the proposals suggesting drastic modifications of specific clauses:

i)   That the Indian Railways Act IX of 1890 was to apply on these tramways.

ii) A purchase clause, same as agreed to for branch line terms resolution.

109. Railway Projects 'A', no. 47 RP.
110. Railway Projects 'A', no. 48 RP.

iii) The guarantee to be effective for ten years from the date of completion of the whole tramway and to be limited to a definite amount of Capital in rupees.

iv) The interest allowed during the construction was to be charged for a limited period and the maximum commission allowed was not to exceed 2.5 per cent to include all expenses of floating [a company].

v) The share of guarantee of the Local Board was to be met by raising the necessary amount by an additional cess.

vi) That in the next Provincial Settlement with Assam no allowance would be made for any extra-burden imposed by its share of guarantee, and finally the amount paid by the Government as guarantee was to be carried forward as debt by the Company at 3 per cent, to be repaid out of any earnings in excess of 4 per cent.[111]

The response of the Government of India was so discouraging that Jardine Skinner and Company, and Octavious Steel and Company withdrew their schemes. Shaw Wallace and Company pressed for the acceptance of their conditions. The Chief Commissioner would not reconcile to the clause that the share of guarantee to be paid by the local board had to be met by increasing local taxation. He emphatically protested against the inclusion of the last clause in the final order, which was tantamount to abandoning the schemes for the want of a guarantee.

The unwillingness of the government to undertake any financial liability was due to the financial burden faced by it for repairing the damage caused by the earthquake of 1897, to the railways in Assam. It was estimated that restoration

111. Railway Projects 'A', June 1898, nos. 40–57, no. 50 RP, 4 June 1898 from Government of India PWD to the Chief Commissioner Assam.

work would require an additional Rs 50 lakhs. Unless liberal assistance was forthcoming from the imperial revenues, it was impossible for the slender provincial resources to meet the extraordinary expenditure. Thus a well-devised scheme of light railway feeders to enhance traffic on the Assam–Bengal Railway and subsequently its earnings, were lost. The issue of the light railways was reopened in 1912, by Sir Archdale Earle, Chief Commissioner, after the completion of the Dhubri–Gauhati extension.

Generous financial settlements that had been made for the reorganized province of Assam in 1912, made it possible for the Chief Commissioner to provide for a guarantee, without exceeding the admissible annual expenditure. The system of permanent Provincial Settlements, initiated by the government offered ample scope to the provincial administrative head, to adjust future expenditure with the rate of expansion of provincial revenues.[112] He tried to convince the Government of India that under no circumstances would the burden of meeting the guarantee for railway projects fall on the imperial revenues.

At the Commissioner's Conference in 1908–10, it was decided to re-survey the light railway projects submitted earlier between 1897 and 1899. The Mangaldai Tramway Project was dropped as the Eastern Bengal State Railway extension to Tangla was taken up on practically the same alignment.

In Sylhet, the Srimangal–Manumakh tramway was considered redundant as a branch line was constructed between the Assam–Bengal Railway's line and Fenchuganj. It commenced a survey on the line from Madna via Habiganj to Shaistaganj in 1910–11. The Habiganj–Shaistaganj section was recommended as a feeder branch line for the Assam–Bengal Railway.

112. Financial 'A', file no. BT/114 F, June 1912, no. 1190 F, 17 June 1912.

The Longai Valley project between Juri and Hathikhira and the extension into the Chargola Valley was recommended at the Chief Commissioners Conference, 'that it was absolutely necessary for the Chargola Valley gardens [to] have an exit by rail or road'.[113]

The three lines in Cachar were also re-surveyed. At the conference, the Hailakandi line was considered to be of immense value to the Surma Valley and hence it was proposed that it be taken up as a branch line. Except for the Katakhal–Lalabazar Railway, which was taken up as a branch line, the rest of the schemes did not materialize due to the war situation. Thus, the scheme of a well-developed feeder system in the tracts teeming with produce could not be marketed for lack of connectivity with the trunk line. The Assam–Bengal Railway continued as a financial burden, with its earnings barely reaching 3 per cent.

The Dwara–Therria tramway project suffered at the hands of the Imperial Government, for its refusal to give a guarantee. Following the abandonment of the Cherra–Companyganj Railway, the Viceroy sought the opinion of the Chief Commissioner, on the possibility of constructing tramways required to open out the area south of the Khasi and Jaintia Hills. A syndicate represented by G.L. Garth, proposed to construct a twenty-eight-and-a-half miles long metre gauge line from Dwara on the Surma river via Therria to Uthmar.[114] He also suggested that in the event of the railway being sanctioned, a company should be formed for working the coalfields and lime quarries at Maolong. The Secretary of State objected to a grant

113. *List of Light Railway Projects in Eastern Bengal and Assam: Corrected upto 31st August 1911.*
114. Railway Projects 'A', February 1902, nos. 2–5, 'Notes', Gen'l no. 13706 RP, from Assam PWD, no. 4448, 5 November 1901, para 1.

from the provincial revenues unless the scheme could find a place in the 'Imperial Programme'.

Garth later modified his scheme by omitting the third section of the line from Dwara to Maolong. On the altered alignment, the line would run from Dwara to Maolong for thirteen miles, with a branch from Maolong to Therria of five miles. The gauge was later altered to 2 feet 6 inches.[115] Garth was informed that as the demand on the railway programme was so heavy for other provinces, there was no prospect of finding a place for the project in the programme in the near future. Assam had already received a large sum of railway grants for upkeep of the Assam–Bengal Railway, leaving very little scope for accommodating fresh projects.

In May 1902, the Government of India authorized by a draft order, the construction of a railway from Dwara–Bazar via Maolong to Therriaghat.[116] The mineral concessions desired were granted to the Maolong Lime and Coal Company and linked with the railway company. The project was primarily conceived for developing the mineral resources of the area. It was expected to provide concomitant commercial and administrative advantages to the province.

The capital for the project was to be in the form of a loan of Rs 10 lakhs. In 1904, the thirteen mile long section between Dwara and Maolong, with a one-and-a-half mile quarry siding not originally provided for, to the face of the coal head was constructed. An additional sum of Rs 3 lakhs was required for completion of the project. The promoters asked the local

115. Railway Projects 'A', February 1902, nos. 2–5, 'Notes', Gen'l no. 13706 RP, from Assam PWD, no. 4448, 5 November 1901, para 1.
116. Railway Projects 'A', October 1904, nos. 1–3, no. 2168/3853PW, from Officiating Secretary to the Chief Commissioner of Assam in the PWD to the Secretary to the Government of India in the PWD, Shillong, 29 July 1904.

government to guarantee an amount of Rs 3 lakhs at 4 per cent per annum for a period of twenty years.[117]

Awaiting approval of the Secretary of State, the Government of India allowed the local government to guarantee 4 per cent on a loan of Rs 3 lakhs. Initially the Secretary of State took exception to the grant, but on a special request from the Government of India and the local administration, they were permitted to guarantee interest at 4 per cent per annum for a period of ten years, on a debenture loan of Rs 4 lakhs.[118] The promoters failed to raise the loan and consequently in December 1907, approached the Assam Government to sell the line, as neither the imperial nor provincial government could advance funds for its purchase or completion. The company went into liquidation, and subsequently in 1911, H.V. Low and Company purchased the rights and concessions vested to Garth's syndicate, for Rs 1,75,000 and spent Rs 75,000 in endeavouring to complete the line.[119] They failed to complete it and in 1912, a group of investors in England chiefly members of the two families connected with mineral extraction in the locality, formed the Khassia [sic] Hills (Assam) Company Limited. The capital was fixed at Rs 9,00,000 of which Rs 7,50,000 was issued to complete and work the line as well as the limestone deposits at the terminus of the railway. The line was completed in 1914. Disaster struck shortly afterwards in the form of heavy rainfall which caused many breaches in

117. Railway Projects 'A', October 1904, nos. 1–3, no. 2168/3853PW, from Officiating Secretary to the Chief Commissioner of Assam in the PWD to the Secretary to the Government of India in the PWD, Shillong, 29 July 1904.

118. Railway Projects 'A', April 1905, nos. 10–15, no. 47RP, 29 March 1905, from the Secretary Railway Board to Chief Commissioner Assam.

119. Projects 'A', May 1916, no. 373-P/1–9, from the Managing Agents, Dwara-Therria Light Railway to the Secretary Railway Board, 8 January 1910.

the railway embankment. The loss was minimal. However, funds were not available for undertaking the repair work, nor could the company raise additional funds for the purpose. Their agents, Gladstone Wyllie and Company proposed to the Government of India, that the Assam–Bengal Railway should execute the repairs and provide additional equipment and work the line. The Assam–Bengal Railway meanwhile undertook the survey of a metre gauge line on the Sylhet–Dwara route. They agreed to restore the line only in case of an imperial guarantee, but the scheme never materialized and fell through. Thus, a railway aimed at tapping the limestone deposits of Khasi Hills was lost. In 1942, the Assam–Bengal Railway with a route length of about 1,113 miles was amalgamated with the Eastern Bengal Railway and was named as the Bengal and Assam Railway.

5
Labour

One of the results of industrial development in India under the colonial government was the creation of a large workforce. India's development as an agrarian and raw material adjunct resulted in structural changes in the traditional agrarian economy. The suppression of the traditional handicrafts industry rendered a large chunk of people involved in them without a means of livelihood. The traditional agricultural sector was too overcrowded to leave any scope for absorption of this surplus labour force into this sector. Under the new land settlement rules, a peasant failing to pay his revenue dues was dispossessed of his landholdings, forcing him to seek employment elsewhere. This gave rise to a growing army of landless people seeking alternative avenues of employment.

With such a large labour force at its disposal, the colonizers embarked upon a plan to utilize this growing army of landless people in various productive ventures built with British capital. The sectors where the labour were employed were plantations, mines, factories and the transport industry, more so the railways. An entirely new class of industrial workers emerged in the Indian social milieu. A new economic system emerged, which was based on the exploitation of wage labourers by the capitalists.

A study of the railways as an industry would be incomplete without taking into account the human effort behind their development. Industrial development in Assam, as has been mentioned earlier, centred around the tea, coal and petroleum industries. Labour was a major component in these industries, but the availability of labour for wages was a scarce commodity in Assam. Certain socio-economic factors were responsible for this phenomenon. The proportion of the indigenous population to the total area of the province was very little.[1] The native population were inclined to cultivate for their subsistence, producing very little marketable surplus. The minimum needs of the population were met within the village. Unlike the rest of India, there was no pressure on agricultural lands, as there was an abundance of wastelands. Therefore, peasants were not attracted to labour for wages during their off season, to supplement their earnings. According to the Census of 1881 about 84.2 per cent of the population, were engaged and supported by agriculture and a mere 1.8 per cent were engaged on earthwork and general labour.[2]

The first tea garden became operational in 1839. It was difficult to induce local people to work on these gardens and until 1843, Chinese labourers were imported for the gardens.

1. The growth of population during the last four decades of the nineteenth century was practically arrested. The Burmese interlude caused a steep fall in population, estimated at 75 per cent by Pemberton. Cholera and smallpox as epidemics assumed devastating proportions in 1839, 1847 and 1852, largely reducing the local population.
2. *Census of India: 1901*, vol. IV, Assam, part I, report by B.C. Allen, p. 162.

After dispensing with their services, Cacharis came to be employed on the plantations till 1859. With an increase in acreage under tea and adoption of more labour intensive methods of production, the greater demand for labour could not be met locally. Labour began to be imported for the tea gardens from the congested districts of Bengal and Bihar. Indentured labour came to replace free labour. Plantation labour became the exclusive property of the planters, and were not available for work outside their gardens.

Local Assamese labour was hard to come by for constructing roads. The Nagas and the Khasis were occasionally available, convicts were also used. An explanation offered by the British to this aversion is reflected in an observation of Sir George Campbell:

> that somehow people have to look on all Government workmen as impressed labourers. It matters not if they are offered double rates obtainable elsewhere; they are still disinclined to take service as it lowers their social position.[3]

An accusation levelled against the Assamese peasantry's aversion to hard work was that they were 'lazy and unenterprising'. Aversion to hard work was also attributed to the habit of smoking opium. However, it was difficult to accept the accusation fully, as it was this very lot of people who were credited with building large embanked roads, tanks and temples at the behest of their Rajas. In such a situation however, the colonial government was faced with an acute shortage of labour rendering its developmental projects very expensive because of having to import labour.

Railways in Assam were pioneering works, because of the immense difficulties faced in their construction. It meant the

3. Hunter, *A Statistical Account of Assam*, pp. 46–7.

employment of a very large number of ordinary unskilled labourers throughout the entire length of the railway. Over the rest of India these labourers were recruited from amongst the poorer classes of cultivators. Since the railway authorities in Assam could not rely on such a pool of agricultural labourers, they had to depend largely on the import of a labour force. Unskilled labour for earthwork and cuttings were imported from other provinces of India, while skilled workers or plate-layers for laying rails and crossings accurately, were imported from England for the Assam–Bengal Railway.[4]

Very little information about the employment of railway workers is available for the three short feeder railways at Dibrugarh, Tezpur and Jorhat. Generalized information like 'a labour force to be insisted before the working season had expired' was available as regards the Dibru–Sadiya Railway.[5]

For constructing the trunk railway from Chittagong to Tinsukia a large number of labourers had to be imported. For convenience in construction, the entire length of the railway was divided into three sections. Section I between Chittagong and Badarpur traversed the populous districts of Bengal. For this section the workforce was entirely recruited from amongst the local population. The other two sections between Badarpur and Makum, and Lumding and Gauhati were practically devoid of population. The line through North Cachar Hills was not only unhealthy and inhospitable, but afforded neither labour nor food supplies.

Contractors imported a large proportion of the labourers for this line. Many came voluntarily from the Makran Coast near Karachi, Kabul and the North-West frontier.[6] Initially

4. Gawthropp, *Story of Assam Railways*, p. 16.
5. Ibid.
6. Railway Construction 'A', April 1897, nos. 256–259, enclosure no. 2 to Railway despatch no. 39 of 1897, para 24.

attempts were made to import men from the labour districts of Bihar, from where the bulk of the plantation labourers came. The attempts were unsuccessful, as they appeared 'to suffer far more from the effects of the climate than the better-fed Mussalmans from the Western Frontier'.[7] The cost per head of importing coolies from the distant North-West Frontier was between Rs 30 to Rs 40. The coolies travelled at their own risk and were usually employed on daily wages or petty contracts.

Labourers for Assam plantations were strictly imported till 1870 through licenced contractors or *arkattis*. By an amendment of the Emigration Act in 1870, licenced gardens' *sardars* and *sardarnis* were permitted to recruit labourers directly. Further, in 1873 by another amendment, free recruitment was allowed on a short-term contractual basis. It was under this new 'Emigration Clause' that labourers for the railways in Assam were recruited.

Between 1895 and 1897, there was a marked increase in the number of free immigrants recruited by contractors, due to a demand for construction on the Assam–Bengal Railway. It rose from 15,054 in 1895 to 95,014 in 1896, slightly declining in 1897 to 54,934. During the corresponding period, recruitment through *sardars*, licenced contractors and special agents was 21,234 in 1896 and 39,657 in 1897.[8]

WAGES

There was a marked difference in the wages of indentured and free labourers. The wages of indentured labour was controlled by various acts and statutes, with a view of economizing on

7. Railway Construction 'A', April 1897, nos. 256–259, enclosure no. 2 to Railway despatch no. 39 of 1897, para 24.

8. Revenue 'A', Proceedings, November 1898, General Department, Emigration Resolution no. 2421, Calcutta, 2 August 1898.

the expenses of the planters. The minimum wages were Rs 5 for men and Rs 4 for women and children above twelve years of age. Child labour received Rs 3 per month. A free labourer employed on public works in 1864 earned Rs 7 per month.[9]

A railway coolie in 1895 earned between 6 to 8 annas per day, giving a wage rate between Rs 11–4–0 and Rs 15 per month. This calculation seems to be exaggerated, as a railway coolie in 1897 is said to have earned close to Rs 6 per month. This rate was later enhanced to Rs 8 per month. This increase was designed to attract labourers' in spite of the high mortality amongst the workers, which had been a discouraging factor. The rates furnished were for unskilled workers employed for earthwork and cuttings. Skilled labourers for plate-laying and tunnelling were imported from England at a wage of Rs 9 per month.[10]

The wide discrepancy in the earnings of an 'Act' coolie and a free labourer created serious problems. Many of the indentured workers on plantations escaped to work on the railways.[11] During the construction of Assam–Bengal Railway, many leading planters of the province in a memorandum to the Assam Administration accused the railway contractors of enticing coolies from the tea gardens by 'offer of higher wages for employment in the railway'. Wier, the manager of Kalline tea estate, in a statement showed that 77 Act I coolies had deserted his garden in 1897. In 1898, the number of Act coolies who deserted was 43 while there were 14 Non-Act coolies.[12] The nature of the desertions was so grave that in one

9. Hunter, *A Statistical Account of Assam*, p. 121.
10. Revenue 'A', Proceedings, November 1898, General Department, Emigration Resolution no. 2421, Calcutta, 2 August 1898.
11. Revenue 'A', August 1899, nos. 41–42.
12. Ibid.

of the gardens, the cultivating force was reduced to 25 men only.[13]

HEALTH AND SANITARY CONDITIONS

It has been mentioned earlier that there was a high mortality rate amongst the labourers employed on the construction of the Assam–Bengal Railway on the Badarpur–Lumding and Lumding–Dimapur section. These labourers were not imported under any Immigration Act. There was an absence of strict supervision over the labour imported for the railway. It was in violation of the strictness impressed upon private employers for carrying out their responsibilities towards labourers under their control. Under the provision of the Emigration Act of 1882, it was binding upon the employer to ensure proper sanitary conditions in the localities where labourers were settled, in order to minimize the mortality rate. In Assam particularly, efforts were made to ensure proper health conditions of the imported labour employed on tea gardens, oilfields and coalmines.

On the Assam–Bengal Railway, the contractors imported labour directly and therefore it was not binding on them to follow the stipulations of the Emigration Act. The agents of the railway company had no control over the labourers. No attempts were made to ensure proper health and sanitary conditions of the coolies employed on the railways. Very often, such unhealthy conditions led to an outbreak of epidemics amongst them.

H.J.S. Cotton (Chief Commissioner) on a tour of the province of Assam was concerned at the irresponsible attitude

13. Revenue 'A', August 1899, nos. 41–42.

of the railway contractors in not making proper sanitary arrangement to prevent epidemics. He observed:

> I found that hundreds of railway coolies amounting to several thousands in the aggregate, were coming into Gauhati by steamers every day, but that no arrangements were made for their reception or medical observation ... This was obviously a most unsatisfactory state of things and usually calculated to spread cholera.[14]

The large mass of labourers, numbering a few thousands, were housed in the most insalubrious localities along their worksites, with hardly any provision being made for their sanitary welfare. This resulted in excessive mortality amongst the labourers. Without any binding legal sanctions on the employing contractors, the sick were not given adequate medical attention. Many of them became destitute or permanently incapacitated, they were not repatriated, and left to fend for themselves. To redeem the situation, the government issued orders compelling the contractors to accept responsibility for ensuring better health of the labourers and to help repatriate sick and destitute coolies. The orders could not be executed in. the absence of any legal machinery, except through the agent of the railway company, who could exert a certain degree of departmental pressure. The company, already burdened with excessive expenditure on the line, was unwilling to shoulder on extra responsibility in treating the sick coolies as it would be a charge on the capital expenditure of the railway. The temporary nature of the workforce, and the fact that they did not come under any Emigration Act, resulted in the irresponsible behaviour of the railway contractors and company agents.

14. Home 'A', September 1901, 'Note on Sanitary Arrangements for the Prevention of Cholera Among Railway Coolies at Gauhati', by H.J.S. Cotton, 22 March 1900.

The issue was debated considerably within the local administration. Finally the Chief Commissioner issued an order, wherein the entire medical arrangements for that portion of the railway which was within Assam were placed under the general supervision of the Principal Medical Officer of the province of Assam.[15] A proportionate share of the expenses was to be borne by the railway company.

LABOUR POPULATION

In 1881, about 20,000 persons were engaged in the construction of the Assam–Bengal Railway in North Cachar Hills. The total labour force engaged on the two sections of the Assam–Bengal Railway within Assam was 31,583.[16] The same figures were registered in the census of 1891. However in 1897, in the northern section of the railway between Lumding and Tinsukia alone the presence of 35,000 labourers was registered during the working season.[17]

Labour had to be imported during the construction of the Dhubri–Gauhati extension of the Eastern Bengal Railway. The area through which the railway passed, was not as unhealthy as the hill section and the Nambor forest area. Construction being phased out over a longer period, mass immigration was not required. Recruitment procedures were however largely hampered by the provisions of the Emigration Act of 1901.

The Emigration Act of 1901, stipulated that all recruitments

15. Home 'A', September 1901, nos. 55–56, 'Note by Chief Commissioner on Sanitary Arrangements in Railway Camps'.

16. Railway Construction 'A', April 1897, nos. 256–259, enclosure no. 2 to Railway despatch of 1897, Assam–Bengal Railway, section III.

17. In the Census of 1901, about 6,214 persons from Punjab and 1,407 from Bombay came to Assam. Attracted by the Assam–Bengal Railway *Kabulis* and natives of Baluchistan were enumerated in the census in North Cachar Hills and they probably worked on the railways.

henceforth were to be made by *arkattis* or garden *sardars* or through the Labour Supply Association. None of these agencies were suitable for recruiting coolies for the construction of a railway. The formulators of the Act did not perceive the implications of the provisions of the Act on public works operations. The Eastern Bengal Railway requested for the withdrawal of the Assam Labour and Emigration Act VI of 1901 from the districts of Kamrup and Goalpara, the area covered by railway operations. The Indian Tea Association raised serious objections to the proposed withdrawal and the scheme was thus stalled. The Eastern Bengal Railway therefore, had to depend largely on local labour for its construction, which was taken up in phases.

Special Land Settlements for Railwaymen

Labour was not only required for the construction of railways, but for annual maintenance of its permanent way. It was a difficult proposition to import small groups of men annually for the purpose, as it would involve considerable expenditure.

Land was acquired in stretches along the railway line. On completion of the Assam–Bengal Railway, it was considered desirable to lease out these lands adjacent to the railway and encourage settlement. It was of importance to the railways and the local government to encourage settlers and establish a population with the view 'of opening up the country and creating a labour force upon which to draw in cases of emergency'.[18] Some workmen on the railway had already temporarily established themselves close to the railway line.

18. Railway Construction 'A', January 1909, nos. 175–178, General no. 973 RC no. 268C of 15 April 1907, from Agent, Assam–Bengal Railway to the Consulting Engineer to the Government of India for Railways.

The railway company, which was in closer contact with the labourers, was in a better position to induce them to settle on railway lands on temporary terms. The local government was impressed upon to frame rules for settling this group of labourers on the land either temporarily or permanently.

A study of the agricultural conditions of the Kopili Valley in 1900 revealed, that 'small bodies of pioneers' settled the tract between Lanka and Kampur stations of the Assam–Bengal Railway. These men had come for employment on the Assam–Bengal Railway and were still more or less connected with it. B.C. Basu, Assistant to the Director Land Records, recorded his observation on the issue:

> At Kampur I found two Hindustanis who grew wheat, barley and peas . . . At Lanka I found a compact settlement of nine families from different parts of Bihar and North-West. Some of them are still employed on the railway . . . They are extending cultivation and seem to be well pleased with the prospect . . . At Chamburigaon near Lanka, I found three Punjabi families who are cultivating land in addition to following their pursuits. They are men of moderate means and they wish to apply for a grant but would require pecuniary assistance from Government.[19]

In 1902, the Chief Commissioner of Assam was authorized by the Government of India to offer 'to the contractors, labourers and employees of the railway in Assam, settlements of wastelands along the tract, on either side from Lumding to Nowgong and on one side to Golaghat'.[20]

19. Revenue 'A', October 1900, nos. 81–82 dated 17 May 1900, 'Report on the Agricultural Conditions of the Kopili Valley which it Proposed to Throw Open to Colonization'.

20. Revenue 'A', June 1908, nos. 91–107, 'Colonization of Wastelands', from F.J. Monohan, Commissioner Assam Valley Districts to Secretary Board of Revenue.

The terms of the grant were designed thus: Land was offered in parcels of 10 to 50 acres, larger allotments permitted in special cases. It was rent-free for the first five years, after which it would be assessed at 2 annas per acre for the next five years, and at 4 annas per acre for the next ten years. At the end of this period, the land was liable for assessment under ordinary rules. The grant was not transferable till the end of twenty years. The grant was liable to cancellation in the fifth, tenth or fifteenth year, if the lessee did not clear a fifth, a quarter or a third of the total area.[21] The government in addition offered pecuniary assistance to the cultivators.

The railway company was asked to widely publicize the terms of the settlement and encourage its employees to take up land on the termination of their employment. In 1903 by a modified order, the area covered by the concession was identified between Jamunamukh and Bokajan stations. Bona fide settlers, other than railway employees, were offered the concession. The eastern limit for the settlement was fixed at Nowgong district.

The initial response to the settlement policy was not very encouraging. In 1905–1906, twenty-five acres of land were settled under the scheme, which gradually increased over time. In 1911–12, 1,400 bighas, (a bigha being approximately 0.367 acre), were settled in Lumding block alone. A marked increase in the area settled under the rules by railway coolies was visible in 1913–14 in Sibsagar district. They increased from 1,237 to 3,810 acres.[22] After 1913, large-scale migration of cultivators from Mymensingh took place into Nowgong district. Separate

21. Revenue 'A', June 1908, nos. 91–107, 'Colonization of Wastelands', from F.J. Monohan, Commissioner Assam Valley Districts to Secretary Board of Revenue.
22. *Report of on the Revenue Administration of Assam Valley Districts: 1911–1912*, p. 4.

statistics on settlements under the scheme are not available, as their lot had been reflected along with other migrants thus: '... in Nowgong cultivators from Bengal, ex-railway coolies and people of that class have taken up over 10,000 acres'.[23]

In North Cachar Hills, attempts were made in a small way to attract settlers in the vicinity of the Assam–Bengal Railway. The Chief Commissioner after an inspection of the North Cachar Hills sub-division expressed his desire to open it up to colonization:

> I may shortly publicize a scheme for offering land on very favourable terms to bona fide foreigners who have come here in the service of the railways.[24]

The Deputy Commissioner was authorized to issue a proclamation on the following conditions: Land would be liable to survey and assessment after three years of its occupation. At the time of survey, the government reserved the right to dispossess men who were speculators or middlemen and settle them instead with actual cultivators. The holding of 2 *hals* (0.32 acres) of rice land could not be exceeded without special permission from the Deputy Commissioner. Any possession in excess of the stipulation was liable to resumption at the time of survey.[25] The scheme had teething problems, as the government did not find the railway company a suitable agency to effect such land settlements. The government decided to demarcate the actual land required for purpose of railways and relinquish the rest. It was also stipulated that all lands temporarily settled earlier were resumed. Friction between the local

23. *Resolution on the Land Revenue Administration of Assam: 1913–1914*, p. 5.
24. Ibid.
25. Revenue 'A', March 1903, Notification from Deputy Commissioner Cachar to the Secretary to the Chief Commissioner Assam, 17 January 1903.

administration and the railway company was on account of the company overruling the stipulations set by the government. It created complications, as under the Government of India Act 1909, North Cachar was declared a Scheduled District. Settling non-natives was possible only with a special permission from the Deputy Commissioner. The situation reached such an impasse that the Government by an order in 1911, instructed that the railway company was expressly prohibited from leasing out land in North Cachar Hills.[26]

The labourers who came for employment on the railways from distant places in India were absorbed as cultivators into the population of Assam. They contributed successfully to the colonization of the rain-shadow Kopili Valley by introducing crops hitherto unknown in Assam, best suited to the dry areas of the valley like wheat, peas, barley and sugar cane. This was a step towards commercializing agriculture within the province, since they oriented their growing towards creating a surplus. Railway stations served as exporting centres, where agents of buying firms bought the produce. This obviated the necessity for a producer to reach a trading centre to dispose surplus produce. It completed the process of integrating the economy of Assam with the international market system.

As mentioned earlier, colonization disrupted traditional socio-economic structures, creating new ones. The emergence of the working class was the result of a new and subordinated socio-economic structure. Railwaymen were an important component of the industrial workforce. Table III gives the number of industrial workers in India from the 1931 census.

26. Along the Assam–Bengal Railway, another colonization scheme was launched. Certain forest tracts in the Diphu and Nambor forests were cleared. The land was offered to Assamese cultivators for ordinary cultivation. Railway coolies were excluded from the scheme.

As can be seen the second largest component was that of railwaymen.

TABLE III: Census of Industrial Workforce in India in 1931[27]

Factory workers	2,036,758
Miners	423,458
Railwaymen	701,307
Water transporters	361,000

RAILWAYMEN AND THE NATIONAL MOVEMENT

The history of the Indian national struggle has shown the important role of the working class at each successive stage. In the pre-1914 period, the working class followed the National Movement, with the exception of the 'Bombay General Strike' of the working classes, against Tilak's sentence.[28]

The real awakening of the working class came about in the wake of the Non-Cooperation Movement launched by Mahatma Gandhi in 1920. The spell of Gandhi acted as a spring shower on all dormant social forces within the country, which included labours urge for emancipation from exploitation. Plantation labour in Assam had attained a considerable degree of political maturity, which crystallized into a labour movement by the 1920s. This was evident from a chain of labour strikes that broke out in both the Brahmaputra and Surma Valleys in 1920.

In the non-plantation sector, railway workers played a significant role in the labour movement within the province. Consciousness within this group gradually grew as Gandhi

27. Palme Dutt, *India Today*, pp. 385–6.
28. Ibid.

took over the leadership of the national movement. Gandhi's visit to Assam in August 1921, provided additional impetus to the Non-Cooperation Movement in Assam, as well as to the working class movement.

The most momentous event of the non-cooperation period occurred in the Surma Valley. It was the famous Assam–Bengal Railway strike under the leadership of J.N. Sengupta.[29] The strike was in sympathy with the plantation workers of Chargola and Longai in the Surma Valley. Faced with a price rise in the post-war period, the plantation workers demanded higher wages. When their demands were not met, they took to a mass exodus to their homes. The large number of workers who gathered at Chandpur railway junction *en route* to their destinations, were subjected to barbaric atrocities by the Gurkha Regiment in full view of the railway officials. The railwaymen at Chandpur and Laksham railway junctions spontaneously struck work in protest against the outrage. The strike subsequently spread over the entire length of the Assam–Bengal Railway. Steamer workers also joined the strike in sympathy. This historic strike lasted for two-and-a-half months, involving some eleven thousand employees of whom about four thousand five hundred lost their jobs.[30]

The strike was of immense historical importance, being the first sympathetic strike ever organized in the country. It exhibited the rising solidarity amongst the working classes within the provinces of Assam and Bengal.

The workers of the Dibru–Sadiya Railway went on a strike in 1920 demanding a fifty per cent increase in their salaries.

29. 'Labour Movement in Assam', *Political History of Assam Documents 1939*. Letter from Kedarnath Goswami, a public man and journalist from Moranhat.
30. *Amrit Bazar Patrika*, 20 May 1921.

The strike went on for ten days, virtually paralyzing the railways and its allied concerns. The authorities were compelled to come to terms, effecting a salary hike between thirty to thirty-five per cent.[31] The workers went on strike again in 1928, demanding a wage hike. With work disrupted for a fortnight, and the company reeling under heavy losses, the management agreed to a fifteen to twenty-five per cent increase in wages.[32]

In 1938, the Dibru–Sadiya coal-handling workers at Dibrugarh ghat were discharged from service following their enrolment as Congress members. A movement called the Dibru–Sadiya Railway Boycott Movement followed and ran for over a month.[33]

In course of the movement the Dibru–Sadiya Workshop Union was formed. The union threatened to strike in sympathy with coal-handling workers. The movement involved the arrest of Congress and labour workers. Huge public demonstrations were organized and the police and labour clashed. The company had to yield and the discharged labourers were reinstated.

The period between 1942 and 1946 was extremely volatile, when the centralized All India Railwaymen's Federation intensified its agitation over important railway centres. The period witnessed a series of railway strikes all over the country including the Assam–Bengal Railway.

31. Dipankar Banerjee, 'Genesis of Labour Movement Among Non-Plantation Workers and Wage Earners in Assam', *Proceedings of the North-East India History Association*, Agartala 1985.

32. Ibid.

33. 'Labour Movement in Assam', *Political History of Assam Documents 1939*. Letter from Kedarnath Goswami, a public man and journalist from Moranhat.

Conclusion

The labourers employed on the railways in course of their construction were 'Non-Act' labourers, imported by contractors in their individual capacity. Many of them came to seek employment of their own accord. Lack of organized recruiting, and the nature of the workforce being temporary, has made it difficult to get accurate data on the number of labourers employed during construction.

Once the railway network became fully operational, labour was employed on various sections for its working and maintenance. To create a labour pool, it was essential to encourage settlement of ex-railway coolies, as local labour was hard to come by. The government, therefore, opened up certain tracts along the railway line to encourage settlement of railway coolies as cultivators. This not only increased the land revenue base of the province by the colonization of its wastelands, but was also a step towards commercializing agriculture. The raw-material potential of the province was enhanced. The railway coolies who had come from outside were assimilated into the local cultivating class.

Their role in the labour movement, which swept over the rest of the country, was significant. Though not integrated into the All India Railway Movement till the Quit India Movement, its singular role in the strikes paralyzing the colonizers operations is significant.

6
Railways and their Relations with Other Industries

The tea industry was the earliest and major beneficiary of the influx of foreign investments in Assam. The industry, which evolved through an experimental phase, was marked by the formation of the Tea Committee in early 1834. In 1836, the Government Experimental Tea Garden was set up, which successfully produced 'Assam Tea' in December 1837. The industry steadily expanded between 1825 and 1859. For the next decade capital flowed into the industry from all quarters, resulting in a period of reckless speculation. The massive inflow of capital into the industry forced a crash in the year 1866, consequently pushing the industry into a state of depression.

The industry began to steadily recover from 1869, which was marked by an increase in acreage and production. Between

1881 and 1891, the acreage under tea increased from 93,802 acres in 1881 to 204,682 acres in 1891.[1] The average investment per planted acre was calculated at a rate of approximately Rs 600 before 1872. For the period between 1872 to 1901 the average investment was calculated at Rs 1,000 per planted acre.[2] About four-fifths of the capital employed by the companies was owned by the Europeans.

The tea industry with its record of three decades of steady growth provided the necessary impetus for improving the existing means of transport to boost its marketing facilities. In the preceding two chapters, the role of the planters as a pressure group for introduction of daily steamers as well as railway has been highlighted. Feeder railways catering exclusively to the tea industry were constructed. Apart from the 'tea factor', the construction of railways in Assam was linked with exploiting the mineral resources of Assam, especially coal and petroleum.

COAL

The existence of coal in Assam had been known since 1825.[3] The issue of opening up the coalfields was taken up at the Coal Committee which assembled at Calcutta in 1840. Following the summary examination of coal outcrops in Upper Assam by J.G. Medlicott of the Geological Survey of India in 1865, the areas were subsequently surveyed in 1874–75 and 1875–76 by F.R. Mallet. The coalfields identified were Makum, Jaipur, Nazira, and Desoi.[4] Several attempts were made to

1. Guha, *Medieval and Early Colonial Assam*, p. 189.
2. Ibid.
3. Barooah, *David Scott in North-East India*, p. 111.
4. Revenue 'A', Proceedings May 1874, 'Coal in Assam' from Secretary to the Chief Commissioner to the Secretary, Government of India, Department of Revenue Agriculture and Commerce, no. 129 of 15 May 1874.

work these coalmines but lack of labour and inadequate transport facilities rendered the attempts unsuccessful.

In 1874, the Chief Commissioner of Assam in his correspondence to the Government of India, apprised them of the increasing demand for coal in the tea industry and more so by steamers:

> The development of the river steamer trade is necessarily dependent on the supply of coal. There is very little wood growing close to the main river banks though there are great forests inland . . . The result is that though excellent coal is procurable in the lower ranges of the Naga Hills along the whole of its southern boundary . . . Yet the steamers in Upper Assam are supplied with coal brought over a distance of 8,000 miles to Dibrugarh . . . The tea industry will soon arrive at a point where hot air must be substituted for charcoal in leaf drying . . . Further steam power is steadily taking the place of manual labour for leaf rolling and other processes in all large concerns. The tea interests then require a cheap supply of coal, as much directly for manufacturing purposes as indirectly for communication with their markets and world outside.[5]

Investors were unwilling to sink adequate capital for developing the coal resources of Assam for lack of labour and proper navigational facilities. The provincial authorities were keen on developing coalfields and proposed constructing a light railway to connect the coal deposits to the Brahmaputra.[6]

A light railway to open up the coalfields of Makum was conceived as an integral part of the Dibru–Sadiya Railway. In 1879, Shaw Finlayson and Company, as promoters, expressed a desire to construct a 'branch line to the Makum coalfields, from the Dibru–Sadiya Railway'.

5. Revenue 'A', Proceedings May 1874, 'Coal in Assam' from Secretary to the Chief Commissioner to the Secretary, Government of India, Department of Revenue Agriculture and Commerce, no. 129 of 15 May 1874.
   6. Ibid.

The promoters sought a guarantee of Rs 80,000 for the main line and Rs 35,000 for the branch line to the coalfields. The government offered a reduced guarantee of Rs 20,000. The offer was unattractive to the promoters, thus they alternately proposed for a 'collateral advantage or monopoly of the entire coalfields, for a short term or a part of the coalfield for a long term of years'.[7]

Unable to raise funds on the terms offered by the government, the investors demanded nothing short of a monopoly of the coalfields for a period of twenty years. Even though the concessions claimed were considered extremely liberal, they were accepted by the Chief Commissioner on the following considerations:

> but as the circumstances of Assam are peculiar in almost the entire want of internal communication. We were anxious to open out the vast wealth now lying unproductive in the extreme north-eastern corner of the Indian Empire and in order to induce private capitalists to devote a portion of their surplus capital to develop the resources, it seemed to us desirable to deal with the matter in a liberal spirit at the outset.[8]

The promoters of the Dibru–Sadiya Railway insisted on the inclusion of the coal concessions as:

> the sole means of attracting shareholders and filling the subscription list . . . the Old Company had to abandon the scheme because they put forward the railways unassociated with coal timber and petroleum.[9]

7. Railway Construction 'A', November 1879, nos. 71–74, no. 6 'A', dated 12 August 1879, from T.J. Willans, Officiating Secretary to the Chief Commissioner to the Secretary, Government of India, PWD.

8. Railway Construction 'A', nos. 27–32, December 1881, no. 120 RC, dated 15 October 1881.

9. Gawthropp, *Story of Assam Railways*, p. 12.

The final agreement was signed between the Assam Railways and Trading Company and the provincial government in 1881.[10] The document contained three separate indentures. The second indenture incorporated the right to open and work the Makum coalfieds. It also empowered them to 'thereto have and enjoy the sole and exclusive privilege to search and dig for coal and iron ore which they may obtain therein and thereout . . .'[11]

With the coal element being the life of the project, the Assam Railways and Trading Company commenced work in right earnest on the Ledo Colliery in 1882. George Turner, a Staffordshire mining engineer, pioneered work in the coalmines in Assam.[12] He arrived at Ledo with fifty British workmen of various trades. Initial attempts at inducing the Nagas to work the coal outcrops did not yield the desired result. Therefore, they decided to recruit Indian mine workers from the Bengal coalfields. The miners initially found it difficult to work the coal mines in the 'South Staffordshire' method.[13] Colliers therefore had to be imported from England during the 1882–83 season, who trained the Indian miners in the new method within a short span of time.

The Ledo mines became operational in early 1883.[14] Two mines were worked at Ledo — Upper Ledo and Ledo Valley mines. The output during its first year was 569 tons. The men at the colliery restricted extraction, as the railway line to despatch coal to the main line had not been completed. With

10. Shaw Finlayson and Company, the first promoters of the Dibru–Sadiya Railway, sold off their concessions to the Assam Railways and Trading Company.
11. *Dibru–Sadiya Railway*, p. 57.
12. Gawthropp, *Story of Assam Railways*, pp. 28–9.
13. Ibid.
14. Ibid.

the last rail on the line laid on Christmas Day 1883, the first coal train was despatched in early 1884.[15]

In 1884 the two mines produced 19,597 tons. In the decade between 1885 and 1895, the output registered a fourfold increase from 36,816 tons to 165,775 tons annually.[16] The corresponding period witnessed an export of surplus coal from the province. In 1884–85, 462 maunds (17.1 tons) of coal were exported. In 1885–86, 191,701 maunds (7,042.1 tons) were exported, of which 36,136 maunds (1,327.45 tons) went to Calcutta, 48,571 maunds (1,784.25 tons) to Goalundo and 7,000 maunds (257.14 tons) to Serajganj.[17] The direction of the exports was an indicator, that all coal was supplied to the ports; the steamer companies were the primary consumers.

Work on the Tikak colliery was commenced and was completed in 1884 and production started in October of the same year. The weekly production of the mines was 1,200 tons. In 1885, the mine produced 75,000 tons annually, which rose to 100,000 tons three years later.[18] In 1883 the Assam Railways and Trading Company took up construction of the seven-mile long Ledo–Tikak–Margherita Colliery line. It was taken up without financial assistance from the government, and was completed in 1884, under the terms to the concessions granted to them by the indenture of 30 July 1881. The line, which was a tramway, was an exclusive venture of the collieries. It used wagons from the main line and did not pay any rent against it. In 1897, it was integrated and worked as a branch line to the trunk route of the Dibru–Sadiya Railway on certain

15. Gawthropp, *Story of Assam Railways*, pp. 28–9.
16. *Report on the Administration of Assam* for various years from 1885 to1895.
17 Ibid.
18. Gawthropp, *Story of Assam Railways*, p. 29.

conditions.[19] The Namdang and Tirap mines under Haly's Coal Grant, were opened in 1896, making their total number of mines five, including the earlier ones. The major users of coal from these mines, were the railways, ocean and inland steamers, tea, jute and other factories.[20]

In 1899, the Assam Company of Nazira, in Sibsagar, was granted concessions to extract coal in the Dikhu or Nazira coalfield. The coalfield was situated in the Naga Hills district, close to the boundary of Sibsagar, between the rivers Tapias and Jhanzi.[21] The mines were quarried at Telphoon and Geleki within the Naga Hills. In 1899–1900, the mines yielded 24,835 maunds (912.31 tons) and 917 maunds (33.69 tons) respectively. There was no further extraction from these mines after 1900, though the company held the coalfields under the lease for a long time.[22] A company, designated as the Nazira Coal Company was formed in 1910 to work the deposits on the east of the river Dikhu.[23]

This company worked the Borjan mines in the Naga Hills in 1915, which yielded 2,872 tons in its maiden year of production.[24] A telpher line was constructed from the mines to the siding at Naginimara on the Assam–Bengal Railway. It signed a contract with them for marketing its production over an extensive area of the line.

19. Railway Traffic 'A', June 1897, nos. 81–95, no. 577, dated 7 February 1897.

20. *Report on the Administration of Assam 1897–1898*, p. 115.

21. Assam Secretariat Proceedings, Revenue 'A', 1897, nos. 2–16, no. 74 Survey-4745R, Shillong, 13 November 1896.

22. Operations at Telphoon were handicapped due to the ignition of one of the seams, during the rain through spontaneous combustion. The Naga Hills concession had to be abandoned permanently, as sufficient coal was not found to warrant any further expenditure.

23. *Report on the Administration of Assam: 1907–1910*, p. 28.

24. Ibid.

Railways and Coal Exploration

The exploration of coal became intricately linked with the expansion of the railway network. During the construction of the hill section of the Assam–Bengal Railway, the engineers were constantly on a lookout for signs of coal outcrops. However, no outcrops or seams of any real value were discovered throughout the stretch of the railway in North Cachar Hills. The existence of coal in the Naga Hills, Mikir Hills and Nambor Forest within reasonable distance of the Assam–Bengal Railway was known from the records of Mallet, Bruce, T.H.D. La Touche, Medlicott and others, published in the *Memoirs of the Geological Survey of India*, (various volumes).

It was of immense importance to the railways to discover workable coalmines as far south and as near as possible to the lines of the railways. Initial attention was directed to the Mikir Hills and Nambor Forest district. F.H. Smith of the Geological Survey of India surveyed the locality in 1896–97.[25] Coal beds were found in the valleys of the Diphu and Jamuna, and at Longloi Hill, twelve miles from Lumding. Coal from these outcrops was reported to be of little value to the railway, because of its poor quality and inaccessibility of the sites. The river Nambor's outcrops, about six miles off the Borpathar station on the Assam–Bengal Railway, were reported to be of inferior quality. Smith also reported the existence of coal in considerable quantities on the rivers Jeheuri and Koliani, in the hills west of Golaghat.[26]

In 1901–1902, H.S. Attfield, obtained specimens of the Mikir Hills coal from two of the three exposures at Borpathar,

25. Railway Construction 'A', June 1909, General no. 6656/2 RC, Notes by Agent, Assam–Bengal Railway, 'On coal investigation in Assam', by the Bengal Railway.
26. Ibid.

analysis revealed that the coal deposits were of poor quality, therefore further investigations in the area were abandoned. The services of Dr Saise of the East Indian Railway were sought to explore outcrops in the Diphu and Lumding areas. Cursory investigations confirmed that the sites were of little value as workable deposits. Consequently, all investigations on the sites were abandoned.

The Assam–Bengal Railway in its quest for coal finally turned their attention to examining the coal seams in the Naga Hills. It deputed an assistant engineer, Coxc to be assisted by Horne, District Locomotive Superintendent. During the same period, Simpson was deputed by the government to report on the quantity of coal in the same district.[27] The initial attempt was to examine 'the southern portion of the Jaipur field, extending some two miles south of the Disang river and the Nazira, within the Assam Company's grant.'[28]

Investigations revealed the existence of good quality coal, of workable thickness along the hills south of the river Disang at Borhat and the vicinity of Borjan opposite the Nazira station of the Assam–Bengal Railway. The coal seams at Borhat were five miles off the railway station, while the Borjan outcrops were some ten to twelve miles off the railway, the last five miles being over a difficult tract.[29]

The most important survey in that region was that of the vast and promising coalfields in the Tiru and Suffrai Valleys, situated north-east of the Borjan field. They were an extension

27. Railway Construction 'A', June 1909, General no. 6656/2 RC, Notes by Agent, Assam–Bengal Railway, 'On coal investigation in Assam', by the Bengal Railway.

28. Ibid.

29. Railway Construction 'A', June 1909, General no. 6656/2 RC, Notes by Agent, Assam–Bengal Railway, 'On coal investigation in Assam', by the Bengal Railway, pp. 6–10.

of the Nazira outcrops. Most of the coal seams were located within the Naga Hills, which was outside British territory. A detailed survey of the sites could not be launched without an adjustment of the frontier line between the Naga Hills and British Indian territory. The coalfields were situated south-east of the Assam–Bengal Railway station at *Dhodar Ali.*[30] The approximate road distance from the station was fifteen miles.

However, in the cold season of 1907–1908, a survey party under the general supervision of Stapytton, an assistant engineer, was sent out to survey the Suffrai river and its tributaries. In addition, a mining geologist, Dr Bleeck of Calcutta was employed under private interests to 'examine' and report on the coal bearing areas of the Suffrai–Tiru Valley.[31] The sites primarily investigated were at Chota Towcock, a right bank tributary of the Suffrai, the bed of the Suffrai and the Toungsa stream and a right bank tributary of the river Tiru.[32]

Coal outcrops in these localities stretched over many miles along the general strike, from the north-east to the south-west, forming a chain of coalfields. As the hills were of lesser height, the bulk of the coal that was found, was below the level of permanent saturation. It had to be worked either by vertical shafts or along the line of dip with the help of pumping machinery. Analysis of the coal samples from the sites reported that the average of fixed carbon was 59 per cent and the average ash content was 1.5 per cent. The coal in all respects was the same as that of the Makum coal. The investigators pointed out that the profitability of the extraction could not

30. Railway Construction 'A', June 1909, General no. 6656/2 RC, Notes by Agent, Assam–Bengal Railway, 'On coal investigation in Assam', by the Bengal Railway, pp. 6–10.
31. Ibid.
32. Ibid.

be guaranteed, without using diamond drill borings to ascertain the quantity of coal available over the entire area.

Geological surveys between 1865 and 1876, as available in the 'Records of the Geological Survey of India', identified the following coalfields in South Khasi Hills — Cherrapunji, Lakadong, Thanjinath, Lynkerdem, Maolong and Mustoh. The fields were estimated to contain some fifteen million tons of good workable coal. The Cherra–Companyganj State Railway, connecting Shillong and Sylhet across the steep mountain inclines was constructed to exploit and market the limestone and coal deposits in that area. The Cherrapunji coalfields were at a distance of five miles from the mountain tramway. A three-mile long extension from the top of the mountain incline was constructed to tap the coalfields in the Cherra coalfields. With the abandonment of the mountain inclines of the Cherra–Companyganj Tramway, the coalfields were left unexploited.

The Dwara–Therria Railway was sanctioned in 1902, to work the lime quarries and coal mines on the south of the Khasi and Jaintia hills. Along with it a syndicate, the Maolong Coal and Lime Company, was formed.[33] The Maolong mines were worked by the syndicate and it went into production in 1904. A siding of one-and-a-half miles was constructed from Ishamati on the main line to the quarry sidings. The company went into liquidation due to paucity of funds in 1911, and sold their rights over coal and lime to H.V. Low and Company. The company found the Maolong coalfields worthless and resigned the lease. They finally abandoned coalmining operations in the Khasi and Jaintia hills for all times to come.

The railway companies evinced keen interest in exploring

33. Railway Projects 'A', February 1902, nos. 2–5, from G.L. Garth to G.J. Perram, Officiating Secretary to the Chief Commissioner of Assam PWD, 28 October 1901.

as well as exploiting the coal in Assam. The failure of the coal-mining ventures in the Khasi-Jaintia Hills could be attributed largely to the failure of the railway projects in that area — the Cherra–Companyganj Tramway and Dwara–Therria Railway.

The output from the five mines owned by the Assam Railways and Trading Company in Lakhimpur district dominated the coal production scenario in Assam. They monopolized the mining business within Assam for over eighteen years continuously. The Maolong mines were worked in 1904, their production barely exceeding a few hundred maunds, until their final closure. The only other mines worked successfully were at Borjan in Sibsagar district, which was opened in 1911.

Trade

The coal trade, both internal and external was virtually a monopoly of the Assam Railways and Trading Company. It featured as a major item of merchandise over the Dibru–Sadiya Railway. Within the province, the largest consumers of coal were the tea gardens. The Jorhat State Railway and the Tezpur– Balipara Tramway received their supply of coal from the Assam Railways and Trading Company. About two-thirds of the coal went to Bengal through steamers and was sold off at the Calcutta market, while competing with 'Bengal Coal'.

The River and Rail-Borne Trade reports of various years provided data, which contradicted Assam's claim as an exporter of coal. While the Brahmaputra Valley exported coal to Bengal, the Surma Valley imported coal from Calcutta via Chittagong through the Assam–Bengal Railway.

In 1899, while 465,069 maunds (17,084.23 tons) of coal went out of the Brahmaputra Valley, the Surma Valley received 181,458 maunds (6,665.83 tons). In 1900 while 2,315,625 maunds (85,064.07 tons) was exported by river from Upper

Assam, about 255,018 maunds (9,368.04 tons) entered the Surma Valley by rail.[34]

The trend was reasonably reversed in 1905, when 70,000 maunds (2,571.44 tons) of coal was despatched to Sylhet (Surma Valley) from Upper Assam, in exchange for 46,000 maunds (1,689.8 tons) of rice. There was a marked reduction of imports of coal from 92 per cent to 66 per cent.[35] The bulk of the exports from the Assam Valley were carried by the waterways. The Nazira Coal Company redeemed the demand for coal in the Surma Valley to a considerable extent with the opening of the Borjan mines in Sibsagar.[36] These mines were exclusively worked to supply coal to the gardens in Cachar and Sylhet, through the Assam–Bengal Railway.

The Surma Valley received very little of the coal produced in Upper Assam on account of the rivalry on the issue of rates, between the two major railway concerns operating in the two valleys. The Dibru–Sadiya Railway was practically a feeder to the steamers and the interests of the steamer companies largely controlled its trading pattern. The steamers, by quoting low rates on carriage over long distances, manoeuvred the trade to their advantage, to the detriment of long distance railways. The annual consumption of coal on the entire length of the Dibru–Sadiya Railway was approximately 16,000 tons. In 1918, out of the total coal traffic of 537,000 tons on the Dibru–Sadiya Railway, a mere 99,000 tons went over the Assam–Bengal Railway to Chittagong, with the rest passing on entirely to the steamers.[37]

34. *Returns on the Rail and River Borne Trade*, 1898, 1899, 1900.
35. *Eastern Bengal and Assam Administration Report*, 1905–1906, p. 153.
36. Railway Department, Ways and Works 'A', no. 35-W/165, June 1916.
37. Financial 'A', October 1918, no. 291-F-17/1–10, from Secretary of State for India, London, despatch no. 20-Railway, 18 May 1917.

On the issue of rates, the Dibru–Sadiya Railway charged high rates over shorter distances between the mines and the Tinsukia junction of the Assam–Bengal Railway. The freight charge of Re 1–9–0 per maund per mile charged on the length between Tinsukia and the mines, was the maximum rate charged over the entire length of the Dibru–Sadiya Railway, to the steamer ghat.[38] It was a clear case of preferential treatment accorded to shippers by the steamer companies, to the detriment of the Assam–Bengal Railway and those using it.

To sum up, the railways were instrumental in initiating exploration as well as extracting coal from the accessible areas. The companies were keen on exploring possible coal deposits near the lines, for securing a steady supply for institutional consumption, as well as to enhance their coffers through trade. The coal industry evolved and grew as a forward linkage to the railways. The bulk of the cargo on the Dibru–Sadiya Railway was coal, which was a major source of its earnings. It was able to project a profit exceeding 5 per cent within a span of fifteen years. This in turn relieved the provincial government of its share of annual subsidy of Rs 1 lakh payable to the railway, till their earnings reached the 5 per cent mark. The Assam–Bengal Railway neither owned coalmines, nor had access to any workable coalfield close to its line. It also suffered on account of inter-railway rivalry, which was a hindrance in enhancing its earning to reach the 5 per cent mark. The Dibru–Sadiya Railway operated within the framework of Industrial Capitalism and acted as an agency for ensuring maximum exports of minerals from Assam.

38. Somerset Playne, *Bengal and Assam, Behar and Orissa: Their History, People, Commerce and Industrial Resources* (London, 1917), p. 415.

PETROLEUM

The other mineral of importance, found in Assam was petroleum. It was invariably found close to coal bearing areas of Upper Assam. Lieutenant R. Wilcox made the earliest mention of oil springs in 1825, on the bed of the Buridihing [*sic*] at Supkong.[39] When C.A. Bruce was prospecting for coal on the banks of the river Suffrai in 1828, he reported the existence of oil springs in that area. Major White reported several oil springs on the river Namrup below the coal beds.[40] Captain Jenkins while on his tour of Upper Assam in 1838 noticed several oil springs close to the Borhat coal outcrops. Captain Simon Fraser Hannay in 1845 reported oil springs at Nahorpung, near the mouth of the river Namchi [*sic*].[41]

The Geological Survey of India appointed H.B. Medlicott to conduct a detailed survey of the oil springs based on earlier reports. He reported:

> The oil springs on the Makum river are the most abundant, but even here the petroleum is inconsiderable, producing a thin film on the surface of the stagnant pool of dirty white water, the whole ground over an area of many square miles, exhaling obviant gases in numerous pools.[42]

Later F.R. Mallet of the Geological Survey of India during his survey found oil close to Hukanjuri, near Jaipur, at the head of the river Tiru close to the coal beds. He witnessed cracks of massive sandstone oil at Telpung on the river Dikhow and found oil springs, north of Tipam range.[43]

39. H.K. Barpujari, *The Comprehensive History of Assam*, vol. v (Guwahati, 1993), pp. 86–7.

40. Ibid.

41. Ibid.

42. Playne, *Bengal and Assam, Behar and Orissa*, p. 415.

43. Barpujari, *Comprehensive History of Assam*, p. 87.

The government was keen on opening up the oil reserves to private investors. The first prospecting licence was issued to Wagentricher in 1854. The area covered by the licence were the Makum and Bapuso-Pung oil springs, along with the adjoining areas extending to about 200 acres.[44] The licensee did not take active measures to work the oil springs. Subsequently in 1865 F. Goodenough of McKillop, Stewart and Company obtained the grant originally made to Wagentricher. The lease transferred the rights:

> to all petroleum springs, wells and fountains situated upon, within, under and throughout the lands upon each side of the Buri-Dehing river extending in length from Jaipur and Makum and particularly the land near to and surrounding the Cherrapong Hills as far as Jaipur, to the Namchik Pong to the Tirap, Namchik, Jugloo and Teerok rivers.[45]

In 1866, a hand boring well was started at Nahor Pung; the results were unsatisfactory. It was replaced by steam drilling the results of which still remained unsatisfactory. Of the eight holes sunk at Makum in 1867, oil was struck in one hole at a depth of 118 feet.[46] Limited success in the initial operations discouraged vigorous drilling operations at the site. One of the major bottlenecks was the inaccessibility of these oil-bearing tracts. Except for an occasional visit of the river steamer once a month, there was no other reliable means of communication to connect the oil-bearing areas to the world outside.

Balmer Lawrie and Company, as managing agents of the Assam Mineral Oil Company applied for a lease of the oil-bearing tracts in January 1878.[47] In 1880, they were given the

---

44. Playne, *Bengal and Assam, Behar and Orissa*, p. 415.
45. Ibid.
46. Gawthropp, *Story of Assam Railways*, p. 44.
47. PWD, Railway Branch, Railway Construction 'A', nos. 27–32, December 1881, from Government of India to the Secretary of State for India.

rights to extract mineral oil at certain specified localities in the Jaipur sub-division of Lakhimpur district, for a term of 50 years on the payment of a royalty. The Makum Petroleum Licence granted to the Assam Railways and Trading Company originated independent of the railway scheme. In 1880 Balmer Lawrie and Company drew attention to the fact, that the area over which they were given oil-prospecting rights, was the same as that included in the Makum Coal Licence of the Assam Railways and Trading Company. They urged upon a clear demarcation of the boundaries of the lease, to avoid overlapping. To resolve the issue, the Government decided to transfer the petroleum licence to the Assam Railways and Trading Company.[48]

The underlying concern in handing over the petroleum licence to the Assam Railways and Trading Company was influenced by the desire to develop the mineral bearing areas adjacent to the coalmines of the company. Accordingly, in 1882 a concession was acquired by the Assam Railways and Trading Company, to extract mineral oil. The area defined by the concession was thirty square miles at Makum, situated on the south bank of the Dehing bridge. This included the sites worked earlier by Goodenough.[49] The company, during the first few years of its existence, was pre-occupied with opening up of railways and collieries. The first oil wells in the area were drilled in 1887–88 on the south bank of the river Dehing.[50]

The railway engineers, while laying the colliery line, found evidence of oil in the Digboi area. Consequently, in 1888, the company applied to the government for a licence to extract

48. PWD, Railway Branch, Railway Construction 'A', nos. 27–32, December 1881, from Government of India to the Secretary of State for India.
49. Ibid.
50. Playne, *Bengal and Assam, Behar and Orissa*, pp. 415–17.

petroleum within the Digboi oilfields. Both the provincial government and the Government of India did not respond positively. However, the company continued its quest for oil at Barbhil station in Digboi. Oil was struck at the site at a depth of 187 feet on 19 October 1889.[51] A dense jungle existed between the railway line and the oil wells. To work the oil wells effectively, a siding was constructed to the oil well, connecting it with the Digboi station of the Dibru–Sadiya Railway.

A syndicate known as the Assam Oil Syndicate was granted a lease for oilfields covering the area adjacent to the Assam Railways and Trading Company's oil wells in 1893, who in the meanwhile, built a small refinery at Margherita, to which oil was sent from Digboi. The boring operations were relatively successful. In 1893, there were six wells, which rose to eleven wells the following year.[52] Lack of capital, machinery and transportation hindered further development of the industry.

The Assam Railways and Trading Company came to realize that handing over its management to a separate organization could best ensure profitable development of the oilfields. The company promoted a separate organization, known as the Assam Oil Company in 1899. The Assam Oil Company received official sanction and the Assam Railways and Trading Company's oil concessions at Digboi and Makum as well as the rights of the Assam Oil Syndicate were transferred to it.[53] This marked the beginning of systematic exploration of oil in Assam. Boring operations were carried out on the Canadian system, which was later discarded for the percussion system.

51. Playne, *Bengal and Assam, Behar and Orissa*, p. 418.
52. Gawthropp, *Story of Assam Railways*, pp. 46–7.
53. The Assam Railways and Trading Company did not totally relinquish their interests in oil as they held a large number of shares in the Assam Oil Company. Two board members of the Assam Oil Company were from the Assam Railways and Trading Company.

The Digboi crude was particularly rich in wax, the bulk of which was exported. However, candles of good quality were turned out at the Assam Oil Company's factory at Margherita. The kerosene oil extracted, though not of the highest grade, was extensively used in Assam. Small quantities of benzene and petroleum were also produced. The company manufactured tins at their factory, for storage and transportation of petroleum and its by-products. Refining of crude was done in small quantities at the factory in Margherita till 1903, but the limited production from this refinery was unable to meet the requirements within Assam. Setting up of a larger refinery at Digboi in 1902, increased production of refined mineral oil in Assam.

Production and Trade

Before 1900, the mineral oil requirement of the province was largely met through imports from Bengal. Eighty-seven per cent of the oil imported from Calcutta entered Assam by the river route. Small quantities of oil were however brought in by the rail-route via Chittagong. In 1900, while 327,646 gallons entered the province through the waterways, 13,721 gallons were brought in by the railways. Import into the Surma Valley was practically monopolized by boats. In 1902, about 162,322 gallons entered the Surma Valley by the river route and 32,172 by the rail route.[54]

Production at the Digboi refinery went up rapidly from 882,578 gallons in 1900–1901 to 1,756,759 gallons in 1902–1903.[55] A decrease of 37 per cent in value of the mineral oil imported into the Brahmaputra Valley was registered in the same year. It was largely due to increased internal consumption of the produce from the Digboi refinery. The principal

54. *Administration Report of Assam: 1900–1903.*
55. Ibid.

mode of transportation of mineral oils within the Brahmaputra Valley were the railways. The Dibru–Sadiya Railway carried locally all the mineral oil originating on the railway. Very little of the mineral oil traffic passed on to the Assam–Bengal Railway. In 1917 the Dibru–Sadiya Railway carried 17,564 tons of mineral oil over its stretch of 104 miles, with a mere 461 tons passing on to the Assam–Bengal Railway,[56] who however carried 28 per cent of the kerosene oil into the Surma Valley.[57]

Completion of the entire stretch of the Assam–Bengal Railway served as an inducement to the Burma Oil Company to extend its business into Assam. The railway practically monopolized the Burma Oil Company's trade with Assam, prior to an increase in berthing facilities at Chittagong port. The annual import of mineral oil by the railway constituted about 27 to 37 per cent of its total traffic. A large proportion of these imports were in the Surma Valley.[58]

The Burma Oil Company was keen on extending their area of operations into Assam. Badarpur a junction on the Assam–Bengal Railway was a site where it was granted a prospecting licence in 1915. Within two years of its operation, it was reported that, 'oil suitable for use as fuel in its crude state was obtained in commercial quantities at the Burma Oil Company's wells at Badarpur'.[59] The war situation hampered its initial operations. Large-scale extraction of crude oil from the Badarpur oilfields was reported in 1921, when their share of crude production stood at 8,151,322 gallons. The crude oil

56. Financial 'A', October 1918, no. 291-F-17/1–10, from Secretary of State for India, London, despatch no. 20-Railway, 18 May 1917.

57. *Administration Report of Assam: 1902–1903.*

58. Ibid.

59. *Administration Report of Assam: 1916–1917*, p. 25.

was shipped to Rangoon — their headquarters — through Chittagong, for refining, by the Assam–Bengal Railway using an average of eight, eleven-ton tank wagons a day.[60] The balance was shipped by boat and used as engine oil by the tea estates in the Brahmaputra and the Surma Valleys.[61]

The role of railways in transporting mineral oil was very significant in the 1940s, when there was an acute shortage of transport capacity. To ensure a steady supply of aviation fuel and motor spirits for the air and land forces, the capacity of the railways was utilized to the utmost limit. An alternative route was developed to transport oil from Digboi. It was sent up to Tezpur by river and thence on to the Rangiya–Rangapara north bank railway to the extreme north-east corner of Assam, the hub of all military activity. The total weight of kerosene and petroleum carried by the railways during 1940–42 was an indicator of their immense role. They carried 141,307 tons of kerosene oil, 41,854 tons of petrol, and military traffic of 28,971 tons in 1941–42.[62] Before the construction of oil pipelines, crude oil was primarily transported by railways.

Since its inception, the oil industry was inextricably linked with the first railway project in Assam. The industry could not have developed and thrived in the remote corners of Assam, had the railways not opened up communication networks within the region. The net earnings of the railways increased because of their carrying mineral oil.

60. Medhi, *Transport System and Economic Development in Assam*, p. 149.

61. The railway charged each wagon Rs 50 per round trip of approximately 500 miles, an equivalent of one-eighth *pie* per maund of oil.

62. Medhi, *Transport System and Economic Development in Assam*, p. 149.

TEA

The role of the tea industry as a pressure group for introducing railways into the province has been discussed earlier. It becomes imperative to assess the role of railways in the expansion of the tea trade. In the pre-railway era, rivers were the primary channels of both internal and external communication. Steamers were the sole means of long distance and bulk transport. Roads for internal communication were extremely unreliable, subject to the vagaries of nature. The introduction of railways in Assam largely reduced the uncertainties of internal communication.

The Dibru–Sadiya Railway was constructed largely at the initiative of the planters. Tea featured as an important item of traffic on the railways, which combined with the steamer companies and passed on all the traffic to them for external trade.

The Jorhat Provincial State Railway was constructed to transport the produce from the gardens in its vicinity to the steamer ghats for export. The Tezpur–Balipara Tramway carried tea from the gardens to the river. The three railways served as feeders for the steamers.

The Assam–Bengal Railway was taken up with a view of providing an outlet for the tea from Upper Assam through a single transhipment. As the section between Badarpur and Chittagong was opened to traffic in 1897, the railway gradually took over the tea trade in the Surma Valley. The Assam–Bengal Railway carried 92,929 maunds (3,413.73 tons) of tea out of the 1,009,691 maunds (37,090.82 tons) of tea sent out of Assam.[63]

In 1902, with the opening of the entire length of the Assam–Bengal Railway to traffic, tea exports registered an

---

63. *Assam Administration Report: 1897–1898.*

increase of 38 per cent. It obtained 60 per cent of the tea trade in Sylhet, as most of the gardens were close to the railway line. Tea featured as a major item for export from Assam, through the port of Chittagong, and usually constituted between 50 to 60 per cent of the total exports through the port.

TABLE IV: Exports from Chittagong to Foreign Ports[64]

Years	Value (Rs lakhs)
1901–1902	55.59
1902–1903	75.01
1903–1904	125.10
1904–1905	145.10
·1905–1906	155.79

The merger of the provinces of Eastern Bengal and Assam in 1906 resulted in the enhancement in the value of tea exports by 7 per cent through the port of Chittagong. The figures in Table IV indicate the growth of tea trade through the port.

They indicate a threefold increase in the value of exports within the span of five years. To expand the tea trade with foreign ports, a six-weekly steam-shipping service was arranged between London, Middlesbrough and Chittagong by the British India Steam Navigation Company.[65] Further in 1908, an agreement was made between the Assam–Bengal Railway Company and the Clan Line Steamers for through booking of goods from Europe via Chittagong, to and from stations on the railway.[66]

64. *Eastern Bengal and Assam Administration Report: 1905–1906*, p. 151.
65. *Eastern Bengal and Assam Administration Report: 1908–1909*, p. 31.
66. Railway Traffic 'A', April 1908, nos. 24–27.

In spite of the rapid expansion of direct exports of Assam tea, the port of Chittagong could not become an alternative to Calcutta. Tea from Jorhat, Tezpur and one-third of the produce of Upper Assam and a bulk of the tea from Cachar, continued to take the river route to Calcutta. This was because the Dibru–Sadiya Railway, Jorhat Provincial Railway and Tezpur–Balipara Railway despatched their produce to the steamers.

Table V shows a comparison of the exports through the ports of Calcutta and Chittagong respectively.

TABLE V: Comparative Statement of Exports
of Tea through Calcutta and Chittagong[67]

Year	Through Calcutta	Through Chittagong
1911–12	1,886,769	723,195
1912–13	1,579,375	740,987

The figures indicate that the port of Calcutta continued to receive the bulk of the tea for exports, over 60 per cent. Most of the tea on this route went by river. The small length of the railway lines, exclusively catering to the tea gardens, were feeders for the steamers. They operated under agreements with the river steamers to transport their cargo at cheap rates.

To counter this rate competition between the steamers and railways, a network of tramways was proposed to link the tea producing areas to the trunk route. Such projects were planned for the tea producers of Mangaldai, Sylhet and Cachar. They did not materialize for want of government securities.

In Sylhet, the Kushiara–Kulaura–Sylhet and the Akhaura

67. *Administration Report of Assam*, 1911–1912 and 1912–1913.

branches of the Assam–Bengal Railway were constructed with the sole object of attracting tea traffic on the trunk line.

The railway companies were instrumental in developing their own tea estates. The Assam Railways and Trading Company evinced keen interest in setting up plantations close to its railway settlements. In 1890, it acquired land for the Margherita Garden.[68] The garden was later handed over to the Makum (Assam) Tea Company, which was promoted by it.

In 1908, the Assam Railways and Trading Company obtained about 2,000 acres of land at Namdang. They developed the garden, formed the Namdang Tea Company and handed over the management of the garden to that company. In 1919, a new garden was developed between the Digboi and Tingrai stations.[69] In 1928, the Namdang Tea Company absorbed the garden. In 1950, the total area belonging to the Namdang and Makum companies was some 5,000 acres, yielding over 6,250,000 lbs annually.[70] The Assam Railways and Trading Company not only developed collieries and oilfields but developed independent tea estates.

Import of Labour

A vital component of the plantation industry was its large labour force. There was a dearth of local labour and the planters had to import labour from the neighbouring labour surplus provinces of Bengal, Bihar and Orissa.

Labourers for the plantations were transported largely in country boats, which was later supplemented by steamers. Flat boats were attached to the daily steamers for facilitating import of a large number of labourers. At times, large steamers

68. Gawthropp, *Story of Assam Railways*, pp. 49–50.
69. Ibid.
70. Ibid.

were specifically allocated to carry batches of labourers accumulated at transit stations. To maximize the space allotted to each coolie, the contractors engaged in transportation sought a reduction of the space allotted to each coolie on the steamers. It was fixed in consultation with the provincial government at ten feet per coolie in the cold weather and twelve feet during summer. This caused a great deal of inconvenience to the coolies. The planters were concerned at the slow pace of emigration and the high mortality rate in the steamers.

Famine conditions prevailed in most parts of the recruiting districts in 1897, causing a large-scale influx into the plantations of Assam.[71] Inadequate sanitary arrangements at the recruiting centres, and overcrowding in the steamers, resulted in a lamentable outbreak of cholera. Using an all rail route could redeem the situation. Section I of the Assam–Bengal Railway between Chittagong and Silchar, was sanctioned as an official route for coolie traffic, immediately on its opening.

The rail route from Goalundo, a debarkation point on the Eastern Bengal Railway, via Chandpur to Karimganj was opened to coolie traffic in 1898. Coolies for the tea gardens in Sylhet and Cachar usually took this route. Of the 2,542 coolies imported, 272 took the rail route.[72] In Sylhet, all the gardens in Habiganj and South Sylhet imported coolies through this rail route. In 1903 it was reported:

> The Assam–Bengal Railway is now largely used to convey coolies to the tea gardens of Surma Valley. Of the 3,370 coolies imported into Sylhet, only 1,610 passed through the river depots, the remainder having been brought into the district by means of railway, while of the 1,241 immigrants into Cachar, 613 were imported by railway and 628 by steamers.[73]

71. *Assam Administration Report: 1897–1898.*
72. *Assam Administration Report, 1899–1900.*
73. *Assam Administration Report, 1903–1904.*

The mortality rate amongst coolies was reduced to a large extent after they started using the rail route.[74] On completion, Section III of the Assam–Bengal Railway between Nazira and Gauhati in 1901, was opened to coolie traffic.

The planters of Sylhet and Cachar were keen that the provincial government arrange with the railway administration to facilitate the transit of labourers. They urged for the issue of through tickets for coolies to all stations in Sylhet and Cachar from stations on the East Indian Railway. It was proposed that a daily train operate between Asansol, a station on the East Indian Railway, and Goalundo on the Eastern Bengal Railway and thence to Chandpur, which was the Assam–Bengal Railway terminus on the river Meghna.[75] The Assam–Bengal Railway and the East India Railway issued tickets to garden coolies, on the presentation of a credit note signed by the manager or superintendent of any tea garden in Assam.[76] East India Railway also reduced its third class fares to one rupee eight annas per mile for coolies travelling over 100 miles, to encourage recruitment of labourers by garden *sardars*.

A significant increase of emigrants was registered from Chotanagpur, Santhal Parganas, Central Provinces and Madras after the opening of rail routes. In 1914, the rail route from Calcutta via Dhubri to Amingaon was declared open for coolie traffic. The government declaration stood null and void, as

74. No deaths were reported in transit on the railway, with only one death reported on the steamers in 1903.

75. Revenue 'A', February 1905, nos. 263–295, Assam Secretariat Proceedings, from Agent Assam-Bengal Railway, nos. 72–3 Revenue-245, dated 10 January 1905.

76. Intricately linked with the issue of transit of coolies was the demand of the planters of Cachar and Sylhet for withdrawal of the Act I of 1882. They believed it would accelerate the pace of free immigration into the plantations. Certain clauses were amended to entirely free *sardari* recruited coolies from the enforced stoppages *en route* to Assam.

the Eastern Bengal State Railway was not willing to make special arrangements for coolie traffic.

Railways were therefore instrumental in accelerating the import of labourers by providing cheaper means of transportation. This contributed to a reduction in the costs of obtaining labour. Generally on all items of traffic on railways, there was a war of rates amongst various railways. On the issue of coolie traffic however, rivalry on rates was replaced by close interaction amongst the railway companies. They were willing to reduce rates, at the cost of their revenue receipts. Here they acted as agents for promoting colonial interests and helping the plantation industry which was the centre of huge capital investments.

TIMBER

An ancillary industry closely linked with the railways was the timber industry. Assam has been endowed with invaluable and varied forest resources. The eastern fringes of the province, coterminous with the boundary of Goalpara district had tracts of fine *sal* (*Shea robusta*) forests. The timber was of immense commercial value. Exported to the treeless plains of Lower Bengal, they earned a handsome revenue for the province. The entire lot of timber was exported as house-posts or short logs of seven feet, for conversion into planks for house building.[77]

Sal trees were also found in the lower slopes of Garo Hills, the northern slopes of the Khasi and Jaintia Hills and the north-western face of Mikir Hills. A few clumps were found as far east, as the river Borelli [*sic*] in Tezpur. These forest tracts were easily accessible and could therefore be easily exploited.

77. Revenue 'A', Proceedings, April 1900, nos. 50–64, Assam Secretariat Records, pp. 2–3.

The timber species mainly found in the forest tracts in Cachar were *ajhar* (*Lagerstroemia reginea*), *sam* (*Artocarpus chaplasha*) and *nahar* (*Mesua ferrea*). Of these, *sam* and *ajhar* were floated down the river to Sylhet for boat building.

Upper Assam too had large tracts of evergreen forests, totally unexplored in the pre-railway era. The timber was of excellent commercial quality. The remoteness of the tracts, limited transportation facilities, scarcity of labour near the forests, ignorance about the quality of timber, coupled with a bias amongst traders for *sal* and teak hindered their commercial exploitation.

The local demand for timber from these forests was not developed. In most cases, it was confined to the supply of timber and wood to the plantations for building purposes, manufacturing tea-boxes and charcoal making. The wood for charcoal making was obtained from government forests as well as the forest tracts beyond its confines. There was a demand, though on a limited scale, for timber to make dugouts.

The maiden attempt to exploit the forests in Lakhimpur district was linked with the first railway in the province. The promoters of the Dibru–Sadiya Railway insisted on the inclusion of a clause in the contract for free use of timber.

Timber was a prime necessity in the planning of a railway. During its initial phase of construction approximately a quarter million sleepers were required. Besides timber was required for construction of bridges and in considerable quantity for the collieries. The promoters declared that their prime objective was: to render government forests accessible, suitably use timber for sleepers, tea chests and building purposes.

The Forest Department assented to the proposal and the timber concession was incorporated as an integral part of agreement with the Assam Railways and Trading Company.

The company was allowed to 'fell, use or export all timber and trees on lands lying 1½ miles on either side of the main and branch line'.[78] In lieu of the monopoly, the company paid a fixed royalty to the government.

In 1881–82, considerable quantities of timber were extracted from the forests in Sibsagar district. This was largely because of the demand for sleepers by the Jorhat Provincial Railway for the Jorhat–Kokilamukh line.

Sawmills were set up under private ownership for converting timber into marketable products. They were engaged in felling, logging and dressing trees for sale as timber. They produced tea chests from *simul* (*Bombax malabarium*) and other soft woods.

The sawmill industry languished under hardships like dearth of labour and improper transport facilities. Within a few years of operation, accessible forests were denuded, reducing its supply of raw material. Extracting timber from inaccessible areas involved additional expense, which reduced the profit margins of the industry. Tea boxes technically known as 'shooks' were produced locally at the sawmills. These shooks were not popular amongst the planters, who complained that they failed to meet the specifications demanded by the traders at London. Without the patronage of the planters, the local shook industry did not take off.

The early demise of the local shook industry was largely because of imported tea boxes. Garden managers in all cases were bound by agreements with agents at Calcutta. The agents at Calcutta represented the interest of the plywood factories in England. The following extract clearly reflects the situation:

that imported purchases are due to the action of the Calcutta

78. *Dibru–Sadiya Railway.*

Agents of the tea estates who receive a commission on first purchases made and again on sale to the tea gardens . . . [79]

The import of three-ply chests struck a death blow to the tea-shook industry. During the First World War, when supplies of three-ply chests from Europe was interrupted, the local saw-mills began to revive but for a short duration. This temporary interruption in supply not only resuscitated the local shook industry but also encouraged the growth of the plywood industry. Between 1917 and 1924 four plywood factories, including two owned by the Assam Railways and Trading Company were set up.[80] The ventures achieved a reasonable degree of success at an early stage.

The role of the railways in extracting, marketing and use of timber is significant. The Dibru–Sadiya Railway opened up the virgin forests for commercial use. The railway used timber for building purposes, in its collieries, primarily for sleepers and maintenance works. The *uriam* (*Bischofia javanica*) tree found in abundance in Lakhimpur district was used for sleepers.[81] Contractors were employed to obtain sleepers from the forest belt within six miles on either side of the railway line. The sleepers were not only used locally, but also sold to the Jorhat and Tezpur Railways at 15 annas per sleeper. The gregarious *hollong* (*Dipterocarpus macrocarpus*) found in abundance in Upper Assam was also used for sleepers. This widely despised timber was found to be an excellent raw material for plywood manufacturing. For productively utilizing *hollong*,

79. Revenue 'A', Proceedings, March 1899, nos. 38–40, no. 46TR, from Conservator of Forests Assam to Secretary of the Chief Commissioner of Assam, 5 December 1898.

80. Gawthropp, *Story of Assam Railways*, pp. 32–4.

81. It was stated that 60 to 120 metre gauge sleepers could be extracted per tree. The cost of conversion and delivery at Dibrugarh steamer ghat was estimated at Re 1 and at Gauhati at Rs 1–3–0 per sleeper.

the directors of the Assam Railways and Trading Company decided to set up a plywood factory. The necessary machinery was imported in 1922 and production began in 1924. After initial teething problems, the company achieved its desired production target. The annual output of the factory was five million square feet of plywood.[82]

The Assam–Bengal Railway, an extensive railway undertaking of 958 miles, however did not contribute to the growth of the local sleeper industry. Instead, the railway administration laid down rigid specifications, which the infant sleeper industry was unable to meet. An instance of the rigidity is evident from an incident in 1883, when Dear and Company was given a contract for supply of *sal* sleepers from the Goalpara forest range. The Assam–Bengal Railway Company rejected 7,000 sleepers of the 50,000 sleepers supplied. Middlemen delivered sleepers of *jarrah* wood from Australia and *pyinkado* from Burma at Gauhati.[83] The company neither granted special facilities to the local industry, nor encouraged them in any way. Their policy was clearly in favour of imported sleepers which brought with it benefits to the timber traders.

The Assam Railways and Trading Company on the other hand persisted with its efforts in improving the sleeper industry. In collaboration with the Assam Oil Company at Digboi, they experimented with the treatment of sleepers with creosote, to render them free from pests and white ants. This

82. Gawthropp, *Story of Assam Railways*, p. 34.

83 The railway, it is stated, paid Rs 3 per sleeper for *pyngadu* delivered at Gauhati in 1893, while they declined an offer by the Forest Department of Assam for delivering 30,000 sleepers at Gauhati at Rs 2–6–0 per sleeper. The Assam–Bengal Railway earned a notorious reputation of demanding delivery at their yard at Gauhati, with the contractors having to pay for transit.

treatment enhanced the life span of the sleepers. Encouraged by the experiment at Digboi, the provincial government sanctioned a Soft Wood Creosoting Plant at Naharkotiya [*sic*] in 1926. The plant became operational in 1929, when it produced 225,000 treated sleepers. The plant proved equally valuable to the railway company and the Forest Department. Table VI provides production figures for five years.

TABLE VI: Production of Softwood Sleepers, 1929–1933[84]

Year	Production of Softwood Sleepers
1929	220,000
1930	270,000
1931	131,067
1932	191,592
1933	170,000

The figures show a steady decline in production from the third year of its production. This was primarily due to the low rates offered by the Railway Board for softwood sleepers, to balance off the fall in prices of hardwood sleepers. As production declined steadily, doubts were harboured on the feasibility of renewing the contract. The plant was finally closed down in 1933.[85]

The extension of the Eastern Bengal Railway between Dhubri and Gauhati created a demand for sleepers. The forests of Eastern Bengal which included those in Lower Bengal and Nepal, supplied the bulk of the timber to Bengal. This forest

84. *Assam Administration Report*, 1929–1930, 1930–1931, 1931–1932, 1932–1933 and 1933–1934.
85. *Assam Administration Report: 1933–1934.*

tract was practically denuded of mature timber. Therefore, the timber from Assam found a steady market in Bengal. Encouraged by such prospects the provincial government decided to undertake commercial exploitation of the Goalpara *sal* forests.

It was proposed to introduce a portable tramway within the *sal* forest ranges at Goalpara, which would be laid on a flat traction with steel sleepers. The mode of its operation was to be on traction by elephant or the men on their way to and from work. Initially about two-and-half miles of the portable tramway was sanctioned. The area chosen for the portable tramway was between a forest working circle and a suitable floating stream close to it. The Goalpara Forest Tramway was extended annually by lengths of three to four miles until it covered the entire Western Forest Circle. Trade in *sal* timber from the Goalpara range expanded, as the Eastern Bengal Railway purchased sleepers for its metre gauge and broad gauge lines. In 1910, the Conservator of the Western Forest Circle, received orders for supply of sleepers worth Rs 2 lakhs, for both the gauges from the Eastern Bengal Railway.[86]

The Forest Department encountered extreme hardship in employing the requisite number of labour for hand traction. Consequently, in 1913 steam locomotives replaced hand traction. Streams within the forest range were used for floating timber. Exceptional floods in 1921 rendered the Garufela stream useless for floating logs, when a proposal was mooted to connect the forest tramway to stations on the Eastern Bengal Railway to redeem the situation. The necessity of such a connection is evident from this passage:

> The extension of the tramway to the railhead will obviously develop the earnings of the Forest Department and will

86. Forests 'A', June 1928, Assam Secretariat Proceedings, pp. 18–19.

ultimately benefit the Local Bodies by increasing the Provincial resources from which they draw an appreciable portion of their revenues, and apart from the development of the provincial financial resources the proposed tramway will immediately benefit the district of Goalpara by developing the local timber and ancillary trades and providing increased employment in the district.[87]

The alignment chosen for the feeder forest tramway connection to the trunk line was between Kachugaon on the forest range to Fakiragram on the Eastern Bengal Railway. The connection was completed in 1924.

In most parts of the province, railways gave a boost to the development of the timber industry. They were a major contributor in the evolution of the sleeper industry and later on in the growth of plywood factories in Assam. The Forest Department immensely benefited because of enhanced royalty receipts and returns on direct sales.

AGRICULTURE

The most important natural resource of Assam was its soil. Except for a limited stretch of the country in the south, the entire Brahmaputra Valley was a fertile alluvial tract. The soil being rich in potash and lime was responsive to manure and irrigation. Crops like paddy, wheat, cotton, tea, banana and tobacco could be easily grown on this soil. The low-lying, inundated areas yielded a good crop of jute and mustard. The prospect of developing the agricultural potential of Assam attracted the attention of Captain Jenkins. He was keen on commercializing agriculture and enhancing raw material exports from Assam.

87. Forests 'A', June 1928, Assam Secretariat Proceedings, pp. 18–19.

The economy in pre-colonial Assam was predominantly agricultural. It was characterized by production at a subsistence level, rather than market-oriented surplus production. Colonial Assam witnessed a massive rise in population through immigration into the plantations. The existing level of production in the province was unable to meet the requirements of the expanding population. Food grains especially rice, therefore, had to be imported.

Large tracts of agricultural land in the province were lying waste. The sparse indigenous population cultivated a miniscule proportion of the land, with little effort made to bring new areas under the plough. During the early years of British rule in an effort to monetize the economy and increase their land revenue base, they made a large increase in the revenue demand, and changed its mode of collection.[88] Instead of setting the economy on a path of recovery, agriculture stagnated. A survey in 1899 revealed that close to 6,500,000 acres of land suitable for production of rice, jute, corn, and other cereals were lying waste.[89] Wastelands, if brought under the plough, could not only meet the deficit food supply, but also become a source of agricultural wealth for the province. To the colonialist, 'the millions of acres of culturable land now lying waste represent millions of rupees which might be dug out of the soil, but are now wrapped in a napkin'.[90]

Henry Hopkinson, Chief Commissioner of Assam, did not favour large scale import of labourers into plantations as the production of food grains was insufficient to feed the growing

88. For details on revenue administration see Dharma Kumar, 'The Fiscal System' in *The Cambridge Economic History of India*, vol. II.

89. Revenue 'A', November 1998, 'Note by the Chief Commissioner of Assam on the Extension of Cultivation of the Wastelands of the Province', pp. 4–5.

90. Ibid.

population. A significant proportion of the revenues were spent on importing food grains from Burma and Bengal. The issue of developing the wastelands by settlement of surplus population from the overcrowded tracts in other parts of the country, found an audience with the Government of India.

The views of the Government of India found expression in the speech by Sir Patrick Playfair, a Mercantile Member of the Council, in the Budget discussion of the Imperial Legislative Council in 1897. He emphasized the importance of settling immigrants on the cultivable wastelands of Assam for providing relief from recurring famines and scarcity in Bengal.[91]

Jute

Closely linked with the scheme of colonization was the issue of exploring the prospects of cultivating jute in the wastelands of the province. A worldwide demand for jute necessitated the expansion of its cultivation. The production of jute in Bengal had reached the point of saturation, with practically no scope for further expansion. Certain portions of the province were suitable for cultivation of jute and thus jute traders turned towards Assam.

The Chief Commissioner of Assam considered the approaching completion of the Assam–Bengal Railway as an incentive for evolving an appropriate plan to attract settlers for the purpose. He emphasized the suitability of certain tracts for jute cultivation, which could not be initiated except by importing expert jute cultivators from neighbouring Bengal.

The issue of raising jute in Assam as a successful commercial crop was first raised in the Bengal Chamber of Commerce on 28 April 1897:

91. Nag, *Roots of Ethnic Conflict*, p. 89.

the special interest of Mr Cottons' (Chief Commissioner of Assam) description of the Assam country has to me [*sic*] its suitability for jute cultivation and any encouragement given by the Government in this direction will be gladly welcomed by those interested in the trade.[92]

The Director of Land Records and Agriculture was issued instructions in 1897 by the Chief Commissioner to conduct a detailed survey on the prospects of jute cultivation in Assam.

It was found that jute was grown to a greater or lesser extent in all the plains districts of the province and the plains portion of the Garo Hills. The only districts producing jute on a considerable scale for export were Sylhet and Goalpara, being contiguous to the great jute producing districts of Bengal. Small quantities of jute were exported from Garo Hills, Kamrup and Nowgong.

On the issue of suitability of the wastelands for cultivation of jute, he reported:

The extensive tracts of sandy alluvium covered with a light deposit of silt, which are found on both banks of the Brahmaputra appear to be in all respects similar to *char* lands on which the crop is so successfully cultivated in Bengal . . . where numerous channels communicating with the Brahmaputra by which it is intersected, afford an abundance of pure water for steeping which is so indispensably required for production of good quality jute.[93]

On the existing facility for transportation, he said, 'ample facilities exist for conveyance of jute by boat from the *chars* bordering the Brahmaputra to the different steamer ghats'.[94]

92. F.J. Monohan, *Report on Jute Cultivation in Assam*, Shillong, 7 February 1898.
93. Monohan, *Report on Jute Cultivation in Assam*.
94. Ibid.

Any scheme for the colonization of Assam would depend on providing greater facilities for movement of immigrants and removal of produce. The river steamer rendered invaluable service in inter-provincial trade.

The tracts of wastelands identified as suitable for jute cultivation, on the Gauhati branch of the Assam–Bengal Railway were between Nowgong and Kamrup. After a detailed survey, the specific areas identified were along the valleys of the Kopili and the Langfer to the south of Nowgong district along the railway line.

As the immigration scheme was being given its final shape, agriculturists, from Eastern Bengal steadily made their way into Assam. Initially the Assam–Bengal Railway brought in colonizers predominantly from Cachar, Sylhet and Mymensingh. The migrants from Mymensingh had previous experience of growing jute.

Following the merger of Eastern Bengal with Assam in 1905, there was a steady flow of migrants from the districts of Eastern Bengal into Nowgong and Goalpara. In 1907, it was reported that 'jute cultivation which has now become established in all parts of Assam Valley extended very considerably during the year'.[95]

Table VII shows a threefold increase in acreage during the decade. Except for 1914–15 when there was less production, there was a fivefold increase in the quantity exported. Out of the total acreage of 105,098 the shares of the districts were as follows — Goalpara (45,904), Sylhet (16,000), Kamrup (12,564), Darrang (11,941) and Nowgong (12,086). The cultivation of jute was thus limited to a few districts. The extension of its cultivation was largely due to immigrants from

95. *Eastern Bengal and Assam Administration Report: 1907–1908.*

Bengal.[96] The cultivator could obtain land suitable for cultivating jute at rates as low as Re 1–2–0 to Rs 2 per acre.

TABLE VII: Showing Acreage and Quantity
Exported between 1905 and 1915[97]

Year	Acreage	Quantity Exported (in maunds)
1905–1906	37,430	299,221
1906–1907	48,860	465,912
1907–1908	95,755	534,726
1908–1909	69,953	632,790
1909–1910	83,495	689,294
1910–1911	77,827	627,052
1911–1912	94,927	630,123
1912–1913	98,351	837,826
1913–1914	101,285	1,121,182
1914–1915	105,098	897,639

In 1915 the Dundee Chamber of Commerce instituted an enquiry into the possibility of extension of the areas under jute cultivation, as it was threatened by a short supply of material. It was mentioned in the report published in 1910 that:

> this tract is capable of supporting at least one million acres of jute without unduly straining the proportions between jute and other crops . . . Mussalman cultivators are steadily moving from Dacca, Mymensingh, Pabna and Rangpur in the land along the fertile *churs* [sic] in Goalpara in Assam where there were now over 70,000 immigrants from these districts.[98]

96. Revenue 'A' Agriculture, July 1915, no. 783TR, dated 23 September 1914, from Secretary to Government of Bengal, Revenue Department, to Secretary Government of India, Department of Revenue and Agriculture.
97. Ibid.
98. Revenue Department, Agriculture 'A', February 1916, nos. 10–19, pp. 28–41.

Completion of the Eastern Bengal Railway connection with Gauhati in 1910 facilitated the large-scale immigration of cultivators into the province.

Trade: The fibre was taken to the nearest marts, of which the most important were at Sirajganj [*sic*] and Narainganj. There they were sold to *farias* or *paikars* who frequented these marts.[99] They disposed off the produce to wholesale dealers from whom they received advances. As there were no jute mills in Assam, the fibre was pressed into baling blocks at the baling factories at Narainganj and shipped to Calcutta. At times, they were dispatched to Calcutta in large drums of loosely twisted fibre.

The bulk of the jute was sent to Calcutta by steamer from Lower Assam and Goalpara. As early as 1911–12, when trade in the commodity was in its infancy, of the total exports of 650,000 maunds (23,877.63 tons), 550,000 (20,204.15 tons) went from Lower Assam (including the Garo Hills.)[100] In 1913–14, it was registered that in terms of value Lower Assam exported jute worth Rs 100.25 lakhs in contrast to Surma Valley, which exported Rs 12.89 lakhs. Upper Assam contributed only Rs 9.39 lakhs to the export trade. The steamer companies under agreements with the jute balers at Narainganj and jute manufacturers at Calcutta carried almost all the jute, most of it in coordination with the Eastern Bengal Railway, which is evident from the following extract:

> Government is of course aware that the development of this important traffic (jute) has been brought about by the river steamer companies, working in conjunction with, and feeding the Eastern Bengal Railway.[101]

99. *Administration Report of Assam: 1911–1912.*
100. Ibid.
101. Ibid.

In 1898, the Assam–Bengal Railway proposed a railway line of on the left bank of the Meghna, between Goalundo and Narainganj, and a branch line from Hajiganj on the Assam–Bengal Railway.

The Bengal Chamber of Commerce, along with the Indian Jute Manufacturers Association and the Calcutta Baled Jute Association opposed the proposal. The grounds cited for opposing the proposal was that line would be of little utility for developing jute traffic through the port of Chittagong. The two principal river steamer companies, the Indian General Steam Navigation Company Limited and River Steam Navigation Company Limited also opposed the move.

Production and export of jute linked the economy of Assam with world markets. The expansion of the market in the inter-war period is available from the following table.

TABLE VIII: Exports of Jute in the Inter-War Period[102]

Year	Export of Jute (in maunds)
1933–34	1,840,597
1934–35	2,229,540
1935–36	1,829,010
1936–37	3,950,038

The province, because of the export in jute received a share of the net export duty. In 1934–35, the share of the net export duties was 50 per cent. It rose to 62.5 per cent in 1937–38. The share was merged with the provincial revenues.[103]

102. PWD, Railway Projects 'A', May 1899, nos. 1–16, no. 14, from Macniell and Company, Agents, River Steam Navigation Company Limited, to Secretary, Government of Bengal, Railway Department.
103. 'Duty on Jute', *Assam Gazette*, Part-IV, April 1937.

The railways, by opening up wastelands provided the basic infrastructure for the jute industry to develop in the province. Without large-scale migration of cultivators from Eastern Bengal, through the Assam–Bengal Railway and the Eastern Bengal Railway, the jute industry could not have taken off. Jute was an important item of freight over the trunk railways connecting the province with Calcutta, with very little of it going towards Chittagong.

Rice

While deliberating on the issue of framing rules for encouraging colonization of the wastelands of Assam, the colonizers perceived that uncultivated land, suitable for rice cultivation was practically unlimited. Assam could be transformed, they believed, into a province exporting rice to Bengal, rather than receiving it.

The import of rice to feed the large immigrant population employed in the tea industry was 'an intolerable and unnecessary drain' on the resources of Bengal as well as a serious tax on the tea industry. The following figures are an indication of the rice imported into the province.

TABLE IX: Husked Rice Imports into Assam[104]

Year	Brahmaputra Valley (in maunds)	Surma Valley (in maunds)
1880–81	405,459	103,559
1881–82	405,459	28,895
1882–83	482,677	26
1883–84	412,959	55,964
1884–85	379,677	4,635

104. *Report on the River Borne Trade of the Province of Assam: 1884–1885.*

Imports at that time were by boats from the Chittagong division into the Surma Valley, and from Eastern Bengal into the Brahmaputra Valley. Figures over two years show a decrease in imports. The decrease in the Surma Valley was attributable to a large increase in production. Figures for the exports of paddy from the province are available for the corresponding period.

TABLE X: Paddy Exports (unhusked rice)[105]

Year	Brahmaputra Valley (in maunds)	Surma Valley (in maunds)
1880–81	227	163,260
1881–82	2,410	1,051,860
1882–83	3,603	2,494,025
1883–84	64,787	1,725,791
1884–85	160,557	1,818,115

The striking feature of the trade statistics for 1884–85 was that there was a considerable increase in exports of paddy, with the export trade reaching such a magnitude, that it showed prospects of rivalling exports from the Surma Valley.

An increase in the exports of paddy was marked by a commensurate decrease in the import of rice, 84 per cent of the exports from the Brahmaputra Valley went into Northern Bengal and 90 per cent from the Surma Valley was supplied to Chittagong.[106] Thus, the province of Assam started becoming a major exporter of paddy. By the 1890s, production of rice within the province had stabilized. The proportion of the

105. *Report on the River Borne Trade of the Province of Assam: 1884–1885.*
106. Ibid.

export of paddy to imports of rice was generally in the proportion of 60 per cent. Between 1905 and 1911, when Assam was merged with Eastern Bengal, the trade statistics for Assam are not available separately.

A striking feature of the trade was that paddy was exported, while rice was imported. Vested interests did not allow the growth of rice mills within the province. In 1919–20, about five oil mills and nine combined oil and rice mills were set up in the Assam valley.[107] Alongside this development, there was a large reduction in the imports of rice, while the exports included not only paddy, but rice as well.

About 92 per cent of the husked rice that entered the Surma Valley — Sylhet and Cachar — was carried by the Assam–Bengal Railway. It also carried a large proportion of the paddy exports from the Surma Valley, with some of the traffic going by river. However rice from Lower Assam, Nowgong and Goalpara was dispatched to Calcutta through steamers. Rice constituted 73 per cent of the total cropped area as cultivation expanded, an indicator of the agricultural prosperity of the province. Spring rice, mainly grown in Sylhet, was extended to Goalpara by the immigrants from Mymensingh. Extension of cultivation took place in practically all the plains districts of Assam, being most marked in Sylhet, Nowgong, Lakhimpur and Garo Hills.

The Assam–Bengal Railway was used for large-scale migration of cultivators from Cachar and Sylhet to Nowgong.[108] Completion of the Eastern Bengal connection with Calcutta resulted in an influx of settlers from East Bengal particularly

107. *Assam Administration Report: 1919–1920.*
108. In 1915 when the hill section of the Assam-Bengal Railway was closed due to floods, the influx of immigrants into Nowgong was reduced. Though the section was reopened the following year the influx did not take place on the earlier scale and it gradually diminished.

Mymensingh into Goalpara, Nowgong, Kamrup, and Mangaldai. The railways, with its role of transporting a cultivating population, immensely increased the agricultural potential of the province. It transformed a subsistence economy into a surplus economy, with its produce finding its way to the rest of the country and outside too.

Cotton

Cotton was another important raw material exported from Assam. This commodity was primarily grown in the hill districts of Assam. In the plains districts patches of cotton were cultivated in some areas.

The only district in the Assam valley which grew cotton was Nowgong. This was due to the fact that Mikir Hills (Karbi Anglong) was within its boundary. The Mikirs (Karbis) grew cotton not only for domestic consumption, but also for export. Similarly, the area under cotton cultivation in Cachar was high, as the North Cachar Hills sub-division was within its confines. Here the Hill Kacharis, Nagas and Kukis largely grew cotton for export as well as for local consumption.[109]

The Garos grew cotton in very large quantities and supplied it to Goalpara and South Sylhet. The Khasi and Jaintia Hills met the requirements of South Kamrup and North Sylhet. The Naga Hills exported cotton mainly to Sibsagar and partly to Nowgong. The North Cachar Hills' cotton went to Nowgong and also to the plains of Cachar. The Mikirs supplied the bulk of the cotton supplied to Nowgong and Darrang.[110] A considerable degree of inter-district trade therefore existed. Inter-provincial trade, though on a smaller scale, was mainly with

109. H.S. Darrah, 1885, 'Cotton in Assam', *Note on Some Industries of Assam from 1884–1895* (Shillong, Assam Secretariat Press, 1896).
110. Ibid.

Calcutta, and took the river route. All the cotton that went to Calcutta was from the Garo Hills. The Lushai Hills' cotton found its way to the Chittagong division of Eastern Bengal by the river route. The limited scale of inter-provincial trade was through the waterways.

When the Assam–Bengal Railway was opened up to the Surma Valley, Cachar became the terminal market for the cotton from the Tripura Hills and from the Lushai Hills. This is evident from the trade reports of 1900–1901:

> The increase (in cotton exports) . . . from the Surma Valley to the excellent outturn of this crop in Hill Tipperah [*sic*] and to the greater facilities for export afforded by the opening of the Assam–Bengal Railway.[111]

The enhanced cotton export was attributable to the discovery that all the varieties of cotton produced in Assam had a coarse staple, but were rich in lint. This made them immensely valued in Europe for mixing them with wool for producing carpets.[112]

In the North Cachar Hills, the assembling centres were terminal markets as well. These were Lower Haflong, Haflong Railway Station, Mahur, Maibang, Hathikali, Langting and Mupa, which were all stations on the Assam–Bengal Railway. However, in other districts the assembling centres and terminal markets were not the same. Cotton from the Mikir Hills was assembled at Panimur and Amring, and exported through Lanka and Jamunamukh railway stations in the Nowgong district. The other assembling centres were Daigroom Bazar, Lanjan, Borpani, Umpnai, Amguri, Kuthorie and Kaziranga. Terminal markets on the Assam–Bengal Railway were

111. *Administration Report of Assam: 1901–1902.*
112. *A Survey of the Industries and Resources of Eastern Bengal and Assam: 1907–1908*, Shillong, 1908, p. 4.

Furkating, Sarupathar, Noajan [*sic*], Bokajan, Diphu, Dhan-siri, Lumding, Jamunamukh and Chaparmukh.[113]

Lushai Hills' cotton, which earlier went by country boats, found an outlet through the Surma Valley. Cotton was sent to collecting centres at Silchar, Lalaghat, Lalabazar Karimganj, Longai and Kalkalighat from all the markets in the Aijal [*sic*] sub-division. From the river ghats, they were dispatched to railway stations at Katakhal, Silchar and Karimganj. Cotton from the Naga Hills was collected at Mirapani, Gauranga and Wokha. The exporting centres of the Naga Hills' cotton were Furkating, Jamuguri, Sarupathar, Noajan, Bokajan and Dhan-siri on the Assam–Bengal Railway. For Tipperah (Tripura) the terminal centres were the railway stations of Balla, Bhanugarh, Manu and Juri.[114]

As exports increased, a cotton ginning and baling factory was set up in Assam in 1926. Within a span of five years, the number rose to three. Petty rural traders, called *farias*, col-lected the cotton from the assembling centres; they immedi-ately sold it off to the *mahajans* or merchants who came from the terminal markets at the railway stations. These merchants offered advances through the *farias* to the cotton cultivators to sell their cotton at low prices. The merchants then sold it to the brokers of large buying firms, the predominant one being Ralli Brothers. Chottelal Sheth at Silchar was the broker for stations between the North Cachar Hills and Kulaura, and Dutta Brothers of Bhanugarh was the broker from Kulaura to Haraspur stations.[115]

Cotton, which was merely a hill produce, came to feature as an important item of export as the railway network

113. *Report on the Marketing of Cotton in Assam: 1942*, pp. 13–14.
114. Ibid.
115. Ibid.

expanded. Assam cotton reached world markets and fulfilled the colonial desire of securing cheap cotton from India. The railways played an important part in helping to open up the hill tracts and the hinterland to the Chittagong port.

OTHER INDUSTRIES

Certain ancillary industries came up due to the railway establishments. The construction of the railways created a substantial demand for bricks. In 1890, the Assam Railways and Trading Company established The Brickworks at Ledo, which produced bricks fired in a 'Bull's Kiln'. To ensure continuous production the company in 1926 purchased a new brick-making plant and arranged for the setting up of a 'Continuous Manchester Kiln'. It went into production the following year, with an annual output of fifty lakh bricks.

Another ancillary was The Railway Workshop. The Dibru–Sadiya Railway set up this pioneering railway workshop in 1881. The Assam–Bengal Railway established railway workshops at Lumding and Sibsagar. These workshops were primarily concerned with repair works.

The railways were instrumental in promoting the all round development of the province of Assam. They set the economy of Assam on a path of capitalistic development. The provincial economy got integrated with world trade cycles with its primary role becoming a raw-material adjunct, for British manufacturers and traders.

7

Socio-Economic Impact
of Railways

Sociologists consider a social structure to be a nexus of relationships maintained by the will of the social beings living in it. It is like a web, which comes into existence as it is spun, persists through generations, and is shaped by the attitudes of its component beings. Seemingly sacrosanct permanent structures are subject to constant change; growing, decaying, finding renewal, accommodating themselves to variant conditions, and suffering vast modifications in the course of time.

Sociologists have broadly identified and classified the permanent conditions of social change as:

    i) change in nature or physical environment: external causality,

    ii) change in biological conditions: internal causality,

    iii) change in utilitarian, and particularly technological order, and

    iv) change in the cultural order.

Leaving the debate over the relative importance of each of these conditions in initiating social change to the sociologists, the scope of this book concentrates on technology as an instrument of social change.

The approach of viewing social change through technological innovations is of immense significance in this modern age. Technological changes move continuously and unidirectionally, making it possible to trace their influence. The effects are concrete, measurable and demonstrable, offering prospects of their study to the scientific mind. The rapid changes in our society are related and largely, though not solely, dependent on the development of new — techniques, inventions, modes of production, and standards of living. The process propelled by external change, initiates a social response where the component beings develop a congenial way of adapting to the changing environment. Each technological advance provides new opportunities and establishes new conditions of life.

It may be too much to say that every major problem in modern society is initiated or at least strongly affected by technological change. Its concomitants are so visible and far-reaching that it has inspired doctrines attaching primary importance to technology as a direct or indirect determinant of social change. The deterministic theories of Karl Marx and the American sociologist Thorstien Veblen attach primary importance to the changes in the technological order, minimizing the role of other components affecting social change. It is for the sociologists to debate the limitations of such a viewpoint and assign due importance to the different orders. Nevertheless, the role of technology as an initiator of social change cannot be undermined.

A study of *imperialism* and *colonialism* involves an understanding of the interplay of complex forces rather than mere forcible projection of political and economic interests of a dominant power over another. The complex relationships that evolved between the 'metropolis', which was the centre or the core, and 'satellites', which were on the periphery; was largely influenced by the transfer of technology from the former to the latter. Technologies originate within a specific socio-economic and cultural context. Hence, the imposition of the technologies of the metropolis on the satellites, affect the latter adversely.

Recent researches have drawn attention to the close links between commercial interests, technological changes, and government policy decisions in the early years of British rule in India.[1] Transfer of technology to India during the colonial period were in the areas of agriculture and communication. Railways were among the new technologies of the Victorian Age, which made a considerable impact on Indian society. The nature and extent of its impact on the social structure of Assam has been examined here.

The impact of the railways from a purely economic perspective can be explained in terms of the growth and expansion of industries; the provision of a cheap and quick means of transportation; the opening of new markets; the encouragement of internal and foreign trade; the stimulation of agriculture; the direct encouragement to engineering industries and their working; and, a general improvement in all economic spheres.

This model was based on the experiences of the American economy, where railways were the sole powerful initiator of economic growth. The most useful impact was that it lowered transport costs, brought new areas and products into local

1. Deepak Kumar and Roy Macleod (eds), *Technology and the Raj: Western Technology and Technical Transfers to India 1700–1947* (Delhi, 1995), pp. 8–9.

markets and widened existing markets. It enlarged the export sector, which in turn generated capital for internal development. It also accelerated growth in sectors like coal, iron and engineering. The effects of railway construction in America could be sustained with the support of social and political institutions. In America, the railways were constructed to handle new traffic and were considered as the harbinger of civilization. In Europe however, as the Industrial Revolution preceded the introduction of the railways, they were built to accommodate the existing traffic.

Railways in India were not developed as in Germany and Japan to foster industrial progress. They were an inevitable consequence of the capitalist exploitation of India by the British. Western imperialists concentrated on creating an infrastructure within the external economies by building railways. The British introduced railways in India, to meet the ever-increasing demand for raw materials for machines and creation of a market for their machine-made goods. Commercial interests dominated other factors. This policy was entirely in accord with the practice of viewing colonies as satellites to the metropolis and consequently restructuring their economies on western lines. The impact therefore, of the railways in India, could not be the same as in America.

Marx, while commenting in his article, 'The Future Results of the British Rule in India', perceived that the introduction of railways would play a 'regenerating' role within India at the initiation of the colonial policy makers. On the role of railways in India, he made an important declaration. It was on the economic future of India as visualized by him in the aftermath of the introduction of railways:

> I know that the English millocracy intend to endow India with railways with the exclusive view of extracting at diminished

expenses the cotton and other raw materials for their manu-
factures. But when you have once introduced machinery into
the locomotion of a country, which possess iron and coals,
you are unable to withhold it from its fabrication. You cannot
maintain a net of railways over an immense country without
introducing all those industrial processes necessary to meet the
immediate and current wants of railway locomotion and out
of which there must grow the application of machinery to
those branches of industry not immediately connected with
the railways. The railway system will therefore become in
India, truly [a] forerunner of modern industry . . . Modern
industry, resulting from the railway system will dissolve the
hereditary divisions of labour, upon which rest the Indian
castes, those decisive impediments to Indian progress and
Indian power.[2]

He visualized railways as an initiator of economic as well
as social progress, injecting the country with the inherent
strength to fight the colonial state. The unfolding of events in
its aftermath was contrary to Marxs' expectations. The 'external economics' impact of the railways was not achieved; instead it ensured greater and better political control and more
commerce. It belied the expectation of Marx that railways
would contribute and become the 'leading sector' of the Indian
economy.

The impact of railways in India has been an issue of intense
debate amongst economic historians. One school, representing the colonial viewpoint, highlights the enormous benefits of railways. To them the network of easy and extended
communication converted India from a mere geographical
expression to a well-knit and consolidated political unit. The
efficiency of the army and civil administration, the pillars of

2. Karl Marx, 'The Future Results of British Rule in India', in Marx and
Engels (eds), *On Colonialism* (Moscow, 1981), p. 84.

British authority in India increased. The economic sphere was revolutionized. Railways diminished the isolation of the village-based self-sufficient economy. Agricultural production was diversified and extended, catering to the demands of the external economy. There was expansion of exports and imports, with a tendency towards equalization of prices along the network of railways. Reduced transport costs, brought in concomitant benefits. It facilitated distribution of food grains in times of famine.[3] Socially, acute conservatism and barriers of caste and prejudices were broken down, with increased interaction amongst the public travelling on railways. Its social benefits in terms of integrating the people was highlighted by Mahatma Gandhi:

> Trains and steamers are the best media for the practical education of millions of travellers in spotless cleanliness, hygiene, sanitation, and camaraderie between different communities of India.[4]

The opposing viewpoint, reflecting the ground reality presents the viewpoint of Indian nationalist historians. In real terms, the effects were not as revolutionizing as claimed by the British. Whatever little benefits accrued were overshadowed by the harmful effects of the railways.

The first deleterious effect of the railways as viewed by nationalist historians was on industrial activity. Indigenous industries declined under commercial exploitation of the East India Company. Interruption of the internal trading network

3. For details refer, Dharma Kumar *et al.*, *The Cambridge Economic History of India: 1757–1970*, vol. ii; D.R. Gadgil, *The Industrial Evolution of India in Recent Times: 1860–1939*; V.B. Singh (ed.), *Economic History of India: 1857–1956*; Bipan Chandra, *The Rise and Growth of Economic Nationalism in India: 1880–1905* and Vera Anstey, *The Economic Development of India*.

4. J. Johnson, *The Economics of Indian Rail Transport* (Bombay, 1963), p. 60.

through a system of town and transit duties led to a segment-
ation and contraction of existing markets. Heavy duties on
inter-regional movement of goods damaged the local production base as well. Under the administration of the Crown, the
interests of the manufacturer in England dominated economic
policies and little was done to foster new industries. On the
contrary, the influx of machine-made goods sealed the fate of
indigenous textile industries and retarded their progress. The
population engaged in indigenous handicraft industries were
displaced and increasingly turned to the land for a means of
livelihood and became peasants on a large scale, gradually
transforming India into a raw material adjunct.

A 'dependent development' and the possibility of using railways to stimulate new industries was stifled by the London-
based directors of manufacturing firms and that of the railway
companies.[5] A degree of industrialization was initiated by
branching out complementary investments in the coal, iron and
steel, engineering, and chemical industries. Improved transport
facilities stimulated European, rather than Indian industry. The
pace of development of these linkages was however very slow.[6]

The plantation sector, an area of European investment, developed as the new means of communication fostered foreign
trade. Foreign investors multiplied the avenues of exploitation
and garnered the gains from the industrial sector fostered by
railways. A very harmful consequence of the railways was its
role in increasing the drain on wealth in the form of 'Public
Debt'.[7] The development of railways with state aid, guarantees

5. Deepak Kumar *et al.*, *Technology and the Raj*, p. 16.
6. Arun Bose, 'Foreign Capital in India', in V.B. Singh (ed.), *Economic History of India 1857–1957* (Bombay, 1965), pp. 512–612.
7. The origin of this debt lay in the first place in the costs of war and other charges debited to India. They later included the costs of railways and public works initiated by the government.

for private enterprise undertaking them, and direct state con-tracting swelled the debt.[8] The money remitted to England was in the form of interest on guaranteed capital and profits, payments on imported rolling stock, payments for the services of European staff, establishment costs in England and loss on exchange rates. Apart from the financial capital, management of the enterprises, manpower, equipment and skilled labour was imported. Government did little to aid or stimulate the development of heavy industries or impart managerial skills amongst the Indian population.

The second phase of private railway construction under the guarantee system was revived because it was perceived that the railways would help in mitigating famines, by exporting food grains from surplus provinces to deficit areas. Large-scale export of food grains on the pretext of foreign trade resulted in insufficient supply of food grains in normal times. The export trade and improvement of communications tended to diminish the custom of storing food, ingrained amongst the peasants, making them prone to famines.[9] Indirectly too the railways contracted the internal food supply by promoting production and export of commercial crops against food crops.

The railways, though regarded, as a 'magnificent asset' of the government, could not become self-supporting, practically till the end of the century. This was because the commercial potential of the region was not the only criterion in deciding

8. Upto the end of the nineteenth century, 226 million was spent on railways, registering a net loss of 40 million on the Indian Budget. Till 1943–44 the sterling debt due on railways was reported close to 30 million annually. This was transmitted from India to England as railway debt (Palme Dutt, *India Today*, p. 136).

9. In 1897–98, food grains worth £10 millions were exported, while there was a widespread famine in India, when millions of people died of starvation. (R.C. Dutt, *The Economic History of India*, vol. II, p. 401).

the location of the lines. Along with it were added military as well as humanitarian considerations. In absolute terms, the money paid out of the Indian tax revenues to British investors was substantial and in no way commensurate with its benefits.[10]

The railways with their 'raw material exporting bias' encouraged foreign trade at the cost of internal trade and development. India's foreign trade was both a mechanism for transfer of surpluses abroad, and an engine for the development of India's home market.[11] Thus, the railways belied the expectations of the Indian population, as it was under political subjugation. Overall, it perpetuated the backwardness of the Indian economy.

The positive effects of the railways came in driblets. The agricultural sector of the economy was deeply affected by the widening of markets as Indian agricultural cycles became linked to world trade cycles. As a part of the linkage, a farmer's decision about the crops to be planted was effected by prices in international markets, rather than the demands of the internal market. Local specializations in particular crops were largely a product of the facilities provided by the railways. Inter-regional price differences were equalized. The rising Indian entrepreneur, who represented the merchant capital of the country, penetrated the countryside and fostered limited economic growth under colonial constraints.

10. In the period between 1849, when the guarantee was first instituted, and 1909, when the earnings of the railways as a group began to exceed or equal the guarantee, a total of Rs 568 million was paid out as guarantee, John M. Hurd, 'Railways' in (Dharma Kumar *et al.*, *The Cambridge Economic History of India*, vol. II, p. 743).

11. The surplus extracted from India was not the kind, which originated as a spill over of the home market saturated with indigenous products, which permitted a profitable participation in a worldwide division of labour.

IMPACT IN THE BRAHMAPUTRA VALLEY

Apart from the 'strategic' and 'famine' lines, railways in most parts of India were constructed over tracts teeming with agricultural produce as well as population. In Assam, the situation was different as it was a sparsely populated province, producing very little agricultural surplus.

All economic activities in Assam were centred around the plantation industry during the pre-railway era. Railways were planned within the province to further the interests of the tea industry. When the trunk route across the province was conceived, very little information was available on the nature of the terrain. The Assam–Bengal Railway connecting Upper Assam with the port of Chittagong traversed large unpopulated tracts. The portion of the line between Badarpur and Lumding crossed desolate hill ranges, while the portion between Lumding and Gauhati passed through extensive forests as well as grasslands. The colonizers expected that the opening up of these desolate tracts would result in a spurt of economic activity. This was largely in consonance with the Canadian or American model where railways were made over desolate prairies, expecting that an influx of population in those areas would follow in its wake.[12]

Railways did initiate changes in the pattern of trade. The self-subsisting economy of Assam made way for a surplus economy, in line with the system of capitalistic development under colonial rule. Pre-colonial trade in the direction of Bengal was carried on mainly through the river Brahmaputra. In the early years of colonial rule, water communication was made more efficient to meet the demands of expanding trade.

12. Financial 'A', January 1920, no. 173 F-19/1-5, extract from the Proceedings of the Council Meeting on 5 April 1919.

Communication by water in Assam had a lopsided effect on trade patterns as districts close to the waterways garnered the benefits of external trade. Areas away from the navigable rivers could not reap the benefits due to the unreliability of the feeder systems between the producing areas and the rivers. A sparse indigenous population hindered development of resources in many areas.

Assam had immense natural resources in the form of land, forest and minerals. Railways were introduced in the province to exploit these natural resources and to foster the export of raw materials. The role of the railways in the development of forward linkages in the form of the coal, petroleum, timber, and jute industries have been discussed in detail in the preceding chapter. The forces of world markets penetrated Assam, extracted raw materials and made a formative impact on its internal market.

Growth of the Internal Market

Many commercial interests came up once the construction of the Assam–Bengal Railway started. Coal companies at Margherita and Nazira developed to meet the demand for coal in the tea gardens of Cachar and Sylhet, along the Assam–Bengal Railway route.[13] Commercial groups operating at Chittagong port were largely dependent on the upward traffic of the railways. Traders at Chittagong imported salt and sent it up to the province through the railways. They also handled rice imports into Assam as well as the import of corrugated iron. This

13. Ways and Works 'A', 35-W/1–64, June 1916, from G.A. Bayley, Acting Agent, Assam–Bengal Railway to the Secretary Railway Board, no. E-368-2, dated 24 September 1915.

network of trade developed under the patronage of big exporting firms controlled by Europeans.

Petty rice and paddy traders sold their produce at stations on the Assam–Bengal Railway between Chittagong and Badarpur, which was later sold in Upper Assam. Rice production was taken up on a large scale by the end of the nineteenth century in the districts of Assam proper. Consequently, paddy and small quantities of rice were dispatched from stations on the Gauhati–Tinsukia section. Lime and limestone for building purposes and for use as tea fertilizers was brought into Assam by the railways from Sylhet.[14]

The hill section of the Assam–Bengal Railway traversed desolate tracts of North Cachar Hills where the native population was sparse. The government offered land to settlers in the Lower Valleys of the North Cachar Hills along the railway line.[15] Subsequently in 1905, considerable settlements grew along the valleys of the Jatinga, Doyang and Mahur. However, settlement schemes were not opened for long enough, for their effect to be positively felt.[16]

The Assam–Bengal Railway was instrumental in providing primary marketing facilities in the North Cachar Hills. Its effects on the primary traders along the railway were visible, after the closure of the hill section following the devastating floods of 1915. 'In N.C. Hills the villagers who grew cotton and sugar cane were handicapped by the closing of the railways which deprived them of cheap means of transport.'[17] The

14. Ways and Works 'A', 35-W/1–64, June 1916, from G.A. Bayley, Acting Agent, Assam–Bengal Railway to the Secretary Railway Board, no. E-368-2, dated 24 September 1915.

15. *Administration Report of Assam: 1902–1903*, p. 8.

16. *Administration Report of Assam: 1905–1906*, p. 6.

17. *Administration Report of Assam: 1915–1916*, p. 4.

construction of the hill section of the railway helped in the all round development of the hill tracts along its alignment:

> Small traders flourished and made their livelihood by selling vegetables, sungrass, ghee, timber, cattle etc. at railway stations, which was practically non-existent before the opening of the hill section.[18]

The population of the tract responded to the demands of the market economy introduced by the British. The role of the railways in inducing surplus produce into the market is evident from the mushroom growth of weekly markets alongside the line. A small feeder railway like the Tezpur–Balipara [Light] Railway helped improving marketing facilities and promoted greater money circulation amongst the populace as, 'two of the largest markets [were] are those at Amaribari and Bindukiri. . . . Special trains [were] are run from Tezpur to serve these hats and are crowded with shopkeepers and wares'.[19]

In Nowgong district, economic upliftment fostered by the introduction of railways is evident from the following account:

> Cultivation is however beginning to extend near Lumding and to a less extent near Kampur, Jamunamukh and Lanka, and with facilities now afforded it is hoped that the population will increase in the neighbourhood alike. At Chaparmukh the railway taps the trade coming down the Kopili from the Hills . . . the construction of the Kohima–Manipur cart road and the opening of the railway to Dimapur afforded an outlet for the large surplus store of rice grown in the Valley (Manipur Valley).[20]

The increase in the volume of trade over the Assam–Bengal Railway resulted in an increase of exports through the port of

18. *Administration Report of Assam: 1915–1916*, p. 4.
19. Allen, *Assam District Gazetteers*, vol. v, Darrang, p. 181.
20. Allen, *Assam District Gazetteers*, vol. vi, Nowgong, p. 172.

Chittagong. The managing agents of various companies at the port of Calcutta were unwilling to relinquish their hold over the trade from Assam. The Dhubri–Gauhati extension of the Eastern Bengal Railway was constructed to maintain their stranglehold over trade.

The railway, which ran through the north bank of the Brahmaputra, traversed the best-cultivated and thickly populated areas. The line secured the entire tea and rice trade from Mangaldai; surplus rice from Nalbari was sent to distant markets, and it tapped a considerable trade in paddy, raw jute, and timber from Goalpara. All the mustard seed and rapeseed from the Kamrup *Duars* found an outlet because of the railway connection.[21] The railway channelized the existing trade networks and offered additional inducements for market-oriented surplus production. Assam therefore, became a raw-material exporting province, like the rest of the country.

URBANIZATION

One of the most important factors in the growth of towns in India during the colonial period was the construction of railways. Growth was affected in two ways. The advent of railways to a town generally meant an increase in trade. It also had the effect of creating new centres of trade along the tract it traversed. Often the exigencies of railway construction made it necessary that old towns should be left aside from the main line. This naturally meant a diversion of old channels of trade and spelt a decay of old towns.[22]

21. Railway Construction 'A', May 1901, no. 36, 'Note', dated 16 July 1900, by D.H. Lees, Officiating Director Land Records and Agriculture Assam, *On the Proposed Connection of the Eastern Bengal State Railway with Gauhati.*

22. Mirzapur, a key terminus on the Ganges for the inland cotton trade

Assam during the pre-colonial period was 'population poor' in contrast to the rest of India. The few towns which existed were mainly administrative centres.[23] In the second half of the nineteenth century, with the introduction and proliferation of colonial enterprise, the process of urbanization in the Brahmaputra Valley witnessed a slow, yet definite transformation. Railways became a paramount factor in determining the economic geography of the region. They extended and strengthened the existing networks, and offered added advantages of through traffic in an economy, where external trade was entirely dependent on river routes.

Urban centres could be broadly categorized into two groups; (a) focal points of administration and military control, and (b) nodes located at transport junctions. Arterial roads connecting river ports, and junctions of roads and railways, generally fulfilled the role of receiving as well as exporting centres. These centres which served other tertiary functions, survived on their intermediary position, as connecting points between the external and internal economies.

The Dibru–Sadiya Railway turned Dibrugarh into a thriving town and centre of all economic activities in Upper Assam. It was a steamer terminus as well as the headquarters of the Assam Railways and Trading Company. The oil wells and coalmines afforded livelihood to a considerable number of labourers and artisans. Tinsukia developed into an important railway junction and commercial centre between the Assam–

carried by pack bullocks, had been a prosperous town during the cotton boom of the 1860s. When cotton began to be transported increasingly by rail, Mirzapur declined as a trading centre. By 1911, its population dropped to half that of 1881 due to out-migration.

23. Shihabuddin Talish has given an account of the administrative centre at Garhgaon in the year 1662. The city, which was the capital, appeared to the writer as a 'circular wide aggregation of villages'.

Bengal Railway and Dibru–Sadiya Railway, commanding all the principal avenues of trade on the frontier of the province.

Dimapur on the Assam–Bengal Railway also grew into a flourishing commercial centre. It served as an outlet for the produce from the Naga Hills and Manipur. While the Nagas exported cotton from Dimapur, the Manipuris brought down their surplus rice. They also procured foreign goods available at the railhead. In the pre-railway period Dimapur had been an inaccessible area.

Lumding junction on the Assam–Bengal Railway was situated within the Nambor forests. It connected two important branch lines of the railway and grew into a busy station, as a forwarding and receiving depot for all kinds of produce. It developed into an important railway township and a commercial centre.

Gauhati, a centre of provincial administration and a commercial centre since the seventeenth century, became a focal point of trade when connected by the Assam–Bengal and Eastern Bengal Railway systems to the ports of Calcutta and Chittagong respectively.

The hill station of Haflong, situated on the spur of the Barail Range at an elevation of about 2,400 feet, was the construction headquarters of the hill section of the Assam–Bengal Railway which developed into a township. The role of the railways in the growth and development of this town can be assessed from the view expressed by the agent of the railway, while debating the issue of the closure of the hill section in 1915:

> The small Hill station of Haflong cannot be overlooked in discussing this question, as although the place is very small, it provides an inexpensive health resort to the members of the planting community in both [the] Upper and Lower Valleys. Several bungalows have been built and a substantial club has

been made and there is no doubt compensation will be claimed by the owners of this property.[24]

Small townships, more in the nature of distributing centres, grew practically along the entire length of the hill section of the Assam–Bengal Railway.

Effects on the Peasantry and Middle Class

Changing trade patterns, export of surplus food grains and agricultural raw materials, and better marketing facilities were all pointers to the improved condition of the peasantry. The impact of the railways amongst the peasantry needs to be studied in the light of benefits which accrued to them.

While lakhs of rupees were spent in the province during the construction of the Assam–Bengal Railway, the state of material improvement of the peasantry was barely visible. While over the rest of India, railways provided the poor classes of cultivators an opportunity to supplement their earnings, during the off-season in agriculture. A natural result of this sudden demand for unskilled labour was a general increase in wages in that area. It enhanced the revenue-paying capacity of the cultivators. In Assam, ordinary cultivators were averse to working as coolies on the railways.

The daily wage of an ordinary labourer in Nowgong, through which the railway passed, was one anna, while it was five to six annas in heavily populated areas.[25] A railway labourer in comparison received eight annas. Yet there were no takers amongst the local peasantry: this was probably because

24. Ways and Works 'A', 35-W/1–64, June 1916, from G.A. Bayley, Acting Agent, Assam–Bengal Railway to the Secretary Railway Board, no. E-368-2, dated 24 September 1915.
25. Hunter, *A Statistical Account of Assam*, pp. 47–9.

railway work was considered optional, and involved a certain loss of status. Indigenous cultivators failed to respond to the demand for producing more food.

Increased facilities for education resulted in the emergence of an educated middle-class, qualified for white-collar jobs in all sectors, both government and non-government. The nascent Assamese middle-class languished, partly due to the discriminatory policy adopted in favour of appointing Bengalis in the clerical cadre and partly due to their indifferent attitude. They failed to derive substantial benefits from the large administrative establishment of the railways, which employed educated youth.

Europeans manned all superior managerial posts, which were few in number. Only 158 Assamese were employed on the Assam–Bengal Railway, drawing a salary of Rs 30 per month.[26] The pay scale was an indicator that the posts held were in the subordinate category. Table XI shows the total number of natives employed on the Dibru–Sadiya Railway and Assam–Bengal Railway in 1934–35.

TABLE XI: Number of Native Employees
on Various Railways[27]

	Years	
	1934	1935
Dibru–Sadiya Railway	14	16
Assam–Bengal Railway	3,607	3,424

These figures included inhabitants from both the Surma and Brahmaputra Valleys. Over 3,500 'natives' were involved

26. 'The Assam Legislative Council Debates', *Assam Gazette*, part VI, 29 August 1923, p. 54.
27. Ibid.

in skilled work on the railways, between 1889 and 1903, when the Assam–Bengal Railway was under construction.[28] However, the term natives in all probability referred to the imported labour working in the railways.

In the course of the National Movement, there was an increased demand for native employment. The legislators demanded, 'preference to Assamese for appointments and contracts in Government services, railways, steamers and other commercial bodies'.[29] The middle class had hardly any capital to invest in major contracts on the railways, which was generally in hands of non-indigenous people. Petty contracts went to the Assamese entrepreneurs who could not make much headway for lack of entrepreneurial skills.

EMERGENCE OF A NON-NATIVE CAPITALIST CLASS

Between 1871 and 1901, the economy of Assam developed a dual character, where the traditional subsistence, and capital-intensive highly monetized plantation and mining sector developed simultaneously. A few Assamese entrepreneurs invested in plantations, but its benefits did not flow back into that sector.[30] Mustard, an important cash crop, was grown in surplus and the natives of Kamrup monopolized its trade.

The rest of the trade in the province of Assam was in the hands of the Marwaris, locally known as *Kyahs*. They entered

28. *Administration Report of Assam*, for various years between 1898 and 1903.

29. *Political History of Assam*, file no. NL 1908, Newspaper Bundles 3 and 4, Gauhati, December 1931, 'Demand of Assam: Transfer of Sylhet to Bengal'.

30. Sajal Nag, 'Working Class Alienation in Swadeshi and Non-Cooperation: A Reflection of the Class Character of Nationalist Movement in Assam 1905–1924', *Proceedings of the North-East India History Association*, Imphal Session 1983.

Assam along with the British, and in the absence of an indigenous trading class, gained a foothold and virtually controlled all
the means of production in rural Assam. Their operations
ranged from shopkeeping in the remotest areas of Assam, to
trading, moneylending, speculation and acting as agents of the
Raj. The Dacca *beparis* engaged in considerable trade in miscel-
laneous goods. In Dibrugarh, European firms carried out a
large trade in articles used by Europeans. The principal items
exported from Assam were timber, hides, unhusked rice, silk-
cloth, cotton, lac, betel nut, jute, mustard seeds, rubber, tea and
coal. Except for tea and coal, most of the export trade was a
monopoly of the Marwari traders. Imports of rice, salt, pulses,
sugar, European piece-goods, kerosene oil, cement, corrugated
iron and fancy goods were also monopolized by them.[31]

The Marwaris dominated the weekly markets, where they
sold their wares and collected surplus products. They trans-
acted in primary products like, rubber, wax, hand-woven
cloth, elephant tusks, rhino horn and medicinal plants, which
they exchanged for rice and salt.[32] They were practically the
sole exporters from the province. Marwari shops were found
at every *Sadar* (sub-divisional headquarters), tea gardens, and
even beyond the North-East Frontier in the midst of jungles.
Thus, lakhs of rupees, which annually poured into the province, passed into the hands of the Marwari traders and shopkeepers.

The Marwaris also had an indirect way of controlling the
peasantry. In spite of the heavy burden of taxation, the peasantry did little to supplement their income, nor adopt any

31. *Report on Rail and River Borne Trade*, for various years, 1881 to
1915.
32. *Report on the Administration of Assam*, for various years, 1875–76
to 1885–86.

measure to extend cultivation. They increasingly turned for their financial requirements to the Marwari trader, who also indulged in usury. The cultivator was often forced to sell cash crops to them. The *Kyahs* offered advances to the *ryots* to meet their revenue dues, insisting that in lieu they should grow a particular crop (mostly mustard) and supply it at specific rates.[33] Thus, the merchants combined the functions of trade and usury and reaped immense benefits.

Primarily traders, the Marwaris generally did not invest in land. However, in course of time land resources began to be transferred to the Marwaris against the debts of the cultivating class. In 1917 it was registered that an 'increase in land held by Marwaris was chiefly in Sibsagar and Darrang due to mostly acquisition of property by purchase or in satisfaction of Civil Court Decrees.'[34] The decrees were an indicator of the degree of indebtedness amongst the peasantry and their alienation from their primary means of production.

The colonizers were unwilling to encourage possession of agricultural land by non-cultivating classes. Hence, in 1919, the Chief Commissioner approved of the inclusion of an additional clause to the new periodic *pattas*. The clause meant that hitherto transfer of land from a professional cultivator to a person of the non-cultivating class would require prior sanction of the District Officer.[35] This was to prevent expropriation of the cultivators land by Marwaris. By 1921, a positive decrease was visible in the land held by Marwaris because of the new administrative measure.

---

33. The Marwari moneylenders procured mustard seeds at one rupee per maund, when the market prices ranged between Rs 3 to 4.
34. *Resolution of the Land Revenue Administration: 1917–1918*, p. 5.
35. *Resolution on the Land Revenue Administration: 1918–1919*, p. 6.

TABLE XII: Landholding by the Marwaris[36]

Year	Acres
1915–1916	14,252
1916–1917	13,965
1917–1918	15,338
1918–1919	16,311
1919–1920	16,454

COLONIZATION SCHEMES — IMMIGRATION AND ITS IMPACT

While debating on the formulation of a scheme for opening up the vast wastelands for colonization, areas close to the railway line were first taken into consideration. The dense Nambor Forest between Lumding and Golaghat, which had been pierced by the railway, was considered to be of immense agricultural value for ordinary cultivators, hence suitable for colonization.

In pursuance of the scheme the Chief Commissioner in 1897 issued an order to:

> disforest from time to time and settle on certain terms within a convenient distance of the railway line from Bokajan to Jamuguri on decennial leases at the rate of 8 annas a *bigah* with a revenue free term of three years.[37]

In 1900, an area of 100 square miles in the Nambor Forest in Sibsagar district was opened to cultivation on an experimental basis. The scheme was declared to be exclusively for Assamese cultivators. The entire area was divided into three *mauzas*

36. *Resolution on the Land Revenue Administration 1919–1920*, p. 5.
37. Revenue 'A', October 1904, nos. 132–157, no. 34-1625 R of 14 April 1903.

for each of which an Assamese *mauzadar* was appointed, who would receive Rs 50 per month for the first three years. Revenue collection would commence from the fourth year, they were allowed to retain their collections until the fifth year. At the end of the fifth year, they were to receive a commission on their collections. An annual grant of Rs 1000 was to be set aside for the first three years to develop infrastructure like building of new roads within the *mauzas.*[38]

In 1905, another 100 square miles in the Nambor Forest were opened for cultivation. In 1910, a mere 747 acres were brought under the plough. In 1914 while the area under cultivation was 1,348 acres, only 232 colonists had been settled.[39] The pace of colonization was hindered by lack of communication and water. The response to the scheme of colonization was not encouraging and hence it was withdrawn in 1920.

Simultaneously, a survey was undertaken in the valleys of the Kopili and Langfer, south of Nowgong district, along the Assam–Bengal Railway for opening it up for colonization. In course of the survey, it was found that small bodies of men who had worked on the construction of the Assam–Bengal Railway had settled along the line. They were men from Bihar, Punjab and North-West Provinces and had extended cultivation around Lanka and Kampur. Encouraged by the agricultural prospects of the area, the Assam–Bengal Railway in 1902 was authorized by the Chief Commissioner, to offer:

> Contractors, labourers and other employees of the Assam–Bengal Railway for their settlements on the wastelands that are available for cultivation in the tract of the country stretching along the line in either direction from Lumding station

38. Revenue 'A', October 1904, nos. 132–157, no. 34-1625 R of 14 April 1903.

39. *Report on the Revenue Administration of the Assam Valley Districts: 1910–1914.*

towards Nowgong on one hand and towards Golaghat on the other.[40]

It was offered rent-free for the first five years, with a graduated system of assessment until the expiry of a full term of twenty years, when the land came under ordinary settlement.[41]

Colonization by ex-railway coolies was significant. In 1912–13 about 1,399 *bighas* (approximately 514 acres) of land had been settled under the colonization scheme in Nowgong district along the Assam–Bengal Railway. In Sibsagar, 3,810 acres was taken up for cultivation in 1914.[42]

A significant feature of the topography of Assam was the existence of large tracts of cultivable wastelands, which propelled the growth of the plantation sector. Settled at fee simple rates, to encourage European investment the land did not yield substantial revenue. The tea industry thrived in the districts of Lakhimpur, Sibsagar and Darrang because of their topography. It barely thrived in the weather conditions of Kamrup and Nowgong.

The total area of cultivable wastelands assessed in 1897–98 stood at 6,779,978 acres. An area of approximately 5,000,000 acres was available for successful cultivation of food crops, after deducting 178,720 acres under tea and 1,658,078 acres under other crops.[43]

40. Revenue 'A', May 1903, nos. 255–308, Railway Circular no. 1167 of 23 December 1902.

41. The assessment was to be at the rate of 2 annas per acre for the first five years and at 4 annas per acre for a further period of ten years. The grants were liable to be cancelled at the end of the fifth, tenth and fifteenth year, if a fifth, quarter, or a third of the total area was not brought under the plough.

42. *Report on the Revenue Administration of the Assam Valley Districts: 1912–1914.*

43. Revenue 'A', November 1898, nos. 128–133, 'Note by the Chief Commissioner of Assam on the Extension of Cultivation on the Wastelands of the Province'.

Francis Jenkins submitted the first scheme of colonization of these wastelands for ordinary cultivation in 1833. This issue has been discussed in detail in Chapter 1. Bringing wastelands under the plough, he perceived 'would compensate for any shortfall in the quota of land revenue by a falling off in the, peasant land holdings and the concessions to planters, on wastelands'.[44]

Henry Hopkinson was aware of the serious imbalance between the flourishing plantation and the agricultural sector. He urged that immigration into the plantation industry should be discouraged, as the province did not produce enough food grains to feed them. He suggested that cultivators from Bengal should be invited to settle on the wastelands of Assam. It was Henry Cotton, a staunch imperialist who launched extensive investigations to explore the possibilities to extending cultivation in Assam by encouraging immigration of cultivators into the wastelands.

Sir Patrick Playfair, a mercantile member of the Imperial Legislative Council, raised the issue of colonization on 26 May 1897. In his view, it was important to encourage emigration of large bodies of agriculturists to Assam from heavily populated districts in Bengal. He stressed that it would relieve the cultivators from the recurring famines and scarcity in Bengal. The proposal received support from *zamindars* like the Maharaja of Darbhanga, the Chambers of Commerce, the Indian Tea Association and the Indian Jute Manufacturers Association.[45]

The nascent Assamese middle class also supported the scheme of immigration. It was observed by them that, 'the

44. Nag, *Roots of Ethnic Conflict*, p. 87.
45. Revenue 'A', November 1898, no. 130, 'Colonisation of Wastelands in Assam'.

ultimate reclamation of these lands is infallibly destined to [be] a great source of revenue of the Province of Assam'.[46]

The view of Denzil Ibbetson, Secretary to the Government of India, was that the approaching completion of the Assam–Bengal Railway, 'will offer facilities for colonization which never before existed and the present time is therefore, specially appropriate for reconsideration of the subject'.[47]

Henry Cotton in his 'Note on Colonization' exhaustively dealt on the measures to be adopted for encouraging colonization of the wastelands in Assam. Debating on the possibility of importing agriculturists from other parts of India, the choice of the colonizers fell on the 'stout and fanatical Mohammedan of East Bengal', considered to be the most eligible for immigration as they were hard working and prolific cultivators.[48]

The promoters of the scheme realized that the success of the 'colonization project' could only be achieved with improved communication between Bengal and Assam, as well as through the improvement of the internal communication. Success of any developmental scheme in Assam depended on the provision of greater facilities for the movement of immigrants and the transportation of produce. The existing river network was unable to speed up communications. The Assam–Bengal Railway undoubtedly improved the communication network, but its alignment made it difficult to compete successfully with the river routes. While the railway provided the shortest route to the Chittagong port, the dynamics of internal and external trade demanded its connection with the rest of India, more so with the port of Calcutta. In the beginning of the twentieth

46 For details, see Nag, *Roots of Ethnic Conflict*, pp. 87–90.

47. Revenue 'A', November 1898, no. 130, 'Colonisation of Wastelands in Assam'.

48. Nag, *Roots of Ethnic Conflict*, p. 90.

century, there was a demand to connect the terminus of the Assam–Bengal Railway at Gauhati with the Bengal Railway system. The Chief Commissioner, Henry Cotton, wrote on its necessity in 1897, 'It is more important for the development of Assam to connect it by rail with Calcutta and the rest of India than it is to connect it with Chittagong'.[49] On the economic advantages of the Eastern Bengal Railway connection Henry Cotton remarked:

> immense areas of State owned waste lands from which, as population extends, revenue will surely be earned. It is quite conceivable — or may be argued — that even after direct railway earnings and indirect land earnings shall have been raked in by the State, there will still remain a balance of interest charges to be made good.[50]

The push factor for the railway connection with Calcutta was to foster large-scale immigration into the province and enhance its revenue potential. The Eastern Bengal Railway connection to Dhubri was achieved in 1902. However, there remained a gap of 151 miles between Dhubri and Gauhati, which was served by steamers. This gap resulted in delayed transhipment at both ends which acted as a deterrent to free immigration from the over populated districts of Bihar and Bengal to the unpopulated tracts of Assam.

The Consulting Engineer for Railways in Assam, F.J.E. Spring, making an observation on the benefits of the Dhubri–Gauhati extension said that:

> From my point of view and specially now that we have more than completed the original Famine Commission's scheme of protective railways, the immigration problem is of far higher

49. Railway Construction 'A', May 1901, no. 36, dated 14 January 1901, from H.J.S. Cotton to F.R. Upcott.

50. Railway Construction 'A', May 1901, 'Notes', F.J.E. Spring, 23 December 1901.

practical importance to the general taxpayer than the problem of making the railway directly remunerative through its own revenue account. For an improvement in the revenues of Assam, through spread of cultivation to the extent of 4 annas per acre on ten or fifteen million acres, means a great deal more than any possible railway profits.[51]

The profits of the railway was conjectured not just in terms of its direct benefits, but the indirect benefits as well, in terms of encouraging immigration and its role in enhancing the revenue receipts of the province by expanding cultivation.

The role of the Assam–Bengal Railway in facilitating free immigration cannot be minimized. It promoted inter-district migration within Assam, and migration of settlers from the more thickly populated parts of Cachar and Sylhet to several *mauzas* of Nowgong district through which the railway passed. It was evident from a report that, 'the influx of immigrants from Cachar and Sylhet into the Nowgong district was checked by the temporary closing of the Hill Section of the Assam–Bengal Railway'.[52]

The partition of Bengal and the merger of Assam with Eastern Bengal in 1905 started the process of immigration of farm settlers from Eastern Bengal. Between 1905 and 1915, about 70,000 migrants from the districts of Dacca, Mymensingh, Pabna and Rangpur entered the province.[53] In 1911, rail communication between Assam and Bengal was achieved with the completion of the Golakganj–Gauhati extension of the Eastern Bengal Railway. This was followed by a dramatic increase of agriculturists into Assam from the Eastern Bengal districts.

51. Railway Construction 'A', May 1901, 'Notes', F.J.E. Spring, 23 December 1901.

52. *Report on the Administration of Assam: 1915–16*, p. 4.

53. Revenue Department, Agriculture 'A', February 1916, nos. 10–19, Appendix 'A', 'Note on Jute' by R.S. Finlow.

TABLE XIII: Immigration of Farm Settlers of
Various Categories to Total Immigration
into the Brahmaputra Valley, 1881 to 1931[54]

Decade	Eastern Bengal Farm Settlers	Nepalese	Traders/ Artisans	Others
1881–1891	17,300	1,000	3,400	13,400
1891–1900	17,700	9,000	3,400	37,100
1901–1910	74,700	15,000	12,600	23,300
1911–1920	1,95,800	12,000	25,000	84,600
1921–1930	2,26,000	16,000	30,000	149,000

Migration from the Eastern Bengal districts, particularly from Mymensingh, was into the districts of Goalpara, Nowgong, Kamrup and Sunamganj sub-division of Sylhet.

Another group of immigrants who arrived were the Santhals. The earliest attempts to establish a colony for Santhals was taken up under the orders of Sir Stuart Bailey in 1880.[55] In 1897, an area of 3,730 *bighas* was brought under cultivation by a colony of 1,361 Santhals.[56] Until the opening of the Eastern Bengal Railway, small groups of Santhals used to migrate annually. The railways fostered immigration of this group which is evident from the report that, 'immigration increased appreciably in the Eastern *Duars* of Goalpara district, where Santhals continue to arrive from Dumka, Dinajpur and Jalpaiguri'.[57] They were settled mostly in the forest villages.

A large number of Nepali graziers migrated into Assam from Jalpaiguri, owing to an increase in the rates of grazing

54. Cf., Nag, *Roots of Ethnic Conflict*, p. 90.
55. Revenue 'A', November 1898, no. 130, 'Colonisation of Wastelands in Assam'.
56. *Report on the Administration of Assam: 1897*, p. 4.
57. *Report on the Administration of Assam: 1911–12*, p. 4.

tax in that district.[58] They settled in the districts of Lakhimpur and Sibsagar and were instrumental in the economic development of the area. They introduced sugar cane cultivation in the Brahmaputra Valley, about which Somerset Playne reported:

> In Lakhimpur and in the east of Sibsagar and Darrang, cultivation is mainly in the hands of the Nepalese, who plant the [sugar] cane on virgin soil in the forest clearings. The bulk of the crop is grown in patches of one or two *bighas* . . . In Upper Assam and in the hilly tracts in the South of the Surma Valley this nomadic system of cultivation is practised by the Nepalese on land newly reclaimed from the jungle.[59]

The transformed economic prosperity, which began in Assam in the second decade of the twentieth century, was primarily a contribution of the immigrant peasants. They introduced improved methods of cultivation, worked harder and longer, and produced primarily for the market. The government also encouraged the introduction of new cash crops. The immigrants introduced jute and tobacco to the province. Marwari traders too, cashed in on this opportunity, by providing short-term loans to the immigrants for extending cultivation of jute, rice and other cash crops. The area under 'spring rice' that was grown mainly in Sylhet, was extended to Goalpara by the immigrants from Mymensingh.[60]

The immigrant peasants became highly successful due to their hard work and enterprise. This was in sharp contrast to the condition of the Assamese peasantry, which floundered because they failed to respond to the new demands of the economy for the production of surplus, as well as the cultivation

58. *Report on the Administration of Assam: 1912–13*, p. 5.
59. Playne, *Bengal and Assam, Behar and Orissa*, p. 624.
60. Nag, *Roots of Ethnic Conflict*, p. 95.

of non-traditional crops such as jute, tobacco, wheat, sugar cane, etc. Many indigenous farmers sold off their lands to the Eastern Bengal migrants at high prices. In order to prevent this, 'a proposal was mooted in 1923–24 to insert periodic *pattas* in the districts of Kamrup, Darrang and Nowgong with a clause restricting the right of Assamese [peasants] to sell off their lands to immigrants'.[61]

The landless Assamese farmers entered into a vicious cycle of rural indebtedness. The local peasantry could not match the aggressiveness of the Eastern Bengal migrants and their worsening material condition stood out in sharp contrast to the economic prosperity of the immigrants. These migrants who mostly settled in the districts of Kamrup, Nowgong and Darrang, were a cause of concern for the Assamese farmers. Their relationship was far from cordial, resulting in perpetual clashes and confrontations.

Immigration created drastic demographic changes, which tilted the population balance in favour of the Bengalis, the majority of whom were Muslims. Their linguistic and religious differences caused serious ethnic tensions in an erstwhile insular Assamese society, now exposed to an alien cultural element. In the pre-colonial period, indigenous Assamese Muslims were completely assimilated into Assamese society and did not maintain a distinguishable identity. The alien nature and culture of the Eastern Bengal immigrants sparked social conflicts, in the areas where they settled.

Immigration threatened to reduce the Assamese population to a minority. Earlier ethnic conflicts were discernible at the level of the educated Assamese middle class, which faced stiff competition from their Bengali counterparts. This problem

61. Amalendu Guha, *Planter Raj to Swaraj: Freedom Struggle and Electoral Politics in Assam, 1826–1947* (New Delhi, 1977), pp. 204–6.

now spread to the peasantry as well, this issue played a vital role in galvanizing and consolidating Assamese nationalism. Until Independence, the issue of immigration dominated the arena of provincial politics.

EQUALIZATION OF TRADE

A reasonable amount of equalization in inter-provincial trade was witnessed in the districts connected by the Assam–Bengal Railway. Similar developments occurred in the districts traversed by the Eastern Bengal Railway. Different trade blocks within the province connected by the railway, traded items amongst themselves. Statistics for the rail-borne trade between Sylhet and Cachar, along the Assam–Bengal Railway were registered for the first time in 1899. The most important article exported from Sylhet to Cachar was rice 'not in husk' (paddy), to the tune of 19,368 maunds (711.48 tons) against 1,415 maunds (51.98 tons) the previous year.[62] Sylhet thus met the rice requirements of Cachar. The trade between the Khasi and Jaintia Hills, and Sylhet was almost entirely confined to lime that was exported from the quarries in the Khasi and Jaintia Hills. This was transported over the 'plains section' of the Cherra–Companyganj Railway.

In 1900, the rail-borne trade from Lower Assam was 12,264 maunds (450.52 tons) and that from the Upper Assam to the Lower Assam block was 5,823 maunds (213.91 tons). The main exports from Upper Assam to the internal trade blocks were coal and kerosene oil, while Lower Assam re-booked foreign imports of rice and paddy to Upper Assam. Mustard seed and tea were chiefly booked for foreign export

62. *Report on the Administration of Assam: 1898–99*, p. 92.

to Chittagong, while mustard oil was mainly consigned for Upper Assam. Coal, the chief produce of Upper Assam, was re-booked at Dhubri or Gauhati for the Eastern Bengal blocks. The trade therefore was not only internal, but an extension of imports into the province.[63]

The prices of commodities registered a rise during the construction of the Assam–Bengal Railway as a consequence of having to feed a large workforce involved in its construction. Some amount of trade developed along railway stations, where agents of the exporting firms arranged to buy the produce. This obviated the necessity for the producers to go to the trading centres in order to dispose off their surplus produce. This was a feature visible along the Assam–Bengal Railway as well as on the line between Dhubri and Amingaon. Every railway station was virtually a centre for export, as this extract shows.

> The prices of timber, jute, mustard and paddy ruled high. The rise in the prices of these articles has drawn into trade, a number of persons, particularly those living near railway stations.[64]

The export of raw materials and much later food grains, linked the economy of Assam with world markets. The production of crops became closely linked with prevailing prices in world markets. It was reported in 1915 that, 'jute prices fell heavily with the disorganization of trade that marked the early stage of war in Europe'.[65] It was further stated that:

> The outturn [sic] of cotton, which is a crop of some import-ance in the North Cachar Hills was less than the preceding

63. *Returns of the Rail and River Borne Trade of Assam: 1900–1901*, p. 63.

64. *Resolution on the Land Revenue Administration: 1923–24*, p. 2.

65. *Land Revenue Administration of the Surma Valley and Hill Districts Division: 1914–1915*, pp. 1–2.

year. This is attributed to some extent to the falling off in the demand in consequence of the war with Europe.[66]

LIMITED TECHNOLOGICAL CHANGES

Technology, whether as a form of knowledge or a tool is not free. It always manifests political qualities. In colonial conditions, it naturally acquired the contours of colonial power, both in the administrative and commercial spheres. Manifestly, India's burgeoning commercialization of agriculture was neither supplemented nor followed by industrialization. For India to industrialize by using applied sciences, there had to be incentives to invest and innovate. The nascent Indian bourgeoisie could not produce heavy capital goods on a weak and dependent technological base. They faced formidable problems arising from the absence of essential machinery, know-how and trained personnel.

In Assam, the colonial period witnessed a substantial increase in the volume of exports of industrial raw materials, without any commensurate improvement in technology. This can be attributed to an all-pervasive phenomenon of the colonial period, of catering to the interests of the Indian suppliers, British exports and the Government of India's fiscal requirements. Relative retardation in technology has also been assigned to the 'dominant' influence of archaic social institutions and the consequent failure to utilize the available technical knowledge and skills.[67]

For instance, Assam exported mustard seeds in immense quantities and imported it back in the form of mustard oil. The

66. *Land Revenue Administration of the Surma Valley and Hill Districts Division: 1914–1915*, pp. 1–2.
67. Kumar *et al.*, *Technology and the Raj*, p. 27.

seeds were exported to Rangpur, from where it was imported back as oil. This was apparently due to the high yield from the Rangpur oil presses, which yielded 16 *seers*, (a *seer* = approximately 1 kilogram), of oil, against 12 to 13 *seers* of the Assam presses.[68] Attempts to start oil-pressing units at Barpeta met with partial success. In the case of rice, it was exported in the form of paddy and received back as husked rice.

Mustard oil for internal consumption was extracted in indigenous presses called *ghanis*. During World War I, imports into Assam were drastically affected due to the disruption in shipping and the general uncertainties at that time. A Department of Industries was created in 1915, which started operating from 1918. This department tried to infuse new technology in the oil-seeds and paddy husking sectors. In that year, six oil mills were set up in the Assam Valley.[69] The local administration encouraged the setting up of rice mills, in view of the considerable exports of paddy and imports of husked rice into the province. In 1918, there were five rice mills and nine combined oil and rice mills in the Assam Valley.[70] In the post-Depression period, there emerged a group of entrepreneurs amongst the rural rich all over India, which invested their surplus funds in oil and rice mills. Similar developments occurred in Assam. In 1935, over thirty-one combined mills sprung up in the districts of Lakhimpur, Darrang, Sibsagar and Kamrup, a response to the increased production of cash crops ushered in by the immigrants. The business was mainly in the hands of the Marwaris.[71]

As raw cotton exports increased, small power ginning

68. *Report on the River Borne Trade of the Province of Assam: 1884–85*, p. 3.
69. *Report on the Administration of Assam: 1920–21*, p. 20.
70. Ibid.
71. *Report on the Department of Industries Assam: 1934–35*, p. 5.

factories were set up in the province.[72] The Department of Industries surveyed the existing industries and their stage of development. The iron industry in the Assam Valley flourished in the hands of the up-country men (from north and central India). The only industries, which flourished under local enterprise, were the bell-metal, soap-making, pottery and ivory-works. A few sugar factories were set up in Upper Assam and one at Haibargaon in Nowgong. The sugar manufactured was brown in colour and non-crystalline, as the technology was not of a high grade. A redeeming feature of this industry was the involvement of Assamese entrepreneurs.

The bell-metal industry was monopolized by Assamese craftsmen from Sarthebari. The raw materials had to be secured from Marwari merchants who secured a major portion of the profits. The brass industry was also dependent on them for raw materials. Brass workers, mainly Muslims, were called *Morias* in the Assam Valley.[73] This industry stagnated due to the poor quality of the finished products. Ivory-work was indigenous to the Barpeta sub-division in Kamrup. The indigenous pottery was rough and not durable and therefore craftsmen from other provinces captured the pottery market.

GROWTH OF A MIDDLE CLASS

In any society, a viable middle class emerges from the agrarian, the trading and commercial, or the industrial sectors. The colonial system created the base for the growth of new classes, particularly the middle class in Assam.

72. A small power-ginning mill in Golaghat sub-division was owned by Moll Schuttle and Company and managed by T.F. Severine. The capital invested in the concern was Rs 50,000.

73. *Report on the Administration of Assam: 1920–21*, p. 20.

In medieval Assam, there was no social élite other than the nobility. The concept of a *raij mel*, an assembly, to take decisions on various socio-economic matters, prevented the growth of an exclusive élite to take up the leadership of the community. The Bhakti Cult led to the formation of a new socio-religious institution, which became the centre of socio-political power and prestige. This movement gave rise to an élite class, which provided the leadership to society when the British took over.

With the destruction of the medieval economy and its transformation, the former nobility was reduced to a deplorable condition. The colonial economy provided very few opportunities to the Assamese, and the only sector open to those who were educated was that of white-collared jobs. The erstwhile nobility found that these jobs paid adequately and gave them a certain social status. They therefore educated their children and rallied round white-collared jobs. The children of the priests of the Vaishnava *satras* were sent to Bengal for their education. On their return, the majority joined the government sector and became the leaders of the nascent Assamese middle class. The landlords of Goalpara also emerged as social leaders. However, they had to face stiff competition in their white-collared positions from the Bengali's. Thus, the Assamese middle class, a progressive group of intellectuals representing the interests of all the people of Assam, grew under the shadow of the Bengali middle class towards the end of the nineteenth century.

The middle class, which evolved from the erstwhile aristocracy, was responsive to the demands of the market economy. They ventured into making capital investments. A few such as Manik Chandra Barua, began his career as a timber merchant and a tea planter. His timber business collapsed, following which he settled down as a modest planter. Bhola Nath Barua, a close relative of Manik Chandra Barua, began his career at the latter's timber business and rose to become a millionaire timber merchant of Orissa. Dinanath Bezborua established two tea gardens. Lakshmi Nath Bezborua, after marrying into the Tagore family of Bengal, became a timber businessman and settled outside Assam. He began initially as a business partner of Bhola Nath Barua and later set up his own independent business.[74] The natures of these enterprises were unlike the capitalistic ventures that flourished in the rest of India. There were small capitalistic ventures in the sugar industry, like the Gurjogania Sugar Industry near Golaghat owned by Das and Company of Jorhat, and the Baidihi Sugar Works at Jorhat belonging to C.K. Bezbarua.

Outside the purview of the colonial framework, this entrepreneurial class with its roots in the erstwhile aristocracy flourished under British patronage because of their faith in the regenerating role of British rule. A separate class of entrepreneurs did not emerge out of the increased economic opportunities under colonial rule, which could be largely attributed to the lack of enterprise amongst the general populace of the province.

The railway network, which improved communication, was an important factor as far as economic development was concerned but it also hastened political development. A.R. Desai has endorsed this view.

The nationalist movement would have been inconceivable but for the fact that the railways made it possible for the people of different towns, villages, districts and provinces to

74. Nag, *Roots of Ethnic Conflict*, 'Appendix A — Background of Assamese Middle Class Leadership', p. 165.

meet to exchange views and decide upon programmes for the movement.[75]

He further argued that it was a means of disseminating nationalistic ideas through the press, which depended for its circulation on the railways. Various political organizations could not have functioned on a national scale without the railways helping in transporting their delegates.

In Assam, mobility amongst the masses was limited during the pre-railway era. The railway connection and later Assam's political amalgamation with Eastern Bengal, exposed the people of Assam to the National Movement. Initially, the response to the 'Anti-Partition' or 'Swadeshi Movement' was lukewarm, as it was regarded to be 'essentially a Bengali movement'. Subsequently, the Assamese élite took active part in the national movement, joined by the press and other sociopolitical organizations. It was the training ground for political leaders, who for long had faith in the regenerating role of British rule.

Direct communication with Bengal brought the general people into contact with the nationalistic forces operating in the rest of the country, and they changed their attitude towards colonial rule. They raised strong objections on issues like the opium policy and the raising of the grazing tax. They joined the mainstream national movement and participated with immense fervour in the Non-Cooperation and the Civil Disobedience Movements. Simultaneously, they upheld their separate identity, with a parallel movement to sustain it. This phenomenon evolved in the face of the threat perceived by the Assamese people of the cultural and economic hegemony of

75. A.R. Desai, *Social Background of Indian Nationalism* (Bombay, 1976), p. 133.

the alien immigrant population of cultivators settled in the province. This nurtured the growth of a distinct Assamese nationality.

IMPACT IN THE SURMA VALLEY

The Surma Valley comprised the districts of Sylhet and Cachar. Traditionally, there was always a considerable difference in the agricultural and trading patterns between the Surma and Brahmaputra Valleys.

In the Surma Valley, which was essentially Bengali in culture, occupational castes having specialized functions were a feature of its economic organization, unlike that in the Brahmaputra Valley. Here agriculturists formed a separate occupational caste. In Cachar, the peasant proprietor drove the plough, while in Sylhet the poorer middle-classes were engaged in agriculture for wages. Traditional industries in the Surma Valley closely resembled those in the neighbouring districts of Bengal. Weaving was not a household industry like in the Brahmaputra Valley. It was confined to the *Tantis* and *Jugis*, the professional weaving caste. The occupational castes included potters and barbers.

In Sylhet, catching of fish was of considerable importance. In Cachar traditional industries included weaving, the extraction of mustard oil, carpentry, and the making of — rough pottery, bell-metals, iron hoes, *daos*, and simple agricultural implements. In Sylhet, a large number of persons were engaged in the manufacture of ornaments from precious metals like gold, with the goldsmiths being mainly from Dacca and Manipur. Ivory products of considerable value were produced providing employment to a large number of artisans in the town of Sylhet. Iron works were found all over the Surma Valley, the products manufactured at Rajnagar in South Sylhet sub-division being particularly notable.

The peasantry of the Surma Valley had responded to the demands of a market economy, since the early days of British rule. In both Cachar and Sylhet, paddy was sold to the labourers in markets close to the tea gardens. In other parts, growers sold their surplus at markets convenient to them and carried them along the numerous waterways, by boats to Bengal. Most of the purchases were made by *beparis* who brought their boats from Bengal and took paddy from Cachar and Sylhet.

In Cachar the import trade was mainly in the hands of foreign merchants. Internal trade in the district was carried on at markets held on specified days or at permanent shops. Most of the shopkeepers were Bengalis, mainly Dacca *beparis* or from the Upper Provinces. Very few indigenous inhabitants of the district had attempted to appropriate any portion of the profits accruing from retail trade. The number of Marwari merchants was however, very small.

Commercial contacts with their counterparts in Calcutta, Dacca and Narainganj, in the neighbouring districts of Bengal, made the people of Sylhet excellent traders. They retained trade in their own hands and its profits were more widely distributed. The trade of this district was primarily with Cachar, the Khasi Hills, Hill Tipperah [*sic*] and Bengal.

In the Brahmaputra Valley cultivable wastelands awaiting the plough was a predominant feature, while in the Surma Valley there was less cultivable land awaiting settlement. In Cachar, land available for settlement had shrunk with an expansion of the population. Consequently, in 1902, the local administration opened the entire Dhaleswari, parts of the Barak, Sonai and the Inner line Reserves for settlement. The competition for the acquisition of land was so acute that the *beels* (freshwater wetlands) and *chars* (river islands) were brought under the plough and no field was left fallow, unless rainfall was below normal. Sylhet, which was under the Permanent Settlement Rules, did not have cultivable land lying fallow. The people were reportedly energetic and enterprising and agriculture was prosperous.

The opening of the Assam–Bengal Railway through the Surma Valley, coupled with an improvement in steamer communication with Calcutta, stimulated trade immensely. The principal centres of trade in both the districts had been traditionally situated along the river, and their position was enhanced by speedier water communication. As the railway network expanded, primary markets developed, where the producers sold directly to the agents of exporting firms without the aid of middlemen. Every railway station practically became an exporting centre. Railways facilitated inter-district trade as well. After its completion, the Assam–Bengal Railway carried considerable quantities of paddy from Cachar to Upper Assam and from Sylhet to Eastern Bengal. In Sylhet, the peasantry availed the opportunity of supplementing their resources by seeking employment on railway construction sites. Cotton from the neighbouring hill districts was exported from the railway stations in the valley.

As the railway network expanded, the economy became increasingly oriented towards foreign trade. There was an increase in the acreage and the production of paddy. Jute cultivation on unutilized lands increased rapidly. In fact, the effects of the railways were very visible in the Surma Valley. With more connectivity and surplus production, coupled with the commercial aptitude of the people, the peasants of the Surma Valley were in a reasonably better economic position, than peasants in the rest of Assam.

IMPACT ON THE
OVERALL FINANCIAL MANAGEMENT OF THE PROVINCE

The impact of the railways on the provincial as well as the imperial revenues requires mention. Based on the agreements the funds provided for railway construction could be broadly classified under imperial and provincial heads.

The Jorhat Provincial State Railway was constructed from provincial revenues. The interest charges were classed as imperial revenue, with the net receipts going to the provincial government. During the first four years after its completion it earned a revenue of under Rs 40 per mile per week. Its earnings exceeded Rs 40 per mile per week from 1884, and from 1911, its earnings were over 3 per cent per annum.[76] Receipts on this railway were hampered, as it served as a feeder to both the steamer and the railway services. Construction of the Jorhat–Mariani branch line of the Assam–Bengal Railway provided it with outlets at either ends. With traffic drawn in either direction, its receipts in most cases were halved.

The Cherra–Companyganj Railway was also constructed from the provincial revenue account. The interest charges were paid from the imperial funds. The capital costs on the line from its commencement till its abandonment in 1900, stood at Rs 7,68,902. The hill inclines of the railway, an instance of engineering failure, had to be abandoned after the test runs. On the open-plains section the expenditure was Rs 3,38,749, while on the abandoned section it was Rs 4,30,153.[77] The railway was abandoned at a great loss to the taxpayers' revenue.

76. Projects 'A', April 1916, no. 256-P/1–6, 'Notes on Choice of Gauge', Traffic Prospects of Railway Projects in Assam.
77. Railway Traffic 'A', November 1898, nos. 49–50, from Government of India, PWD (Railway Traffic) to Chief Commissioner of Assam, no. 1185 RT of 25 October 1898.

The Tezpur–Balipara Tramway (later Railway) did not receive direct financial help from the government in the form of a guarantee, from either the provincial or the imperial revenues. The corpus fund came from contributions of the tea planters. They raised Rs 75,000 through ordinary shares, while McLeod raised an additional sum of Rs 3,05,000.[78] They also raised funds through preferential shares. However, the Tezpur Local Board was authorized by the provincial government to grant an annual subsidy of Rs 5,000 for a total period of five years. The subsidy continued to be renewed at the end of every five years.

With an increase in mileage, its earnings increased from Rs 80 to Rs 105 per mile per week. In 1901, its earnings on capital employed were 5.29 per cent per annum, which rose to 6.71 per cent per annum in 1904. Over the next two years its earnings were 6.58 per cent and 5 per cent respectively, inclusive of the subsidy.[79] As its receipts, including the subsidy, registered above 5 per cent, the railway was declared a dividend earning concern.

In 1900, a Reserve Fund was created to handle any expense beyond the elasticity of the revenue budget. The subsidy was continued, in spite of it being a dividend earning concern, as it was calculated on the basis of the average dividend on the shares declared at 1.75 per cent. The government was ready to share the burden of the limited finances of the local board as long as the planters received profits on their shares and debentures.

The Dibru–Sadiya Railway, was given a subsidy of 5 per cent, in contravention of the officially approved 3.5 per cent for the rest of the country, for being a 'pioneer railway' over

78. Traffic 'A', June 1915, nos. 167–171, no. 167.
79. Ibid

unknown terrain. An annual subsidy of Rs 1 lakh was to be paid from the provincial revenues until its annual earnings crossed 5 per cent. In 1900, net receipts exceeded 5 per cent and consequently the subsidy was terminated in 1903.[80] The subsidy was renewed in 1911 over the extended portion of the line between Talap and Saikhowaghat. A sum of Rs 5,112 was paid as an annual subsidy until 1921. Saddled with a perpetual annual subsidy from its provincial revenues, it hampered the approval of future railway projects in Assam.

The Assam–Bengal Railway Company was formed on a guarantee of 3.5 per cent for an initial period of six years and at 3 per cent thereafter from the imperial funds.[81] The surplus profits were to be proportionately shared by the company and government. It was tantamount to a perpetual guarantee of 3 per cent, as the government was the owner of the railway, with the company merely acting as an agent for its construction and management.[82]

The Assam–Bengal Railway proved to be a steady burden on the financial resources of the Government of India. On the completion of its entire length in 1903, the infamous hill section alone cost close to Rs 3.5 lakhs per mile. The return on the capital was a mere 0.5 per cent in contrast to the returns on the Eastern Bengal Railway during the corresponding period.[83]

The colossal expenditure on the hill section had serious implications on the financial management of the Assam–

80. Financial 'A', October 1918, 291-F-17/ 1–10, from the Secretary of State, London. Despatch no. 20, Railway, dated 18 May 1917.

81. Sanyal, *Development of Indian Railways*, p. 153.

82. Sanyal, *Development of Indian Railways*, p. 142.

83. Railway Construction 'A', July 1908, no. 1173 RC, dated 2 July 1908, from Secretary Railway Board to Officiating Secretary to the Government of Eastern Bengal and Assam PWD, Railway Branch.

Bengal Railway after its completion. Finances on a completed railway were categorized under two distinct heads, capital and revenue accounts. The capital account represented the amount actually spent on the construction. It also allowed for an inclusion of the amount subsequently spent during the first two or three years of the completion of the construction. Every additional rupee spent on the capital account meant less interest on the capital to the Government of India.[84]

The revenue account was opened after its completion usually for 'maintenance' and 'new works'. This account was usually calculated on its earnings and the guarantee paid by Government of India. In the case of the hill section, allocation of funds between the capital and revenue accounts was difficult to differentiate. Generally, works like repairing slips were classified as new works and charged on the revenue account. However, in the hill section, new works required extra staff and thus it had to be charged on the capital account. The extensive damage on the various stretches of this section because of the nature of the terrain and the recurring natural calamities made all expenses a perpetual charge on the capital account.

In 1895, 129 miles of the railway had been opened to traffic, which earned Rs 64 per mile per week. In 1913–14 with a mileage of 811 miles, it earned Rs 167 per week per mile. It represented a profit of 1.45 per cent, as the proportion of working expenses to its earnings was 67.75 per cent.[85]

84. The interest loss of the government was calculated by taking the difference between the interest that had to be paid on the capital raised, and that which it could have earned till the operation of the 'Revenue account' of the railway became operational.

85. Financial 'A', February 1916, no. 16/I-P, General no. 10663, G. no. 5218 B, dated 6 August 1915, from the Secretary to the Chief Commissioner Assam in PWD, to the Secretary Railway Board.

Higher working expenses in Assam proved to be a handicap for the primary trunk line. Allocations for further railway expansion in the province was reduced as the 'chief railway administration of the Province was not placed on a sound financial footing'. It exercised a detrimental influence on the future of railway expansion in the province.

The short feeder railways were financially sound concerns, ensuring steady dividends to its shareholders. However, the system of subsidy was an immense drain on the limited internal resources of the province and the country at large. The location of the trunk route was not decided on a commercial criterion; therefore, the government was not concerned about the potential earnings and the volume of traffic. The masses were not benefited by the large-scale expenditure on infrastructure development.

Claims that the railways offered a viable alternative to the existing waterways in terms of making them redundant, proved to be a fallacy. In real terms, the Assam–Bengal Railway operated under the strain of severe competition from the steamers. The feeder railways worked in close coordination with the steamers, while inland railway lines working independently faced stiff competition from the steamers. The rivers Brahmaputra, Barak and their numerous tributaries provided Assam with navigable waterways. Introduction of daily steamers on both the river valleys was a great step towards ensuring bulk movement of goods.

The Dibru–Sadiya Railway, the Jorhat Provincial Railway and Tezpur–Balipara Railway were commercially viable lines as they worked in effective coordination with the steamers. They adjusted their rates to cater to the demands of the steamer companies. The companies exercised a great degree of control on the railways, penalizing railways which did not coordinate by adopting block rates. So powerful was the influence of the steamer lobby that issues like the merger of a feeder line with the Assam–Bengal Railway could not materialize. Steamers dominated the entire range of export trade.

The Assam–Bengal Railway, a financially handicapped concern had to encounter severe rail–steamer competition. The Dibru–Sadiya Railway adopted preferential rates in favour of steamer companies on the carriage of coal against the Assam–Bengal Railway and local consumers. The general public was charged, based on the fixed rate on coal transportation over a minimum distance of twenty-five miles and not on the actual distance between the colliery and the destination.[86]

The Dibru–Sadiya Railway shared a junction with the Assam–Bengal Railway at Tinsukia. However, through-traffic over the junction to the all-rail route was very limited. The two main items carried over the Dibru–Sadiya Railway were coal and mineral oil. In 1918, out of the 537,000 tons of coal carried by the Dibru–Sadiya Railway, 99,000 tons went to the Assam–Bengal Railways. Of the 17,564 tons of mineral oil carried by the Dibru–Sadiya Railway a mere 461 tons went to the Assam–Bengal Railway.[87] It can be inferred that the bulk of the traffic in coal and mineral oil went to the steamers. They operated under a system where the Dibru–Sadiya Railway enhanced its earnings by quoting higher rates over its short length, while steamers secured the entire traffic by quoting lower rates. The freight structure was oriented towards encouraging linkages with world markets, working against regional market integration within Assam or India at large.

86. The station-to-station rate of Re 0–1–2 [*sic*] per maund infringed the maximum permissible rate of quarter pie per maund, for distances beyond fifty-six miles. The government justified the rates on the ground that they were small feeder railways.

87. Financial 'A', October 1918, no. 291F-17/1–10, 'Notes'.

The Eastern Bengal Railway too exercised immense influence over trade in Assam, after its operations were extended to Goalundo, a natural junction in the river system of Eastern Bengal. It functioned in conjunction with steamers operating close to its rail network, and it worked to secure all the jute trade from Narainganj and practically all the trade from Sylhet and Cachar.

The Assam–Bengal Railway sought to counter such competition by signing agreements with steamer companies for a combined cargo service between Goalundo and Chandpur. However, the steamer companies did not honour these agreements as they favoured a direct cargo link between Sylhet and Cachar and the coastal trade with Chittagong.[88] This accounted for a substantial diversion of traffic via Goalundo and Chandpur (intermediate steamer points on both the railways) and the reduction of Chittagong's share in the trade. In 1904, it registered a 25 per cent reduction on its receipts.[89]

The position of the Assam–Bengal Railway was redeemed by an agreement in 1907, with the Clan Line Steamers for through booking of goods to Europe via Chittagong, and to all stations beyond Itakhola on the Assam–Bengal Railway.[90] The steamers largely represented the interests of the firms operating at the port of Calcutta, which was a gateway for exports from the North East. Innumerable waterways at practically all pivotal points on the railway made the Assam–Bengal Railway vulnerable to competition of varying intensities. The rate war created an unhealthy competition. The control of the river system on trade was evident from the

88. Railway Traffic 'A', May 1904, nos. 14–28 and no. 6010 of 31 July 1902, from R.S. Stratchey, Agent Assam–Bengal Railway to Agent Joint Steamer Companies, Calcutta.
89. Ibid.
90. Ibid.

river-borne trade statistics. In 1907–1908, 53 per cent of the imports and 45 per cent of the exports went by the river. In 1921–22, when the entire province was covered by a railway network and well connected with the port of Calcutta, river transport continued to dominate and handle 41 per cent of imports and 55 per cent of exports.[91]

An attempt has been made to understand the impact of railways in initiating social change. In terms of Marxian analysis change in technology, which is considered as the 'base', has a determining impact on society — the 'superstructure'. Without taking an extreme position in the debate, it is imperative to mention that technological innovations are nevertheless a major factor in initiating social transformation.

Railways when they were introduced, were identified as an accelerator of economic growth, based on the experience of the American economy — which was sustained by an indigenous political and social support system. The British introduced railways in India as an instrument of colonial exploitation. They were targeted to meet the ever-increasing demand for raw material for their home industries and to push back machine-made goods into the 'satellite' economies like India. The nature of their impact in India under such conditions therefore was bound to be different.

The impact of the railways in Assam has been attempted separately in both the river valleys, where demographic realities were divergent. The Brahmaputra Valley was a sparsely populated region, which was further depopulated by the political turmoil of the late eighteenth and early nineteenth

91. *Report on the Administration from Assam* for various years, 1907–1908 and 1921–1922.

century. In contrast the Surma Valley, which was an extension of the plains of Southeast Bengal, was a substantially populated region. The Brahmaputra Valley witnessed a spurt of commercial activity along the railway network. There was an increase in production, which generated surpluses, visible in the mushrooming of markets along its network. Every railway station was virtually transformed into a primary entrepôt. Trade was directed for foreign markets with hardly any attempt to integrate internal markets. Railways fostered stabilization of prices and equalization in inter-provincial circulation. As it was confined to areas along the railway lines the trickle-down effect to the peasantry was minimal. The colonial period witnessed a substantial increase in agricultural produce with little commensurate technological development.

8
Conclusion

When the British took control of Assam they inherited the social, economic and political structure of the Ahom's, who had entered the eastern extremity of the Brahmaputra Valley in 1228 from Upper Burma. The Ahom's entered a region, which was not politically void. In Lower Assam the erstwhile ancient kingdom of Kamrup persisted in the fragmented form of the Kamata state. Central Assam was controlled by a confederacy of petty land controllers (*Bhuyan Raj*). In Upper Assam the Chutiya and Kachari polity existed on the north and south banks of the Brahmaputra. The region was also inhabited by various tribal groups. The Ahoms had experience of polity formation during their stay in Upper Burma in the form of a *Mung*. The legacy of their politico-cultural tradition helped in laying the foundations of a state, which lasted for 600 years.

They introduced neighbouring communities to their mode of production, represented by their knowledge of wet rice cultivation. Economic patterns stabilized, and with the consolidation of 'state power', trade was extended beyond their

frontiers. Apart from other sources of appropriation of surpluses, trade was used as a means to sustain the surplus. The
Ahoms initiated massive infrastructure projects in the form of
road-cum-embankments. These were meant to serve the purpose of trade as well as help in military movement.

The British annexed Assam when its entire socio-political
structure was in turmoil because of the Moamaria rebellion
and Burmese intervention. The transition to the new socio-
political system introduced by the British was a very painful
one. Assam did not experience the merchant capitalist phase
of British imperialism. It was the ruthless march of British
finance capital, which determined the policies framed for the
annexation as well as the administration of Assam. This phase
was marked by maximization in extraction of raw produce
and creation of limited processing industries. Conditions were
created for pushing finished industrial products into the internal markets and at the same time integrating them with
external world markets. To achieve this end an efficient communication system had to be put into place and sustained. The
existing road network was used in the initial years of consolidation. After this they began rebuilding portions of the ancient
precincts, keeping in mind the requirements of troop movements and for tapping the frontier trade.

The British used the traditional river routes initially for five
decades, to foster extra-territorial trade. The rivers Brahmaputra and Barak had traditionally served as the great high-
ways of the province. The need to develop the communication
infrastructure was a natural corollary to the expanding trade
in raw produce and tea. A major breakthrough was made
when steamers were introduced into the region in the 1880s.
This enlarged carrying capacity as well as increased the speed
of transactions. Linking internal production centres with the

forwarding trade depots at the river ports had to be achieved. This could only be done with the extension of a railway network.

Initial suggestions for a railway network in Assam were met with resistance from the Government of India. The economic potential of the province was not considered profitable enough for the commercial success of the lines.

When the third phase of railway construction was initiated in India in the 1880s, interest was revived for beginning a rail network in Assam. The reasons assigned were the pressures from the plantation sector for connectivity to the nearest port. To these were added the need to explore the coal and mineral oil potential of the region. The political interest in using a railway network in Assam as a base for linking it later with the neighbouring province of Burma (Myanmar) pushed 'Project Railway' in Assam. The railway projects linked were of two categories — one linking specific production centres (tea and coal) to the river landings, the other being trunk lines. Strategic causes were also added to the list, following two petty rebellions in 1890 (Manipur) and 1892 (Adis).

The major trunk route connecting the tea-producing centres of Assam, through the populated districts of Bengal and the port of Chittagong was completed in 1903. Yet by the second decade of the twentieth century the existing trunk route was found to be inadequate for handling trade and immigration. Therefore an alternate trunk line connecting Eastern Bengal and Calcutta to Assam (between Dhubri and Gauhati) was constructed by 1910.

The industrial sector that developed after the coming of the railways was the mining sector, which fulfilled the demands of both the railways and the steamers. The agricultural sector received a boost with the improvement in marketing facilities.

Production and marketing centres mushroomed along railway alignments. Large-scale immigration of cultivators was facilitated by the railways, which brought about demographic changes and transformed the nature of the economy from a self-subsisting one to a market oriented one. In the agricultural sector, the linkage effect was visible in the expansion of the exports in rice and jute. The timber industry flourished. Certain ancillary industries such as saw mills, brickworks and railway workshops converted Assam into a dependent economy rather than initiating any all round development. This phenomenon was visible in the development of railways all over India.

While railways were instrumental in initiating a major shift in the nature of the Assamese economy, they failed to initiate a 'take-off' stage. This was because they operated within the structure of an imposed economy. They played a significant role in the development of forward linkages in industries like coal, petroleum, timber and jute. These linkages did not contribute to a change in the basic structure of the economy, because they operated as enclaves and catered to the demands of the international market. They operated in an environment where the capital, its management, the equipment required and skilled labour were imported from Britain. There was very little emphasis on developing integrated regional as well as intra-regional markets. The alignment for the trunk route did not link the internal production centres to the consumption centres, but linked the ports with the hinterland. Tea, coal and oil, in spite of attracting large-scale investment failed to be leading sectors in the economy of Assam.

Appendices

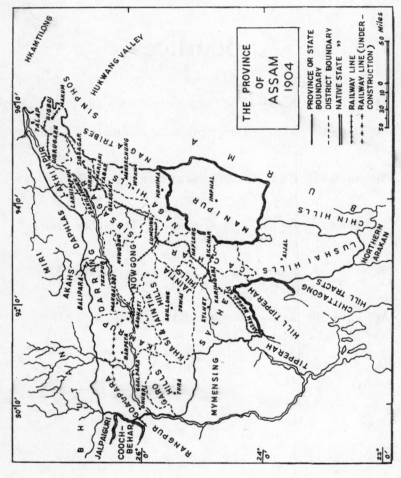

THE PROVINCE
OF
ASSAM
1904

PROVINCE OR STATE
BOUNDARY
DISTRICT BOUNDARY
NATIVE STATE "
RAILWAY LINE
RAILWAY LINE (UNDER –
CONSTRUCTION)

50 30 10 0   50 Miles

HKAMTLONG

HUKWANG VALLEY

SINPHOS

NAGA TRIBES

TALAP
DIGBOI
MAKUM

DAPHLAS
LAKHIMPUR
AKAHS
MIRI
DAPHLAS
DARRANG
BALIPARA
TEZPUR

SIBSAGAR
SADIYA
NORTH LAKHIMPUR
JORHAT
SIBSAGAR
TABAK
GOLAGHAT
DIBRUGARH

NAGA HILLS
MOKOKCHUNG
WOKHA
KOHIMA

MANIPUR
IMPHAL

M A R

SIBSAGAR
NOWGONG
MANGALDOI
NOWGONG
LUMDING
DIMAPUR

N. CACHAR
HILLS
HAFLONG

SILCHAR
CACHAR

GAUHATI
KAMRUP
NOWGONG

KHASIA &
JAINTIA HILLS
SHILLONG
JAINTIA
HILLS

KARIMGANJ
SYLHET

S Y L H E T
SUNAMGANJ

ASSAM BENGAL

HILL TIPPERAH

LUSHAI HILLS
AIJAL

CHIN HILLS
B U R M A

NORTHERN
ARAKAN

CHITTAGONG
HILL TRACTS

TIPPERAH

GOALPARA
DHUBRI
GOALPARA
BARPETA

RANGPUR

GARO
HILLS
TURA

MYMENSING

BHUTAN
JALPAIGURI
COOCH-
BEHAR

96° 0'
94° 0'
92° 0'
90° 0'

26° 0'
24° 0'
22° 0'

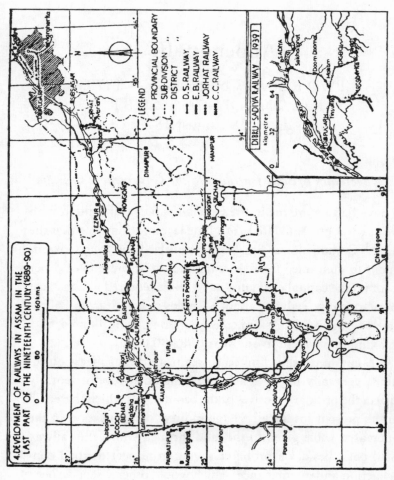

Source: Transport System and Economic Development of Assam, Shyam Bhadra Medhi, p. 66.

Appendix III

PWD Railway Construction — 1879, R.C. 'A' nos. 71–74, no. 128 R, dated 28 August 1876

From
The Secretary of State for India to the Government of India

I have had before me in the Council papers transmitted with your letter no. 166 dated 16th June last informing me that the Chief Commissioner has been authorized by your Government to guarantee for five years interest at the rate of 5 per cent on the capital estimated at 16 lakhs required to construct a metre gauge railway, about 67 miles in length from Dibrugarh to Sadiya in Assam, the guarantee being limited to a maximum payment in any year of Rs 80,000.

A guarantee thus limited is free from the strongest objections generally urged against guarantees. It cannot sensibly affect the ordinary motives of the economy of which there will in its present instance be large indirect compensation in the increased value given to the land through which the railway will pass, besides a probable saving in respect to road construction and maintenance, which would otherwise have been almost certainly unavoidable. Neither am I insensible to the great importance of meeting in a liberal spirit the efforts of the local community in Assam to provide themselves with improved means of communication and I willingly assent to a scheme which appears to involve no objectionable financial liabilities.

It has not been explained by your Excellency how the provincial revenues of Assam will be able to bear the demand made upon them by the guarantee, considering that for some years past they have annually shown a deficit in comparison with the Provincial expenditure, but this is not a point your Excellency's Government is likely to have overlooked and it is presumed that the ordinary Public Works grants will suffice to meet the charge without involving any additional demand on the revenues of India.

Appendix IV

Railway Construction 'A', December 1903, nos. 79–87

Remarks made on the Despatch to Secretary of State while under circulation for signature

Surely the departmental action taken upon the case has been entirely irregular. Sir E. Elles noted with perfect fairness, that he did not think that the Despatch should issue without discussion in the Council. Thereupon someone — I have no idea who — appears to have circulated the case, and I find upon it signatures of three Honourable members. I am under the impression that this was *ultra vires*. I have certainly not known a case circulated without reference to the Viceroy, and shall be glad of an explanation.

As regards the merits of the case, it is one with which I am very familiar, and about which I have frequently corresponded with the Secretary of State. I have travelled, for the special purpose of seeing the line, upon the infamous Hill Section of the railway; and on one occasion I went into the circumstances of its history.

No words can, in my opinion be too strong to describe the careless and the most criminal ineptitude which characterized the earlier stages of this undertaking. The papers put up in this file do not carry us back beyond the formation of the company in 1891, but it is no secret that political considerations were behind the earlier steps. After Lord Dufferin had annexed Upper Burma in 1885 he conceived the idea of connecting Bengal *via* Assam with the new possession. In this premature and fantastic scheme Sir T. Hope, then Public Works Member of Council backed him. The Assam planters foolishly tumbled into the trap and advocated a junction of the Brahmaputra Valley with the Surma Valley, in the interests of their own produce, which was thereby to be transported to Chittagong. When Sir T. Hope left India in December 1887, he reappeared in London as a would-be concessionaire, and made proposals for the construction of a line by a Company. These were discussed for a long time by the Secretary of State, but the negotiations fell through. Then occurred the Manipur outbreak. Once again the Government of India went completely off their heads: the support of Kohima, which was the military base for Manipur, became the supreme consideration: a petty uprising (due to incredible mismanagement) in a quasi-Bengali village of peasants was magnified as a menace to the Empire: and the immediate construction of the Hill section was regarded as an Imperial necessity. The Secretary of State resumed his activity, the proposals of certain English capitalists were accepted, and the Assam–Bengal Railway Company was formed. Mr Guildford Molesworth, supposed to be a capable engineer, travelled over the route and reported favourably upon it and work was begun.

Two years had not elapsed before the Government of India began to learn from their engineers what they were in for, and the costly and the most crazy nature of the undertaking. The years 1893 to 1895 were marked by more than one attempt on their part to get out of the bargain, and to stop altogether, or at least postpone the Hill section. The proposals were steadily resisted by Lord Kimberley and Sir H. Fowler. Lord Elgin's

Government made another attempt in October 1895, but Lord George Hamilton pointed out that this would entail heavy compensation and losses. The Government of India considered this aspect of the case and made out that the losses resulting either from completion or abandonment would approximately be the same. They therefore decided in favour of going on. This was in March 1896.

Since then, so far as I know, all parties, *viz*. the Government of India, Secretary of State, and the Company (to whom it did not so much matter), have torpidly resigned themselves to the situation, which has been marked only by a succession of excesses of expenditure over estimates, without parallel, I should think in the history of railway construction. The process is not yet at the end, though it is nearing completion. The question is whether, having failed to throw up the job in 1893–4–5 and 6 we should do so in 1903.

I think as Sir E. Law says, that a commercial firm would very likely take this step, for they would be accentuated exclusively by profit and loss considerations, and no discredit attaches to an unsuccessful commercial speculation.

The conduct of the Government cannot be determined by the same motives or considerations. We have many interests to consider: the requirements of the province, the rights and obligations of the Company, the attitude of the Secretary of State, the previous history of the case, continuity of policy, and the credit of Government. I would have gladly seen this ruinous folly abandoned at any time during the first ten years after its inception. I deplore the wicked waste of the money of the Indian taxpayer already incurred, and the probable future waste that is to follow. But I do not see that there is the remotest chance of persuading the India Office to back out at this juncture: nor do I think, in view of all that has passed, that we have a sufficiently strong case for asking them to do so.

In these circumstances I recommend that the Despatch be issued.

But if Sir E. Law likes to accompany it by a note of protest, indignation, lamentation or appeal, I have not the slightest objection to his doing so.

Circulate and Council C[urzon],
24-10-1903

Appendix V

Railway Traffic 'A', March 1901,
nos. 41–46 (Notes)

Note, dated 30 July 1900, recorded by Mr W.H. Nightingale, Chief Engineer, Assam, on the Cherra–Companyganj State Railway

I inspected the Cherra–Companyganj Railway on the 21st June 1900, and I regret to say that I found matters had gone from bad to worse since my inspection in November 1898 and the first 3½ miles from Therria are hopelessly ruined. There is no trace of the railway embankment left, and the face of the country has completely changed, there now being nothing but a vast expanse of sand, completely submerged in flood time, and covered with drift timber, where there was formerly a dense tree jungle. The village of Therria has disappeared, and the site of the old station house and the *dak* bungalow is at present a sand bank.

2. Most of the floodwater now appears to come down the Dholoi (or Therria) river instead of down the Dhubri as formerly. Before the earthquake the Therria Bridge on the railway, one span of 60 feet and one of 40 feet, was sufficient to pass the floodwater of the Dholoi. Now that river is about 150 yards broad, bifurcates a short distance above the bridge, one branch flowing north and the other south, of the bridge leaving it high and dry. The two branches unite below the

bridge, and the river flows south, and then in an easterly direction across the railway at mile 2¾. It then joins the Dhubri, forming a lake 300 yards broad and a couple of miles in length, and a branch from this lake again crosses the railway line south of Bholaganj. The workshops at that place have completely disappeared, and the station house lies buried to the eaves in the sand. From the 4th mile to Companyganj the embankment stood fairly well, being breached in only a few places. The rails have been taken up between Therria and the 4th mile to prevent [them] being buried in the sand, as has happened every rain since the earthquake has occurred.

3. There is no doubt that this portion of the line must be abandoned and a new alignment adopted if the railway is to be reconstructed, but looking to the fact that the line has never paid, and that Mr Garth has submitted a project for a railway from Dwarra Bazar to Theria, I am of the opinion that the Government railway should be closed and abandoned altogether. In this case it will be necessary, in order to keep open communication with Sylhet, to construct a bridle path, skirting the foot of the hills and keeping to the high ground to the west of the railway, from Therria to the 4th mile, from which point to Companyganj the embankment is practically intact.

4. The capital cost of the railway from the commencement of operations to the end of May 1900 amounted to Rs 7,68,902, as shown below:

Open Section	Rs 3,38,749
Section abandoned	Rs 4,30,153
Total	Rs 7,68,902

In this sum is included the capital cost of 'Rolling-stock' for the same period, amounting to Rs 92,913, and also that of the ballast and permanent way (including rails), amounting to Rs 1,80,121.

The following is the list of the permanent-way materials:

Rails, 24 lbs to the yard, 21 feet long	7¼ miles
Ditto, 18 lbs ditto, 18 and 21 feet long	1½ miles
Ditto, ditto, ditto	2 miles, 3,681 feet

(The last lot are from dismantled inclines and are stacked at Therria.)

Steel Sleepers, 3½' × 6"	13,200 nos.
Wooden Sleepers, 4' × 6" × 3" (Many of these latter are unserviceable)	5,300 nos.
4 engines	2 unserviceable.
2 composite carriages	1 ditto.
2 upper and lower-class carriages	Damaged.
2 lower class ditto	Damaged.
2 bogie trucks	Damaged.
16 iron wagons	Damaged.
73 iron wagons	Fairly serviceable.

I recommend that all the materials and rolling stock be disposed of on the most favourable terms we get.

W.H. Nightingale,
Chief Engineer, Assam

Appendix VI

Railway Construction 'A', October 1902,
nos. 102–104
Northern Bengal–Assam Bengal Extension to
Gauhati, no. 5302

From
G.J. Perram, Esq.,
Secretary to the Chief Commissioner of Assam, Public Works
Department

To
The Secretary of State to the Government of India, Public
Works Department (Railway Branch)

Shillong, 18 September 1902

Sir,

I am directed to forward a copy of the letter no. 46 of 26 July 1902, from the Secretary of Assam Branch of the Indian Tea Association, communicating the Resolution which the General Committee has recently formulated in favour of the linking of Gauhati with the Eastern Bengal railway near Dhubri by railway.

2. The great advantages which the construction of this line would offer to Assam were strongly represented by Sir Henry Cotton in 1897 and in this Administration's letter no. 3433 of

28 July 1900,when the prospects of the line and its alignment were discussed in some detail. The main argument in its favour is of course that it would facilitate immigration into the province, the urgent need of which an increase in the labour supply, both for the cultivation of tea and for ordinary farming of the country. The number of those who will work for hire in Assam is extraordinarily small. The recent census has disclosed that, taking the whole Assam Valley as a whole, but excluding the tea gardens, only 3.3 per cent of the population belongs to the labouring class, whether as farm servants, agricultural labourers or general labourers. If the westernmost district of Goalpara be excluded, the proportion falls to 2 per cent. It reaches its minimum in the Tezpur district, where they are shown to be only 613 adult male farm servants of ploughmen, and only 580 men of coolie class available for hire, though this is perhaps the locality where cultivation is capable of its largest and most profitable extension. These figures form a very sharp contrast to the statistics of the more densely populated districts of Bihar and United Provinces, where the proportion of labouring population to the total is about 18 per cent. The proportion is as high as this in the comparatively thinly populated districts of the Central Provinces. It is of course owing to this extraordinary dearth of local labour that the Government has been obliged to come to the assistance of those who will go to the extreme of importing coolies by establishing a Penal Labour Law, which, however necessary for the maintenance of the Tea industry, is open to serious objections, and exposes the Government to much criticism. But the country at large has had to procure its labour as best as it could under the ordinary law of the land; and the consequence has been that, in spite of the fact that Assam stands alone among the provinces of India proper in offering scope for colonization on a very large scale, it has,

owing to defective communications practically remained untouched by the people who live beyond its boundaries. There can be no question of the abundance of fertile land. Mr Melitus the Commissioner of Assam Valley Districts, who knows the province well has estimated the area of good culturable waste land at 5 million acres, and if we exclude from consideration the submontane tracts and valleys (such as the valley of the Kopili which was to have been a field of colonization experiment advocated by Sir Henry Cotton five years ago), and confine ourselves to the colonization of the plains lying beyond the limits of the Brahmaputra inundations, there would still remain an area of considerably more than half the extent endowed with a considerable measure of natural fertility, but untouched by the plough. Notwithstanding the existence of this large margin of culturable waste, cultivation in Assam has been expanding but slowly, and the land revenue has shown a disappointingly small increase. It appears to be incontrovertible that scarcity of labour is one of the principal causes of this stagnation. The Assamese are often stigmatised as apathetic and idle. But a very large proportion of the *raiyats* in India derive much assistance in their farming from hired labour — if they do not indeed manage their entire cultivation by its means — and a family which is compelled to itself perform the whole of the field work of its holding is naturally reluctant to undertake [it] in a wider area of cultivation than is absolutely necessary. Mr Fuller was assured by several landholders of position during his recent tour, that they would gladly take up more lands if they could hire ploughmen. The Tezpur people have to hire from Gauhati and pay Rs 10 to Rs 11 a month for indifferent workers.

3. It may perhaps be objected that if so strong a demand for labour really existed, coolies could find their way into the

province. But it is recognized by all who are acquainted with the situation that the conditions of the long journey by river steamer are an insuperable obstacle to unassisted immigration. Whether it be due to apprehension of loss of caste, to the discomfort of voyage, or to the fear that having once crossed the water there will be no return, the fact remains that there has been no natural response to the demand for labour, and the development of the country has not been assisted by the periodical migration of labourers which sustains the agriculture of so many localities — and amongst them the tea gardens in the neighbouring duars of Bhutan Duars. All authorities are agreed that unless direct railway communication is opened with Bengal, no such influx of population can be expected as the province needs for its development, and as would enable the Government to repeal the special Labour Law and place the labour supply upon a free and natural basis.

4. It may be argued that the completion of the Hill section of the Assam–Bengal Railway will afford to the province the communication which it needs. But it appears doubtful whether the circuitous route via Goalundo, Chandpur, and Badarpur will attract labour from the districts which can supply it. The tracts which the Hill section will bring into direct communication with Assam Valley, Cachar and Sylhet districts and the Bengal districts which adjoin them, are as short of labourers as the Assam Valley itself. The labouring class form less than two per cent of the population of Cachar and Sylhet, where indeed it is difficult to hire a coolie to carry a light load under 8 to 10 annas a day. Nor do the adjacent districts of Bengal promise a much better source of labour supply. In Tipperah only 5 per cent of the population works for hire, in Noakhali 10 per cent, and if we cross the Goalundo side of the Meghna we find percentages of 4 per cent in

Faridpur and 7 per cent in Jessore. It is to be noticed that further north, in the country traversed by the east and west line of Bengal and North-Western Railway, there is a striking increase in the numbers of wage-earning population: they amount to over 20 per cent of the total in Purnea and Bhagalpur. [A] number of Sylhetis will, no doubt, cross into Assam Valley and colonize considerable areas, as they have within comparatively recent times colonized the Cachar district, but they will come as petty cultivators, not as labourers. The district from which [it] has obtained its labour supply in the past and into which it must look into the future, lie much further west and taking Asansol as a point upon which they converge the streams of immigration from Bihar, the United Provinces, the route via Goalundo, Chandpur and the Assam Bengal Railway will entail 720 miles of travelling by road and 77 miles by river (costing at present at rates over Rs 10) before the emigrants emerge on the plains of Assam at Golaghat. Travelling by the Bengal and North-Western Railway and the projected link line to Gauhati, the emigrants would have to travel 520 miles of railway, with a saving of Rs 4 before they reached Gauhati, a country where their services would be in demand. If we take Mokameh as the starting point — and the people from its neighbourhood in the Patna and Chapra districts constitute by far the greatest proportion of those who have independently travelled in search of employment — the difference in favour of the northern route is still greater, as Mokameh is nearer Gauhati than Asansol, whereas via Goalundo and the Assam–Bengal Railway, the immigrant would have to cover a distance of 870 miles at the cost of between Rs 12 and Rs 13. Briefly, the northern route would save a distance of 420 miles and a fare of Rs 7 to a passenger from Mokameh. And the longer route moreover is prejudiced by its including the river journey, which, although one of 8 hours only will be attended by some of the difficulties which now discourage immigration to the Assam Valley. The Gauhati route would not improbably be found to be sufficiently cheap to render it possible to import labour for the season on the system which now feeds the tea gardens in the Duars and in Ceylon.

5. It is then a strong argument for the construction of a line between the Bengal and the North-Western Railway and Gauhati that would lead to a more rapid reclamation of the Assam Valley by the relief of the districts in which labour is now underpaid, and that it would offer the Government a prospect of repeal of a special Labour Law, which gives employers powers over their labourers that are capable of being seriously abused, and which fetters the latter to the soil. The financial results of stimulating the reclamation of land may be judged from the fact that the occupation of only half the area, that Mr Melitus takes as culturable with profit, would at existing rates, double the land revenue of the province. But it must not be imagined that the railway has no more immediate prospects. It will traverse one of the most thickly populated tracts in the Valley. The single crop which the Assamese grow for export is mustard. This is now produced in considerable quantities in the inundated country lying between the railway and the river: there are enormous areas of waste land suitable for its cultivation, and in all probability it would be grown in a large scale were it not for the difficulty in exporting it. The railway would carry practically [all] imports of the Valley, and although estimates based upon the existing trade may not provide substantial profits, it seems unlikely that a line [that] would tap a country of great but underdeveloped resources would fail for any length of time to pay a fair dividend. The

officiating Chief Commissioner realizes the magnitude of the expenditure which has been involved by the construction of the Hill section of the Assam–Bengal Railway but he hopes that the Government of India will nevertheless decide that the completion of the provincial railway system by linking it with the Gauhati branch of the Bengal and North-Western Railway, is a project which deserves to be undertaken in the near future.

I have the honour to be,
Sir,
Your obedient servant,

G.J. Perram,
Secretary to the Chief Commissioner of Assam
Public Works Department

Glossary

agar	aloes wood.
Arkattis	licenced labour contractors.
Barua	an officer of rank under the Ahom Government.
barangani	a tax on land.
beel	a small lake; water body; freshwater wetland.
bepari	a merchant, particularly from Dacca.
beesa	a vegetable poison.
Bhakti	a socio-religious movement.
bigah	measurement of land, approximately one-third of an acre.
Brahmin	a Hindu religious preceptor.
Brahmottar	rent free land grant for support of Brahmins.
Britials	goldsmiths.
bund	embankment.
Burgohain	chief amongst the three ministers of the Ahom cabinet.
Bhuyans/ Bhaumik	petty non-tribal armed land controllers.
chars	river banks seasonally submerged in water; river islands.
Chaudhuri	a fiscal officer over a pargana.
coolie	indentured labour employed on the plantations.
crore(s)	Indian term for expressing ten million, written as 1,00,00,000.
Devottar	rent free tenure to support temples.
Duara-Barua	an official in charge of the chief custom-house under the Ahom government.

faringhati	dry land.
gadhan	a tax on land alloted to *paiks*.
ga-mati	land allotted to a *paik* or peasant in lieu of his service to the state.
ghat	a landing place on the river bank.
ghi/ghee	a type of clarified butter used in Indian cookery.
got	a squad or unit of four *paiks*.
Goswami	a spiritual guide.
hat	a weekly or bi-weekly market.
Hira	a potter, who did not use a potter's wheel.
jajmani	relationships based on occupational classes in a traditional Indian village.
Jugis	professional weaving class.
Kalitas	a class of people in Assam belonging to the Kshatriya class.
kala-azar	black fever.
khar	salt obtained by processing plantain trees.
kharikatana	poll tax.
khel	a functional unit or division of population in the Ahom period.
lakh(s)	Indian term for expressing a hundred thousand, written as 1,00,000.
Mahanta	preceptor of Vaishnavism; an important official in the monasteries.
Marwari	a merchant from the Marwar region in Rajasthan.
maund	an Indian maund, which was the standard of weight in British India was equal to 82⅔ pounds avoirdupois, or 40 *seers*.
mauza	a revenue administrative region consisting of a number of revenue villages.
Moria	Muslim brass-workers.
Mufassil	rural.
Nadial	a fisherman.
Narayani	currency coined by Maharaja Nara-Narayan of Koch Behar, 1540–84.

paikar/faria	petty rural trader.
paik	an Assamese peasant whose duty was to render services to the King and State at fixed periods of a year.
pura	a measurement of land equivalent to slightly over three acres (14,400 square yards).
raij	community.
raijmel	village assembly.
Rupee(s)	1 rupee = 16 annas; 1 anna = 4 pice; 1 pice = 3 pies.
rupit	arable land or land on which winter crop or transplanted paddy is grown.
ryot	a peasant whose primary occupation is cultivation.
Sadar	sub-divisional headquarters.
Sadiya-Khowa Gohain	a frontier official posted at Sadiya, in the Ahom period.
Satra	a monastery.
seer	unit of measurement of solids and liquids, approximately one kilogram.
Sicca	currency of the East India Company.
Tanti	professional weaver.
Tehsildar	a revenue officer.
teklah	peon.
til	sesame seeds.
Vaishya-Saud	a trading community.
Wazir-Barua	Ahom custom officer in charge of trade with Bhutan.
Zamindar	a heriditary collector of revenue.

Bibliography

PRIMARY SOURCES

Unpublished Documents

Records of the Government of India (New Delhi: National Archives of India):

    Proceedings of the Railway Branch of the Public Works Department, 1879–1881

    Proceedings of the Railway Branch of the Public Works Department, 1882–1901

    Proceedings of the Railway Branch of the Public Works Department, 1892–1901

    Proceedings of the Railway Branch of Public Works Department, 1902–1904

    Proceedings of the Railway Department of Railway Board, 1905–1910

    Proceedings of the Railway Department of Railway Board, 1911–1920

    Proceedings of the Railway Department of Railway Board, 1923–1924

Records of the Government of Bengal (Calcutta: West Bengal State Archives):

    Bengal Judicial Consultations (Criminal), 1835–1845

    Bengal Secret and Political Consultations, 1827

    Bengal Political Consultations, 1828–1831

    Bengal Marine Proceedings, 1854

Records of the Government of Assam (Dispur: Assam State Archives):

    Letters issued from Government of Bengal, 1833–1864

    Letters issued to the Government of Bengal, 1834–1874

Letters issued to the Board of Revenue for Lower Provinces, 1852–1854
Letters received from Board of Revenue, 1836–1837
Letters issued to District Officers, 1861–1887
Letters issued to Miscellaneous Quarters, 1836–1864

Post-1874 Files:
Bengal Government Papers
Cooch Bihar Commissioner's Office
Goalpara Papers
Assam Commissioner's Office

Assam Secretariat — Public Works Department 1868–1898:
Revenue Proceedings
Home Proceedings
Finance and Commerce Proceedings
Immigration Proceedings
Forest Proceedings
Governor's Secretariat, Files
Political History of Assam, Files

The Proceedings of the Departments between 1905–1912 were titled as Proceedings of the Government of Eastern Bengal and Assam
Goswami, N.N., 'History of Communication Development: North East Region of the Country' (1989).

Published Documents

Government of Assam
Annual Report on the Administration of Assam, (1889–1923).
Annual Report on the Land Revenue Administration of the Assam Valley Districts, (1911–1912).
Annual Report on the River Borne Trade of the Province of Assam, (1882–1896).
Annual Report on the Rail and River Borne Trade of Assam, (1897).
Assam Gazette.
Annual Report on the Labour Immigration into Assam.
A Survey of the Industries and Resources of Eastern Bengal and Assam.

Note on the History of Past Settlements in Assam.
Note on Some Industries of Assam.
Physical and Political Geography of the Province of Assam:
Reprinted from the Report on the Administration of The
Province of Assam for the Year 1892–1893 . . .
Report on Jute Cultivation in Assam.
Report on Land Revenue Administration of Surma Valley and
the Hill Districts.
Government of India
Census of India, 1901, Assam, Part I.
Imperial Gazetteers of India, Volume I, 1885 and Volume VI,
1908.
Statement Exhibiting Moral and Material Progress and Condi-
tions of India.
Gazetteer of Bengal and North East India.

Newspapers

The Statesman, Calcutta (various editions).
Amrit Bazar Patrika, Calcutta (various editions).

Memoir's and Reports

Aitchison, Sir C.U., *A Collection of Treaties, Engagements and*
Sanads, Relating to India and Neighbouring Countries, vol. XII,
Calcutta: Government of India Central Publication Branch,
1929.
Antrobus, H.A., *A History of the Assam Company, 1839–1953,* Edin-
burgh, London: Privately printed T. & A. Constable, Ltd., 1957.
Gawthrop, William R., *The Story of the Assam Railways and Trading*
Company Limited, 1881–1951, London: Harley Publishing Co.
for the Assam Railways and Trading Co., 1951.
Kinney, T., *Old Times in Assam,* Calcutta: Star Press, 1896.
Playne, Somerset (ed.), *Bengal and Assam, Behar and Orissa: Their*
History, People, Commerce and Industrial Resources, London:
Foreign and Colonial Compiling and Publishing Co., 1917.
Dibru–Sadiya Railway, Contracts, Prospectus, Etc., Shillong: Gov-
ernment of India, Public Works Department, 1914.

SECONDARY SOURCES

Books and Journals

Allen, B.C. (ed.), *Assam District Gazetteers*, Government of Assam (all Districts), 1905 onwards.

Anstey, Vera, *The Economic Development of India*, (3rd revised and enlarged ed., reprint), London: Longmans, Green & Co., 1949.

Bagchi, A.K., *Private Investment in India 1900–1939*, New Delhi: Cambridge University Press, 1972.

Banerjee, Dipankar, 'Non-Plantation Labour Movement in Assam: A Study of Assam Oil Company Workers Strike–1939', *Proceedings of North East India History Association*.

———, 'Genesis of Labour Movement Among the Non-Plantation Workers and Wage Earners in Assam', *Proceedings of North East India History Association*, Agartala, 1985.

———, 'Historic Assam–Bengal Worker's Strike (1921): A Survey', *Proceedings of North East India History Association*, Barapani, 1983.

———, 'A Brief Note on the Role of the Congress in the Labour Struggle Assam during 1919–1939', *Proceedings of North East India History Association*.

Banerjee, Tarasankar, *Internal Market of India 1834–1900*, (1st ed.) Calcutta: Academic Publishers, 1966.

Barpujari, H.K., *Assam in the Days of the Company 1826–1858: A Critical and Comprehensive History of Assam during the Rule of the East India Company from 1826–1858, based on original Assamese and English sources, both published and unpublished*, (2d ed.) Gauhati: Spectrum Publications, 1980.

———. (ed.), *The Comprehensive History of Assam: From the Prehistoric Times to the Twelfth Century A.D.*, vol. II, (1st ed.) Guwahati: Assam Publication Board, 1992.

———. (ed.), *The Comprehensive History of Assam: From the Prehistoric Times to the Twelfth Century A.D.*, vol. IV, (1st ed.) Guwahati: Assam Publication Board, 1992.

———, *The Comprehensive History of Assam: From the Prehistoric Times to the Twelfth Century A.D.*, vol. V, (1st ed.) Guwahati: Assam Publication Board, 1993.

Barooah, Nirode K., *David Scott in North-East India: A Study of*

British Paternalism, 1802–1831, New Delhi: Munshiram Manoharlal, 1970.

Bhattacharjee, S., *Financial Foundations of the British Raj,* Shimla: Indian Institute of Advanced Studies, 1921.

Bhuyan, Suryya Kumar, *Anglo-Assamese Relations 1771–1826: A History of the Relations of Assam with the East India Company from 1771 to 1826, based on original English and Assamese sources,* Gauhati: Department of Historical and Antiquarian Studies in Assam, 1949, reprinted Gauhati: Lawyer's Book Stall, 1974.

Bose, Arun, 'Foreign Capital in India' in V.B. Singh (ed.), *Economic History of India 1857–1956,* Bombay: Allied Publishers, 1965.

Buchanan-Hamilton, Francis, *An Account of Assam, with Some Notices Concerning the Neighbouring Territories. First compiled in 1807–1814.* S.K. Bhuyan (ed.), (3d ed.) Gauhati: Government of Assam, in the Department of Historical and Antiquarian Studies, Narayani Handiqui Historical Institute, 1987.

Chandra, Bipan, *The Rise and Growth of Economic Nationalism in India: Economic Policies of Indian National Leadership, 1880–1905,* New Delhi: People's Publishing House, 1966.

Connell, Arthur Knatchbull, *The Economic Revolution of India and the Public Works Policy,* London: K. Paul, Trench, 1883.

Cotton, A., *Public Works in India: Their Importance with Suggestions for their Extension and Improvement,* (2d ed.) London: Richardson Brothers, 1854.

Das, M.N., *Studies in the Economic and Social Development of Modern India: 1848–1856,* Calcutta: Mukhopadhyay, 1959.

Dasgupta, Keya, 'Urban Centres in the Spatial Structure, of the Brahmaputra Valley Under Colonialism', *Proceedings of North East India History Association,* Doimukh, 1994.

Davidson, E., *Railways of India: With an Account of their Rise, Progress and Construction,* London: E. & F. N. Spon, 1868.

Desai, A.R., *Social Background of Indian Nationalism,* Bombay: Popular Prakashan, 1976.

Dowden, T.F., *Notes on Railways,* Bombay: Education Society's Press, 1873.

Dutt, R.C., *The Economic History of India,* (2 vols, bound in one),

Delhi: Low Price Publications, first published 1902–1904, reprinted, 1990.

Dutt, R. Palme, *India Today*, Calcutta: Manisha, reprint,1986.

Gadgil, D.R., *The Industrial Evolution of India in Recent Times, 1860–1939*, (5th ed.) Delhi: Oxford University Press, 1974.

Gait, Edward Albert, *A History of Assam*, Calcutta: Thacker, Spink & Co., 1906.

Ghose, Sarat Chandra, *Lectures on Indian Railway Economics*, Part III, Calcutta: University of Calcutta, 1922–27.

Griffiths, Percival, *The History of the Indian Tea Industry*, London: Weidenfeld & Nicolson, 1967.

Guha, Amalendu, *Planter Raj to Swaraj: Freedom Struggle and Electoral Politics in Assam, 1826–1947*, New Delhi: Indian Council of Historical Research, 1977.

————, 'Land Rights and Social Classes in Medieval Assam', *Indian Economic and Social History Review*, vol. III, no. 3, September 1966, Delhi: Sage Publications.

————, 'Colonisation of Assam: Second Phase 1840–1859', *Indian Economic and Social History Review*, December 1967, Delhi: Sage Publications.

————, 'Colonisation: Years of Transitional Crises' (1825–1840) *Indian Economic and Social History Review*, vol. V, no. 2, June 1968, Delhi: Sage Publications.

————, 'A Big Push Without a Take off: A Case Study of Assam 1871–1901', *Indian Economic and Social History Review*, vol. V, no. 3, September 1968, Delhi: Sage Publications.

————, 'Assamese Agrarian Society in the Late Nineteenth Century: Roots, Structures and Trends', *Indian Economic and Social History Review*, vol. XVII, no 1, January–March 1980, Delhi: Sage Publications.

————, 'Medieval Economy of Assam', Appendix 1, *The Cambridge Economic History of India, 1200–1750*, vol. I, Tapan Raichaudhuri and Irfan Habib (eds), Cambridge; New York: Cambridge University Press, 1982.

————, *Medieval and Early Colonial Assam: Society, Polity and Economy*, Calcutta: Centre for Studies in Social Sciences, by K.P. Bagchi & Company, 1991.

Hunter, William Wilson, *A Statistical Account of Assam*, vol. I, London: Trubner, 1879, reprint Delhi: B.R. Pubishing Corporation, 1975.

Jagtiani, H.M., *The Role of the State in the Provision of Railways*, London: P.S. King, 1924.

Johnson, J. *The Economics of Indian Rail Transport*, Bombay: Allied Publishers, 1963.

Kidron, Michael, *Foreign Investments in India*, London: Oxford University Press, 1965.

Knowles, L.C.A., *Economic Development of the British Overseas Empire*, vol. II, London: G. Routledge, 1930.

Kumar, Deepak and Roy MacLeod (eds), *Technology and the Raj: Western Technology and Technical Transfers to India 1700–1947*, Delhi: Sage Publications, 1995.

Kumar, Dharma and Meghnad Desai (eds), *The Cambridge Economic History of India 1757–1970*, vol. II, Cambridge: Cambridge University Press, 1983.

Levkovsky, A.I., *Capitalism in India: Basic Trends in Development*, Bombay: People's Publishing House, 1966.

Lehmann, F., 'Great Britain and the Supply of Railway Locomotives in India: A Case Study of Economic Imperialism', *Indian Economic and Social History Review*, vol. II, no. 4, October 1965, Delhi: Sage Publications.

Marx, Karl and Frederick Engels, *On Colonialism*, 8th reprint, Moscow, USSR: Progress Publishers, 1981.

M'Cosh, John, *Topography of Assam*, Calcutta: G.H. Huttmann, Bengal Military Orphan Press, 1837; reprint Delhi: Sanskaran Prakashak, 1975.

McAlpin, Burge M., 'Railroads, Prices and Peasant Rationality in India, 1860–1900', *Journal of Economic History*, vol. 34, no. 3, September, 1974, Cambridge: Cambridge University Press on behalf of the Economic History Association.

Medhi, Shyam Bhadra, *Transport System and Economic Development of Assam*, Gauhati: Publication Board, Assam, 1978.

Mehta, N.B., *Indian Railways: Rates and Regulations*, London: P. S. King & Son, Ltd., 1927.

Mills, A.J.M., *Report on the Province of Assam*, Calcutta: Gazette

Office, 1854, 1st reprint Delhi: Gian Publications, 1980, 2nd reprint Gauhati: Publication Board Assam, 1984.

Mukherjee, Aditya, 'Agrarian Conditions in Assam 1880–1890: A Case Study of Five Districts of the Brahmaputra Valley', *Indian Economic and Social History Review*, vol. xvi, no. 2, 1979, Delhi: Sage Publications.

Naoroji, Dadabhai, *Poverty and Un-British Rule in India*, London: Swan Sonnenschein, 1901.

Nag, Sajal, *Roots of Ethnic Conflict: Nationality Question in North-East India*, New Delhi: Manohar Publications, 1990.

———, 'Working Class Alienation in Swadeshi and Non-Co-operation Movement: A Reflection of the Class Character of Nationalist Movement in Assam 1905–1924', *Proceedings of the North-East India History Association*, Imphal Session, 1983.

———, 'Economic Roots of the Regional Class: A Study of Primitive Acumulation of the Marwari Community in Colonial Assam', *Proceedings of the North East India History Association*, Barapani Session, 1984.

Nath, D., *History of the Koch Kingdom, c. 1515–1615*, Delhi: Mittal Publications, 1989.

Prasad, Amba, *Indian Railways: A Study in Public Utility Administration*, London and Bombay: Asia Publishing House, 1960.

Pemberton, R. Boileau, *The Eastern Frontier of India: With an Appendix and Maps*, Calcutta: Printed by order of the Supreme Government of India, 1835, reprint Gauhati: Department of Historical and Antiquarian Studies, 1966.

Raychaudhuri, Tapan and Irfan Habib, *The Cambridge Economic History of India, 1200–1750*, vol. 1, Cambridge; New York: Cambridge University Press, 1982–1983, reprint Delhi: Orient Longman, 1984.

Ramanujam, T.V., *The Functions of State Railways in the Indian National Economy*, Madras: Madras Law Journal Press, 1944.

Robinson, William A., *A Descriptive Account of Assam: With a Sketch of the Local Geography and a Concise History of the Tea-plant of Asam, to which is added a Short Account of the Neighbouring Tribes, Exhibiting their History, Manners, and Customs*, Calcutta: Ostell & Lepage, British Library, 1841, reprinted Delhi: Sanskaran Prakashak, 1975.

Rothermund, Dietmar, *An Economic History of India: From Pre-Colonial Times to 1986*, New Delhi: Manohar Publications, 1988.

Sanyal, Nalinaksha, *Development of Indian Railways*, Calcutta: University of Calcutta, 1930.

Singh, Jai Prakash and Gautam Sengupta (eds), *Archaeology of North-Eastern India*, New Delhi: Har-Anand Publications in association with Vikas Publishing House, 1991.

Singh, V.B., *Indian Economy: Yesterday and Today*, New Delhi: People's Publishing House, 1964.

————. (ed.), *Economic History of India 1857–1956*, Bombay; New York: Allied Publishers, 1965.

Thorner, Daniel and Alice, *Land and Labour in India*, Bombay; New York: Asia Publishing House, 1962.

Thorner, Daniel, *Investment in Empire: British Railway and Steam Shipping Enterprise in India, 1825–1849*, Philadelphia: University of Pennsylvania Press, 1950.

Index

www.pilgrimsbooks.com

For more details about Pilgrims and other
books published by them you may visit our
website at www.pilgrimsbooks.com
or
for Mail Order and Catalogue
contact us at

Pilgrims Book House
B. 27/98 A-8 Nawab Ganj Road
Durga Kund Varanasi 221010
Tel. 91-542-2314060
Fax. 91-542-2312456
E-mail: pilgrimsbooks@sify.com

PILGRIMS BOOK HOUSE (New Delhi)
1626, Raj Guru Road Pahar Ganj, Chuna Mandi
New Delhi 110055
Tel: 91-11-23584015, 23584019
E-mail: pilgrim@del2.vsnl.net.in
E-mail: pilgrimsinde@gmail.com

PILGRIMS BOOK HOUSE (Kathmandu)
P O Box 3872, Thamel, Kathmandu, Nepal
Tel: 977-1-4700942,
Off: 977-1-4700919,
Fax: 977-1-4700943
E-mail: pilgrims@wlink.com.np